THE
LEGISLATIVE
ENCY

14.599

ayne
niversity

lishers

co, London

Sponsoring Editor: Dale Tharp
Project Editor: Penelope Behn
Designer: Katrine Stevens
Production Supervisor: Marion Palen
Compositor: Port City Press, Inc.
Printer and Binder: The Murray Printing Company
Art Studio: Danmark & Michaels, Inc.

THE LEGISLATIVE PRESIDENCY

Library of Congress Cataloging in Publication Data
Wayne, Stephen J.
    The Legislative Presidency.
    Bibliography: p.
    Includes index.
    1. Presidents—United States. 2. Presidents—United
States—Staff. 3. Legislation—United States.
4. United States. Congress. I. Title.
JK585.W34   353.03   77-12925
ISBN 0-06-046964-1

Grateful acknowledgment is made for the use of the following material.

John R. Johannes, "Congress and the Initiation of Legislation," *Public Policy* XX (1972): 284. Reprinted by permission of John Wiley & Sons, Inc.

Doris Kearns, *Lyndon Johnson and the American Dream* (New York: Harper & Row, 1976), pp. 174-75, 177-78, 221-22, 223, 224, 241. Reprinted by permission of Harper & Row, Publishers, Inc.

Richard E. Neustadt, "Presidency and Legislation: Planning the President's Program," *American Political Science Review* XLIX (Dec. 1955): 991, 1015. Reprinted with the permission of The American Political Science Association.

Lyndon Baines Johnson, *The Vantage Point* (New York: Holt, Rinehart & Winston, 1971), pp. 326-27, 328, 447-48, 456, 457. Copyright © 1971 by HEC Public Affairs Foundation. Reprinted by permission of Holt, Rinehart & Winston, Publishers.

John Hersey, "The President," *New York Times Magazine* (April 20, 1975): 40, 76, 110. © 1975 by The New York Times Company. Reprinted by permission.

Louis Maisel, "High Level Domestic Advising: The Domestic Council in the Ford Administration," a paper presented at the annual meeting of the Southern Political Science Association, Hyatt Regency Hotel, Atlanta, Georgia, Nov. 4-6, 1976: 4, 11, 18, 21. Reprinted by permission of the author.

Contents

Preface

The presidency is a multifaceted institution. This is a book about one of those facets: the formulation, coordination, and implementation of legislative policy. Today, executive initiative and involvement is taken for granted. It has become an expectation, made necessary by demands for activitism in a system characterized by its political and constitutional constraints. Congress' seeming inability to provide comprehensive legislative programing and, until recently, comprehensive budgeting has literally forced the president and his staff to develop mechanisms and processes for legislative policy making.

These mechanisms and processes, in turn, have had an enormous impact on the institution and the character of its relationships. They have enlarged the office of the presidency, expanded its responsibilities, increased its influence, and extended its interaction not only with the Congress but with the departments and agencies as well. They have affected the institution's ability to be responsive to public interests and pressures and the president's capacity to lead or be led. They have also influenced the substance of legislative policy.

Describing what these mechanisms and processes are and how they work is a major task of this book; analyzing their effect on the governmental structure in general and the presidency in particular is another important concern. To accomplish these descriptive and analytic goals, Chapters 1 through 6 are organized chronologically on the basis of a functional aspect of legislative policy making.

The book begins with a discussion of the creation of the presidency and the evolution of its legislative role. In examining the constitutional framework in which the institution was established and empowered, Chapter 1 provides a point from which to observe the development of the president's responsibilities and powers. The next five chapters treat separate but not totally independent legislative functions. Chapter 2 explores the White House staff structure, focusing primarily on the relationship between the president and his aides. Chapter 3 examines the clearance and coordination functions in the executive branch, paying particular attention to the role and operation of the Office of Management and Budget (until 1970, the Bureau of the Budget) and its interaction with the White House staff. The development of an annual legislative programing process and the growth of a White House policy staff is discussed in Chapter 4, while Chapter 5 details the organization and operation of the president's congressional liaison office. Chapter 6 looks at the implementation of legislative policy, examining some of the ways in which recent presidents and their staffs have sought to increase their influence over how policy is executed. The enlarged management role of the Office of Management and Budget (OMB) is also discussed in the light of attempts to improve the efficiency of the executive branch of government. The study covers the Truman-Ford period with an epilogue on the Carter transition at the end (Chapter 7).

Chapters 1 through 6 follow a similar format. There is a brief introduction that outlines the general organization and notes the descriptive and analytic emphasis. The body of the chapter discusses the evolution of one aspect of legislative policy making: White House staffing, central clearance and coordination, program development, congressional liaison, or policy implementation. A conclusion at the end of each chapter reviews the highlights of the development, analyzes the relationship between organization (mainly White House and OMB) and operation, and suggests future implications for the contemporary presidency.

The epilogue on the Carter transition (Chapter 7) treats the first nine months of the Carter presidency. It telescopes the major structural and stylistic features of the new administration as well as the processes by which legislative policy have been formulated, coordinated, and presented. It concludes with a synopsis of the president's executive reorganization plan and a discussion of its likely consequences for the legislative presidency.

Most of the information that is presented in the pages that follow comes from interviews with key presidential assistants and OMB officials. In all, over 80 members of presidential administrations from the Truman period to the present were interviewed in sessions ranging from one-half to two hours. While the bulk of these interviews were conducted between 1972 and 1976, some were held as late as July 1977.

Almost all the interviews were tape recorded and subsequently transcribed. Respondents who permitted taping of the interview were promised at the outset that there would be no quotation with attribution without their permission. As a consequence, all quotations in this book that are attributed to statements made during the interviews have been checked for accuracy with the individual concerned and, in a few cases, the grammar has been corrected by the respondent. No substantive changes have been made, however. For those statements where the individual chose to remain anonymous, the material appears in quotation but is *not* cited in the notes at the end of each chapter. All attributed statements, however, are cited in the notes.

The interviews were open ended and focused primarily on the participants themselves. What were their roles in legislative policy making? How did they perceive their own responsibilities? How did they evaluate the roles of others, including the president? What did they see as the principal patterns of interaction and influence? The participants were also asked to discuss the major strengths and weakness of presidential policy making from their perspective; obviously, where they sat affected what they saw.

In the early administrations especially, many of the respondents viewed policy making as an informal process. A phone call to another executive official, a discussion over lunch in the White House mess, a quickly called staff meeting, an option paper sent to or from their superiors were, from their vantage point, often the most typical ways in which decisions were made. When taken together, however, the comments and reflections provided a collective portrait, a picture of a policy process that generally followed certain guidelines, touched certain bases, and operated within certain time frames. It is this process which this book attempts to both describe and evaluate.

In general, the respondents had vivid recall, often remembering in minute detail incidents that occurred 20 to 30 years ago. Most wanted to tell their story, thought very highly of their experience, had great respect for their colleagues, and much admiration for their president. What many of them lacked was a sense of institutional history. A sizable proportion of White House aides admitted to knowing little of what went on before they arrived or after they left. There were some exceptions, but naturally presidential aides displayed most interest, awareness, and emotion where they, themselves, were deeply involved. Theirs were always the good old days. One testimony to this "intoxication effect," as well as to the many contacts made while working in the White House, is that the vast majority of lawyers who were in the president's special counsel's office, the office that was primarily responsible for coordinating and designing legislation until 1965, still work within a five- to seven-block radius of the White House!

To say that past and present presidential aides interviewed were cooperative would be an understatement. They were extremely helpful and very generous with their time. Only three former presidential aides, two who were staffers at the time, did not wish to be interviewed. For current White House assistants who work a 60- to 80-hour week, or even for busy Washington attorneys, to provide a 30- to 60-minute interview is a major sacrifice, but one that they were willing to make. Again and again, presidential assistants sitting in the Ford and Carter White Houses expressed the conviction that the public has a right to know. My guess is that this attitude was more than simply a product of Watergate, more than simply good politics. They believed it. More than most, they were conscious of their charge to be responsive and to maintain the public's trust.

In a democracy it is essential that information be available on how government works, how decisions are made, what forces impact on policy making, and how opinions, especially those from outside the government, affect the formulation and implementation of public policy. We know comparatively little about the presidency; the office has been shrouded in secrecy. The Congress, however, is a more open institution, one that political scientists have examined in greater depth over the last 20 years. One of the objectives of this book is to help rectify the balance in the literature on these two "legislative" institutions.

It is also important to understand shifts of powers and influence between and within institutions. In the aftermath of Vietnam and Watergate, a number of important questions have been raised on the organization and operation of the American presidency. What discretion does a president have and usually exercise in formulating, coordinating, and implementing legislative policy? How can he effect its enactment into law? How does his personality shape staffing relationships and how do these relationships, in turn, affect executive decision making? Hopefully, this book's description and analysis of the legislative presidency speaks to these questions and thereby contributes to the dialogue on how to achieve responsive and effective leadership.

Acknowledgments

In writing this book, I have been particularly fortunate to have had help, advice, and encouragement from a large number of colleagues, students, and friends. Mona Steinbach Wilson typed numerous drafts of the manuscript, often under severe time constraints. She made my task much easier. William Oman offered me guidance and support at a very early stage of this project for which I am grateful. Louis Fisher and Norman Thomas read the entire manuscript not once but twice. I profited greatly from their criticism. This book is more accurate, better organized, and more clearly focused as a result of their very helpful suggestions. Others who read and commented on individual chapters include George Edwards, Hugh Helco, Hugh LeBlanc, G. Calvin Mackenzie, Joe Pika, and Richard Rose. I am indebted to them as well as to the many former and present White House aides who read the portions of the manuscript that pertained to their administration.

Most of all I would like to thank three people without whom this book probably would never have been written. I owe my greatest intellectual debt to Richard E. Neustadt. His insights into the institution of the presidency have guided me from the time I began graduate work at Columbia University. Readers who are familiar with his work will see Professor Neustadt's influence throughout this book.

I was extremely lucky to have met James F. C. Hyde, Jr., when I first joined the faculty of The George Washington University in 1968. An experienced public servant, Jim's encyclopedic knowledge of the inner workings of the presidency provided me with an understanding of the machinery of government that was unobtainable from the literature alone. It was his initial desire to examine the legislative relationships between the White House and the Office of Management and Budget that led to the interviews on which much of this study is predicated.

And finally, I would like to thank my wife, Gayle. Having endured my course on the presidency and my complaints about gaps in the literature, she prodded me with the question, "Why don't *you* write a book?" and then provided constant encouragement while I was doing it. Her stylistic suggestions have made this a more readable work. It is to Gayle that I dedicate this book.

Stephen J. Wayne

CHAPTER 1

Making Legislative Policy: The Development of a Presidential Role

He shall from time to time give to the Congress Information
on the State of the Union, and recommend to their
Consideration such Measures as he shall judge
necessary and expedient; . . . .

Article II, Section 3,
United States Constitution

In theory, the Executive has nothing to do with legislation.
In practice, as things now are, the Executive is or ought
to be peculiarly representative of the people as a whole . . . .
Therefore a good Executive under present conditions of
American life must take a very active interest in getting
the right kind of legislation in addition
to performing his Executive duties . . . .

Theodore Roosevelt,
Autobiography (New York:
Macmillan, 1913), p. 292

As president, within the limits of basic principles, my
motto towards the Congress is communication, conciliation,
compromise and cooperation. . . . I do not want a
honeymoon. . . . I want a good marriage.

Gerald R. Ford,
August 12, 1974

**I have great respect for the Congress, but the Congress
is not capable of leadership. Our Founding
Fathers never felt the Congress
would lead this country.**

Jimmy Carter, as quoted in *The
National Journal,* May 29, 1976
p. 739

INTRODUCTION

The president has always had a legislative role but there has not always
been a legislative presidency. Most of the institutionalized aspects of the
presidency in Congress are of relatively recent vintage (post-World War
II) and coincide with the growth of the contemporary office. They are, in
fact, partially responsible for that growth.

The Constitution requires the president to regularly perform only a
few legislative duties. Designing an annual legislative program and exerting
influence to get it adopted were not part of these original responsibilities.
These functions developed over time and largely as a consequence of the
president's taking the policy initiative. Today, they have become expectations of the modern office and part of the criteria by which administrations are likely to be evaluated.

This chapter deals with the development of these expectations. The
first part examines the constitutional framework in which the presidency
and Congress were cast. It reviews the original design and the assumptions
on which this design was based. In the light of the dual needs to prevent
tyranny and make government work, the chapter discusses the respective
legislative roles and powers of Congress and the presidency. The second
section focuses on the expansion of this role from a presidential perspective. By emphasizing the relationship of strong presidents to Congress, it
illustrates the ways in which chief executives have presented their legislative goals and tried to extend their legislative influence. The institu-
tionalizing of these goals and the exertion of that influence are also
explored.

THE CONSTITUTIONAL PRESCRIPTION—
CONGRESS AS LEGISLATOR

The framers of the Constitution did not envision the president as chief
legislator. They did, however, anticipate that the institution would have
limited legislative functions. Within the framework of the separation of

powers system, the president was given specific legislative responsibilities and powers: to report on the State of the Union, to recommend necessary and expedient legislation, to convene the legislature on extraordinary occasions and adjourn it in cases of disagreement between the houses, and to exercise a qualified veto over bills and joint resolutions passed by Congress. Taken together, these duties were designed to prod and check the Congress but not to usurp its powers. That they could be used as a vehicle for challenging Congress' legislative authority or its role as principal domestic policy maker was not seriously contemplated. In fact, the fear was precisely the opposite. To most of those at the Constitutional Convention, the major problem was to prevent legislative encroachment. The eighteenth century in England and America was replete with numerous examples of the dangers of legislative rule.

Designing an Institutional Framework: The Constitutional Heritage

In the period following the Glorious Revolution in Britain at the end of the seventeenth century, the king's personal influence declined at the hands of Parliament. The burden of many executive decisions shifted from the monarch's control to that of his ministers. He was forced to heed their advice in large part because it was their ability to influence Parliament that would determine if his policy could be implemented.

In America, the governor suffered a similar fate although for different reasons. The position and influence of the colonial governor was adversely affected by the struggle with England. Most colonial governors had been empowered as strong executives with some legislative authority. By the end of the period, the colonial assemblies had become supreme. The governor's power to regulate public expenditures, to initiate and execute policy, to appoint and dismiss public officials, to convene and dissolve the legislature, to assent and dissent to legislation, and to command the military had been limited either directly or indirectly by the assembly's control of the purse. Only the power to pardon, which did not demand the large expenditure of funds, remained unscathed.

The first state constitutions legitimized the governors' weak position, granting the legislatures many of the executive powers they had exercised at the close of the colonial period. In every state but New York, the governors were clearly subordinate to the legislatures. They owed their selection to the legislature; they shared many of their functions with the legislature; they found most of their prerogatives subject to legislative supervision and control. Practically every state constitution denied its executive the sole authority to appoint and remove officers, pardon and reprieve citizens, summon and prorogue the assembly, and veto legislation. While a few states allowed the governor to participate in the exercise of these prerogatives, they permitted him to do so only with the advice and consent of one or both Houses. The one exception was the state of New York where the governor was granted much of the traditional executive authority.[1]

At the national level, there was no independent executive as such, although boards and later departments were created to help in the administration of government. The Continental and later Confederation Congress exercised legislative authority with no effective internal controls. The most basic constraint was the limitation of the powers themselves that were granted by the Articles of Confederation.

The confederation government could not tax, regulate commerce, or enforce its own acts and resolutions. It had the power to contract for the Union but not raise revenue; to conduct foreign relations but not control foreign commerce; to negotiate treaties but not compel their enforcement; to shoulder the country's defense but not independently raise, officer, or finance its troops. These deficiencies eventually proved fatal.

Criticism of the central government was frequently voiced during the Revolution and the postwar period. Congress was accused of being inefficient in operation and deficient in power. How to infuse the system with energy without at the same time creating a potentially tyrannous government was the basic problem which the framers had to tackle in Philadelphia.

The key to its resolution, at least as the founding fathers saw it, lay in the distribution of power within the government and between governments. This distribution of power was thought to be the best protection against tyranny. Charles de Montesquieu in his well-known treatise, *The Spirit of the Laws,* saw the separation of powers within the British system as the reason that political liberty was so well protected and preserved in England. Most of the framers had read Montesquieu and accepted the basic thrust of his argument.[2]

Montesquieu's view was predicated on the belief that social intercourse induces self-interested and self-assertive behavior. He suggested that in society people constantly seek to master and subdue one another.[3] Were they to be completely free, he argued, society would be in a perpetual state of war. Unrestrained freedom for Montesquieu was simply license. To prevent continuous conflict, law must be periodically formulated and continually executed. In such a lawful society, freedom is restricted and thereby becomes meaningful.

Such reasoning extended to legislators, administrators, and judges as well. They too will seek to expand their power—and, therefore, they too must be restrained. By establishing separate government institutions, assigning them specific and distinct powers, and finally safeguarding these powers from usurpation, Montesquieu hoped to preserve constitutional liberty, to keep government free. His genuine fear of the human propensity to dominate led him to the conclusion that the most effective check against the accumulation of power in government was its equitable distribution within the government itself.

The framers accepted the assumptions underlying Montesquieu's logic. They too believed self-interest to be a basic motive and accumulated power a natural but unhappy consequence. To prevent this, they too felt it necessary to distribute power among separate and independent institutions. The structure of their newly devised government and the division of its authority can be understood within this conceptual framework. There were deviations to be sure, but the model served as a basic frame of reference for the Constitution in general and the presidency in particular.[4]

Separating and Securing Legislative Powers: The Original Balance

Article I entrusts the Congress with "all legislative powers herein granted." Section 8 of this article lists the specific powers that were granted, the ones considered both national and legislative in character. Section 9 indicates some of the limitations of that authority (see Figure I-I). Article II grants the president the executive power, but its enumeration is far less detailed.

The task of deciding what was properly legislative and properly executive was not particularly difficult. The framers relied on traditional concepts of authority for their investiture of power. Only where they deviated from these concepts did extensive debate ensue. The general grants themselves aroused little discussion.[5]

Controversy at the Constitutional Convention and during the ratification debates arose over those powers that were shared and/or checked. Prerogatives that allegedly had been most abused in the colonial, revolutionary, and Confederation periods, such as the making of war and the formulation of treaties, fell into this category. While presidential leadership in foreign affairs was considered essential, it was also viewed as potentially dangerous to allow the president to decide important policy matters alone, except in emergency situations, on a short-term basis, and subject to congressional review. The problem was how to combine energy, dispatch, and responsibility, especially in foreign affairs. The solution—joining presidential initiative to congressional declaration or senatorial advice and consent—was thought to provide adequate safeguards against arbitrary executive action and an advisory mechanism for presidents when they got into the policy-making business.

The sharing of authority between the president and Senate, however, was in apparent violation of the concept of separation. It precipitated considerable debate and criticism. The checking of powers, however, met with more general approbation. Negatives were viewed as essential to the maintenance of balanced government. This fine distinction between the

Designation of Powers	Prohibitions and Checks	Provisions for Contingencies
Article I, Section 1 – "All legislative Powers herein granted;"	Section 9 – Congress shall not have the Power to:	Section 8 – "To make all Laws which shall be necessary and proper for carrying into Execution the fore-going Powers ..."
Section 8 – Congress shall have the Power to:	1. Suspend the writ habeas corpus except in cases of rebellion or invasion	
1. Lay and collect taxes	2. Pass bill of attainder or ex post facto law	
2. Coin and borrow money	3. Lay a tax on exports	
3. Regulate interstate and foreign commerce	4. Give preference to the commerce of particular states	
4. Establish bankruptcy laws	5. Draw money from Treasury except by appropriation	
5. Provide for punishment of counterfeiters		
6. Establish post offices	6. Grant titles of nobility	
7. Grant copyrights and patents	Article II, Section 2 – The advice and consent of the Senate required for treaties (2/3) and appointments (majority)	
8. Establish a federal court system		
9. Declare war		
10. Raise, support, and make rules for a standing army and navy		
11. Define and punish piracies		
12. Organize, arm, discipline, and call up the militia		

THE CONGRESS

Designation of Powers	Prohibitions and Checks	Provisions for Contingencies
Article II, Section 2 – Power to make treaties subject to Senate advice and consent	Article I, Section 7 – Veto provision	Article II, Section 2 –
		1. Inform Congress on the State of the Union
		2. Recommend necessary and expedient measures
		3. Convene both Houses on extraordinary occasions and adjourn them in cases of disagreement between them

THE PRESIDENT

FIGURE I-I.   The Legislative Authority

sharing and checking of powers seemed to hinge on whether the exercise of the authority protected or threatened the integrity of the principal spheres. Shared powers such as appointments and treaty making raised serious questions in this respect; checked powers such as the veto did not.

Giving Congress the power to impeach executive and judicial officials and the president the right to veto legislative enactments was defended on the grounds that each was considered a hedge against the balance becoming upset and undone. Although the veto was legislative in character, it had been regarded as a traditional executive weapon, a protection against possible usurpation by the Congress. That executives in the past had also used their veto power to prevent the enactment of legislation they opposed presented a dilemma to the framers. They debated three possible solutions: deny the power to the president, make him share it with a council of judicial officials, or have him exercise it alone. The recent history of legislative dominance made the first and second alternatives unacceptable. Since an unqualified presidential veto was also feared, the founding fathers opted for presidential exercise with the potential of a congressional override by a two-thirds vote. The constitution of the state of Massachusetts had a similar arrangement.

The other legislative duties that were given the president stemmed less from the desire to check the legislature than from the necessities of eighteenth-century government. The obligation to summon and adjourn the Congress in extraordinary circumstances, to inform them of developments between legislative sessions, and to recommend measures for their consideration were duties that the kings of England and the colonial governors had performed. While most state executives lacked the formal authority to exercise these responsibilities, several did so anyway on an informal basis.

The size of the country, the time it took to travel within it, the anticipated length of the congressional sessions (three to four months), and the lack of national newspapers or other efficient means of communication made the recommending and reporting functions especially important. That the president's tenure was continuous and his orientation national made the chief executive the most appropriate person to inform and propose.

By granting these legislative duties to the president, however, the framers had wanted to provide for the contingencies of government, not substitute in the long run and on a regular basis for congressional hegemony over domestic policy making. It is clear that the original design was intended to give Congress the legislative authority that was, in fact, the power to determine national policy. The president had the capacity to stimulate the exercise of this legislative power by his information and his recommendations and to constrain or even negate it by his veto but not to assume it by virtue of any inherent or implied executive or legislative power.[6]

Having the president as a principal legislator or even as a major force in the legislative process conflicted with the notion of separate and independent institutions, each exercising domain over a primary sphere of authority. So long as the role envisioned for the national government remained relatively limited, and the protection and preservation of constitutional liberty remained a primary objective, securing rather than sharing powers continued to be the guiding principle of the new system.

The balance between energy and safety was tilted toward safety on the dual assumption that a great deal of energy was not needed and that authority had to be divided and secured in order to prevent institutional despotism.[7] Once the first of these assumptions began to change, however, the system had to adjust accordingly. How to unify what the Constitution divided, how to induce cooperation between separate and independent institutions, became a critical test for the conduct of presidential-congressional relations.

THE EVOLUTION OF THE PRESIDENT'S LEGISLATIVE FUNCTIONS

Limiting Presidential Involvement: Nineteenth-Century Congressional Relations

Presidential involvement in the legislative process was extremely limited in the nineteenth-century. Not only did the philosophy of institutional separation act as a deterrent to an active presidential role, but the way in which the party system developed, at least before the 1870s, also discouraged most presidents from using the Congress as an arena for exerting political leadership. The disintegration of the Federalist party, the factionalization of the Democratic-Republicans, and the loosely structured Whig coalition provided little incentive for presidents to engage in legislative activity.

Washington was careful not to intrude on the prerogatives of Congress. He recommended only three measures to the legislature—one dealing with the militia, another with the regular army, and a third with a temporary commission to negotiate with some Indians. Each of these recommendations was accepted. And he disapproved of only two bills, one of which he believed violated the Constitution.

While Washington's stance toward Congress was restrained, his department secretaries were more actively involved. During the administration's first term, Congress looked to the executive departments for information and aid when formulating legislation. Hamilton, as secretary of the treasury, was particularly active and influential. He regularly sent requests for appropriations to Congress, testified before its committees, and sought to mobilize support for his financial proposals.[8] Senator William Maclay noted in his journal that "Mr. Hamilton is all powerful and fails in nothing he attempts. . . . Nothing was done without him." [9]

With Democratic-Republican strength growing, the Congress, especially the House of Representatives, took a less sympathetic stance toward the cabinet's legislative involvement in the administration's second term. In 1792, Congress had instituted its first investigation of the executive, an inquiry into General St. Clair's defeat by the Indians. In a straight party vote in 1796, the House of Representatives demanded to see Washington's diplomatic instructions to Jay. By the end of the Adams presidency, partisan differences between a Democratic-Republican controlled Congress and a Federalist executive had turned the cooperative spirit into one of contention.

Presidential-congressional relations improved during the Jefferson period largely as a consequence of Jefferson's position as acknowledged leader of the Democratic-Republican party. Coming into office in the so-called Revolution of 1800, he was the first president to seek and achieve partisan support in Congress. Jefferson helped organize the Democratic-Republican party and made its floor leadership responsive to his interests. He devised a system that had members of Congress reporting secretly to him and working confidentially for legislative proposals he backed and in some cases, had even helped draft.

President Jefferson's cabinet met on a regular basis to consider legislative measures and actually write proposals. The secretaries would transmit these proposals to the appropriate congressional committee. As in the previous administrations, the treasury secretary was the most active of the cabinet officials in the legislative arena. Albert Gallatin, Jefferson's secretary of the treasury, regularly attended congressional committee meetings, guided measures through Congress, and helped the president manage party affairs. He and Secretary of State James Madison frequently talked with members of Congress about policy questions.[10] They worked to maintain party cohesion by participating in the Democratic-Republican caucuses in the Senate and House respectively.

To a large extent, the use of department heads compensated for lack of presidential staff. In the words of James Young:

> [They] allowed Presidents to maintain, for what it was worth, the outward appearance of conformity to community norms which decreed social distance between the President and Congress . . . and it gave Presidents particularly good access to the congressional communities with which department heads had, then as now, much business. The use of executive agents also permitted what neither public messages to congress nor personal transactions between the President and legislators did: a means for presenting and pressing upon Congress legislation in which the President did not want or could not afford to be directly implicated.[11]

For his own part, Jefferson personally entertained congressmen. He held small dinner parties in the White House which were regarded as "the talk of Washington." [12] Ostensibly, politics were not discussed, but Jefferson used these occasions to convey his sentiments and enhance his political capital.

By virtue of his ability to maximize partisan support and even win Federalist backing for some of his proposals, Jefferson was able to affect congressional deliberations and thereby bridge the constitutional and social separation that characterized politics and government during this period. [13] His political skills stood as a model for twentieth-century presidents intent on imprinting their stamp on the legislature but as an exception to the normal course of nineteenth-century presidential-congressional relations.

Jefferson's immediate successors, Madison, Monroe, and John Quincy Adams, were not nearly as resourceful and successful in dealing with Congress even though they utilized many of the same techniques. They too took positions on legislation and had confidential agents in Congress. They too used their cabinet officials in liaison activities; they too had dinner parties although the small, intimate affairs were discontinued in favor of larger and more formal occasions.

But the presidents following Jefferson were less able to utilize tools of executive leadership in the legislature. They could not use their patronage powers as a means of solidifying party support. They lost control of their party caucus to congressional leaders. They did not utilize the veto as a tool of presidential leadership. Madison, Monroe, and John Quincy Adams exercised the veto only eight times.

The decline and disintegration of the Federalist party and the increasing factionalization of the Democratic-Republicans made it difficult for these presidents to mobilize political constituencies in the executive branch or on Capitol Hill. Internal disagreements began developing within their cabinets and this disunity encouraged congressional committee-departmental relations that bypassed the chief executive. Department heads would send reports and information directly to Congress without even informing the president. More and more, these reports tended to reflect department positions rather than presidential views. Some cabinet officers went so far as to actually undercut the president. Young illustrates the problems of President Monroe:

> [His] Secretary of War used his position in the cabinet of a President publicly committed against internal improvements to urge legislation on internal improvements and to wage a presidential campaign on that platform. Monroe's Secretary of State arranged with partisans in Congress to compel the release of an executive report the President had directed to be withheld. His Secretary of the Treasury concealed a budgetary deficit from the President while transmitting the knowledge to Congress, and was driven from the White House by the President, armed with fire tongs, for

insulting language to his chief. Monroe ended his administration not on speaking terms with the head of the Treasury, with whom he communicated through an intermediary.[14]

The growing autonomy of the secretaries reduced the president's influence in and with Congress which, in turn, decreased his incentive for getting involved in legislative policy making. Presidents Madison and Monroe had little choice but to adhere to a philosophy of institutional separation and a political posture of nonintervention. John Quincy Adams quickly found noninvolvement to be a safe and realistic tack to follow. It was not until the administration of Andrew Jackson that a president once again tried to assert strong legislative leadership.

Jackson had less success than Jefferson in using the party as a vehicle for influencing Congress. Lacking a cohesive congressional majority, Jackson was forced to rely on his claim of a public mandate and his use of the president's appointment and veto powers. The use of patronage combined with the increased demands on Congress for government jobs initially produced an instrument of considerable political import for the president.[15] Similarly, Jackson's vetoing of legislation on the grounds of expediency opened up the veto as an instrument of legislative influence. In addition to maximizing the political potential of veto, he also used the veto message as a means both to claim and elicit public support.

The inability of most nineteenth-century presidents following Jackson to control or effectively channel their party's machinery in Congress toward their own legislative goals seemed to preclude a strong exertion of presidential leadership on Capitol Hill. The Democratic presidents had even less political power and popular support than Jackson and, consequently, exercised less legislative influence. The two Whig presidents were philosophically opposed to a presidential role in Congress. Harrison and Taylor in their inaugural addresses both stressed the limitations of the executive's legislative authority.

> [Harrison:] I cannot conceive that by fair construction any or either of its [the Constitution's] provisions would be found to constitute the President a part of the legislative power.[16]

> [Taylor:] The Executive has authority to recommend (not to dictate) measures to Congress. Having performed that duty, the Executive department of the Government cannot rightfully control the decision of Congress on any subject of legislation until that decision shall have been officially submitted to the President for approval. The check provided by the Constitution in the clause conferring the qualified veto will never be exercised by me except in the cases contemplated by the Fathers of the Republic. I view it as an extreme measure, to be resorted to only in extraordinary cases, as when it may become necessary to defend the executive against encroachments of the legislative power or to prevent hasty and inconsiderate or unconstitutional legislation.[17]

Lincoln as a congressman also seemed to support this position, but as president he exercised more power by himself in the absence of the Congress than any previous chief executive. In an 11-week period, he enlarged the military beyond its legal limits and committed it to battle, instituted a blockade of the South, called up the militia, pledged United States credit for a large loan, suspended the writ of habeas corpus, closed the mails to treasonable material, and authorized the arrest of suspected traitors. He then called Congress into special session to legitimize what he had done, justifying his actions to the legislature and the nation on the grounds of the crisis and its threat to the survival of the Union. Lincoln also waited until the adjournment of Congress to issue his Emancipation Proclamation in 1864.

During the congressional session, Lincoln proposed legislative measures and worked to influence their adoption. In at least one instance, he sent a special message to Congress requesting legislation and accompanied it with a draft bill.[18] He also used the threat of a veto to successfully force or prevent changes in pending legislation.

After the election of a majority of radical Republicans in 1864, however, Lincoln's ability to influence Congress declined significantly. His assassination left Andrew Johnson with the unenviable task of attempting to persuade the radical Republicans of the merits of his administration's reconstruction proposals. He was not successful. His eventual impeachment indicated the extent to which presidential-congressional relations had deteriorated during this period. It also revealed how far the Congress was willing to go in imposing constraints on the president.

In 1867, Congress passed the Tenure of Office Act over Johnson's veto. The act prohibited the president from removing civil officers appointed with the advice and consent of the Senate without its approval. If the Senate was not in session, the president could suspend an officer and name an acting replacement. But when the Senate reconvened, acting officials could remain only if the Senate consented. Under the law, the failure of the Senate to consent to an acting appointment would revert the position to the previous officeholder. Johnson's removal of Secretary of War Stanton, without Senate concurrence, was the act that precipitated his impeachment by the House of Representatives. He was acquitted by a single vote in the Senate.

With the exception of the first years of the Lincoln presidency, Congress grew to dominate relations with the president until the end of the century. Its members exercised an increasing interest in and influence over lower-level appointments.[19] Most successful political initiatives emanated from within the Congress. Presidents could muster little support for their proposals. As a consequence, their recommendations to Congress became almost perfunctory and tended to have little impact. Limitations placed on the exercise of executive power worked to discourage presidential requests.

Just about the only effective tool chief executives could employ was the veto. Its use increased sharply during this period. While most vetoes were exercised against private pension bills, some were used to defend the president's authority from congressional encroachment and the president's policy positions from congressional attack. Hayes, for example, negated six laws containing riders that would have restricted his powers as commander-in-chief. Cleveland vetoed several major authorization and appropriation statutes.[20]

Curiously, at the very time Congress was asserting its authority against the president, it was also becoming more dependent on the executive departments for aid in servicing constituency demands. A growing number of personnel requests, patent appeals, pension applications and other pecuniary claims against the government were being brought to the attention of members of Congress who, in turn, were forced to look to the executive branch for help. Providing these services for the legislature quickly developed into an important departmental function, one that brought Congress and the bureaucracy closer together but ultimately proved to be a political liability for the presidency.

"Congressional supremacy," in the words of politics professor Woodrow Wilson, best described the relationship between national legislature and executive branch during the post-Civil War period. Wilson saw power clearly in the hands of the congressional leadership. In his well-known treatise, *Congressional Government,* Professor Wilson suggests that the president was a servant of Congress even in his executive capacity:

> The business of the President, occasionally great, is usually not much above routine. Most of the time it is *mere* administration, mere obedience of directions from the masters of policy, the Standing Committees.[21]

Seeing the veto as the president's major weapon, Wilson argued, "the President is no greater than his prerogative of veto makes him; he is, in other words, powerful rather as a branch of the legislature than as the titular head of the Executive." [22]

Taking the Policy Initiative:
Presidents in the Early Twentieth Century

By the time Wilson became president, conditions had changed and he subsequently had modified his views. Presidents William McKinley and Theodore Roosevelt were able to work with their congressional leadership. McKinley used his popularity among congressional Republicans to assert his influence without arousing their ire; he was the first president to do so successfully since Lincoln. Roosevelt developed a close relationship with Speaker Cannon, consulting him on most major policy initiatives. Cannon's power in the House enabled him to mobilize support for the president's proposals. The close relationship between the Speaker and the president continued until Roosevelt's last year in office.[23]

Theodore Roosevelt's more active involvement in congressional affairs was a product of his personality and his philosophy. Writing in his *Autobiography,* he stated:

> In theory, the Executive has nothing to do with legislation. In practice, as things now are, the Executive is or ought to be peculiarly representative of the people as a whole. . . . Therefore, a good Executive under present conditions of American life must take a very active interest in getting the right kind of legislation in addition to performing his Executive duties with an eye single to the public welfare.[24]

Roosevelt's messages to Congress revealed a larger, more clearly defined program than those of any of his Republican predecessors since Lincoln.

Taft continued to be involved in legislative activities but his more conservative philosophy did not encourage presidential initiatives. Nor did Taft enjoy the same kind of relationship with the congressional leadership, especially the Speaker, that Roosevelt had. In fact, the revolt against the Speaker's power in the House of Representatives in 1910 made it more difficult for a single person in the House to effectively influence its deliberations.[25]

Nonetheless, a more equitable balance in presidential-congressional relations had been achieved, and this caused Professor Wilson to revise his thesis. In a series of lectures at Columbia University, Wilson admitted that the potential power of the president was great. The president could be as big a man as he wanted, Wilson asserted. He could use his position as party and national leader to enhance his political power and thereby exert influence on Congress:

> His capacity will set the limit; and if Congress be overborne by him, it will be no fault of the makers of the Constitution,—it will be from no lack of constitutional powers on its part, but only because the President has the nation behind him, and Congress has not. He has no means of compelling Congress except through public opinion.[26]

Wilson saw the rousing of public opinion as no small advantage in trying to influence Congress. The president, he contended, need not adhere to a literal reading of the Constitution:

> it is not necessary to the integrity of even the literary theory of the Constitution to insist that such recommendations should be merely perfunctory. . . . The Constitution certainly does not forbid the President to back them up, as General Washington did, with such personal force and influence as he may possess.[27]

In fact, Wilson seemed to suggest that as national problems increased, the president would have an obligation to exert his influence. Wilson's remarks were prophetic for his own presidency.

As chief executive, he saw his role as analogous to that of the British prime minister—to propose an integrated set of measures which addressed social and economic problems and to utilize his personal and political influence to get them adopted. Wilson personally supervised the development of policy initiatives in his administration. He chose the priorities, helped formulate the legislation, exhorted and rallied his cabinet, and then collaborated with members of Congress in urging their enactment. As president, he employed many of the same techniques Jefferson and Jackson had used in trying to affect congressional deliberations. He reinstituted the party caucus in Congress; he had cabinet officers explain and help drum up support for his policy proposals. His postmaster general, Albert Burleson, a former congressman, handled the appointment of local postmasters while acting as an unofficial liaison agent in the House. Wilson also had confidential friends on the Hill. Reputedly, John Nance Garner, a congressman from Texas, provided the president with information and support, surreptitiously sneaking trips to the White House into his congressional schedule.[28]

Wilson went to the Congress himself on several occasions. He was the first president since John Adams who personally delivered the State of the Union Address.[29] In tailoring his message to a verbal format, Wilson shortened the speech. He reduced the traditional list of presidential recommendations to Congress to a succinct statement of the goals he intended to achieve. He then employed special messages to highlight individual proposals.

Wilson's tack was to concentrate on one legislative measure at a time. He personally lobbied for his own proposals, utilizing the president's room off the Senate chamber to receive and confer with congressional party officials. The president had a special telephone line installed between the Senate and White House. Occasionally, the administration even supplied its supporters with draft bills and supporting material they could use in congressional committees and on the floor.

Between 1913 and 1917 Wilson's skillful leadership of the Democratic-controlled Congress resulted in the passage of several far-reaching measures. These included the Adamson Act (which provided an eight-hour day for railroad workers), the Underwood Tariff, the Federal Reserve Act, the Clayton Anti-trust Act, and the act that established the Federal Trade Commission. Wilson's personal involvement in the legislative process seemed to augur a further shift in the presidential-congressional balance and one that was not universally applauded. By 1917, some were already sounding the death knell for Congress.

> The private individual of Congress is dead, and it is surely important that there is none to sing his requiem. The traditional separation of powers has broken down for the simple reason that it results only in confounding them. Congress may delay presidential action; but there is evidence enough, even apart from the fact of war, that it is finding it increasingly difficult

ultimately to thwart it. For congressional debate has largely ceased to influence the character of public opinion. . . . Nor is the individual member of Congress alone in his eclipse. The Congressional committees have become less the molders of legislation than the recipients who may alter its details.[30]

After the Senate's defeat of the Versailles treaty and Wilson's failure to rally support, the president's powers looked a little less formidable.

In an apparent reaction to the Wilson presidency, candidate Warren Harding stated that, if elected, he would recommend legislation as the Constitution required but would not interfere with Congress in its deliberations—a promise he later came to regret.[31] Harding's Republican successors, Calvin Coolidge and Herbert Hoover, attempted to steer a middle course between asserting and abdicating their legislative duties. The Congress, however, actually enlarged their role in the legislative arena by its passage of the Budget and Accounting Act of 1921. This act required the president to deliver a budget message and assume responsibility for the financial requests of all executive departments and agencies. While Presidents Coolidge and Hoover did not utilize this budgetary function to extend their legislative influence, subsequent presidents did.

Coolidge and Hoover did have some legislation drafted in the White House ana sent to Congress. Both considered it to be the president's job to try to affect congressional deliberations although neither used Wilson-like tactics to do so. Their conservative philosophy undoubtedly influenced their conception of a limited legislative role for the president. This philosophy, combined with the dispersal of power on the Hill, did not encourage extensive legislative activity on their part.

Extending Presidential Influence: Roosevelt and the 1930s

Franklin Roosevelt, coming into office in the throes of a depression, believed it absolutely essential for the president to take the policy initiative. In his first inaugural address, Roosevelt stated:

> I am prepared under my constitutional duty to recommend the measures that a stricken Nation in the midst of a stricken world may require. These measures or such other measures as Congress may build out of its experience and wisdom, I shall seek within my constitutional authority to bring to speedy adoption.[32]

Having a sizable Democratic majority that was inclined to support policy initiatives and being the kind of person who was not adverse to using his personal influence to get them adopted, Roosevelt quickly and dramatically became deeply involved in the legislative process.

The most immediate problem facing the new president was a crisis that had caused runs on banks and an increasing number of bank failures. The day after his inauguration, the president declared a bank holiday, called Congress into special session, and asked the legislature when it convened 4 days later to pass an emergency banking bill that he and his staff had prepared. The House of Representatives did so in 38 minutes— the Senate in about 3 hours.

The special session, lasting 100 days, resulted in the passage of a series of emergency measures designed by the president and his aides to address the most pressing economic problems. In addition to the banking act, statutes passed during this period included the Truth in Security Act, the Agricultural Adjustment Act, and the National Industrial Recovery Act. Designed both to regulate and stimulate the financial, agricultural, and business sectors of the economy, the legislation also created new executive agencies such as the Federal Deposit Insurance Corporation, Farm Credit Administration, and National Recovery Administration. The establishment of these and other New Deal agencies during the Roosevelt period marked the beginnings of the rapid growth of the bureaucracy which was to have such a profound effect on the president's ability to oversee the implementation of legislative policy.

In the period from 1934–1936 another series of legislative measures designed by the president and his staff was subsequently passed by Congress. Known as the second New Deal, these proposals were distinguished from the emergency legislation of the first 100 days by their orientation away from voluntary compliance and toward more direct help for the small farmers, laborers, and taxpayers, the principal groups in the Roosevelt coalition. The Soil Conservation and Domestic Allotments Act, the Wagner Act, the Social Security Act, and various public works projects provided aid and work for millions of Americans. This legislation also established bureaucratic structures to administer the new regulations and programs. Agencies such as the National Labor Relations Board, the Social Security Administration, and the Works Progress Administration were created.

After 1936, Roosevelt ran into increasing difficulty with conservative Democrats in Congress and was not as successful in achieving his domestic legislative objectives. The war forced both president and Congress to turn to international problems and war-related activity which in turn dissipated some of the tension that had been building between the two institutions. It was left to Harry S. Truman to continue Roosevelt's domestic policy efforts.

In expanding the president's legislative role, Franklin Roosevelt utilized his cabinet secretaries as well as his personal advisors to draft and push for legislative proposals. During his administration a central clearing process was expanded to include policy proposals in addition to budget requests which had to be approved by the president or the budget director.

This enabled the president to oversee legislative policy emanating from the departments and agencies in much the same manner as he could oversee and take responsibility for their financial requests. Roosevelt made greater use of the special message than any of his predecessors. He sent over a hundred such messages to Congress that indicated the need for legislation, frequently contained specific recommendations, and in many cases were accompanied by draft bills.

During the 1932–1936 period especially, Roosevelt was particularly effective in mobilizing support. Unlike Jefferson and Wilson, he did not use the party caucus. Rather, he dealt with political leaders and committee heads on a one-to-one basis. His usual practice was to send a message to Congress requesting specific legislation and then quickly follow with the actual draft bill. Prior to the submission of the legislation, Roosevelt usually made arrangements to have his friends formally introduce the bill. The president also lined up some support for it in both Houses.

Roosevelt continued the practice of sending personal agents to the Hill. Washington lawyers James H. Rowe, Jr., Benjamin V. Cohen, and Thomas G. Corcoran helped lobby for New Deal legislation and also participated in the drafting of some proposals. Roosevelt also had his postmaster general, James Farley, distribute patronage and provide other aid in shoring up votes on critical issues. From Roosevelt's time on, the use of legislative agents by the president became the standard practice.

Finally, Roosevelt realized the potential of the veto both as a positive and negative instrument of presidential power. "Give me a bill I can veto," he is supposed to have told his aides on several occasions. During his years as president, Roosevelt vetoed 635 bills and had only 9 vetoes overridden. By using the veto so frequently, he was able to employ it effectively to prevent riders, amendments, and laws he considered unwise, impolitic, or both.

Roosevelt's contribution to the legislative presidency related more to his level of activity than to any innovation in purpose or technique. Believing it to be a presidential responsibility to formulate national policy, especially during periods of crisis, he placed legislation high on his list of priorities. He submitted more special messages and more drafts of bills and exercised more vetoes than any other president. As a consequence, he expanded the legislative expectations and demands on the presidential office. In the past, such an expansion had produced a reaction by Congress. There was a reaction to the Roosevelt presidency but it was more to Roosevelt personally than to his enlargement of the president's legislative role. In fact, the Seventy-ninth and Eightieth Congresses actually recognized and accepted this enlargement by the passage of statutes in 1946 and 1947 designating presidential economic and national security responsibilities.

Regularizing Presidential Activity:
Post-World War II Domestic Policy Making

The institutionalized presidency follows Roosevelt. It is characterized by the continuation of presidential policy making and the enlargement of the president's policy-making sphere; by the high priority placed on domestic policy objectives, especially during Democratic administrations; by the high level of legislative activity; and by the creation of structures and processes designed to initiate, coordinate, and implement the president's legislative program. The assumption that it was a presidential responsibility to propose legislation and try to influence its adoption was not questioned after the mid-1950s. In fact, the role of policy initiation was seen as a primary obligation of the office, one which could not be shirked without reprobation. In 1947, when Truman asked Congress for legislation to combat inflation, he was criticized by the Republican majority for not presenting a draft bill.[33] When Eisenhower failed to propose a legislative program during his first year as president, he was criticized from both sides of the isle. "Don't expect us to start from scratch on what you people want," an irate member of the House Foreign Affairs Committee told an Eisenhower official. "That's not the way we do things here. You draft the bills and we work them over." [34]

Upon becoming president, Truman quickly assumed the policy initiative. Promising to extend Roosevelt's New Deal, he proposed a variety of legislative measures designed to build on his predecessor's accomplishments. Congress, however, rejected most of his requests. It abolished the Fair Employment Practices Committee against his recommendations, failed to enact his housing program, and rejected his plan for price controls. Truman's only major legislative success during this early period, the enactment of the Employment Act of 1946, extended the president's powers and responsibility to maintain a high level of employment and economic activity.

Faced with a Republican majority in the 1946–1948 period, Truman continued to suggest legislative measures to Congress but the Republicans were unreceptive. Instead, they and southern Democrats together severely cut the president's budget requests, opposed civil rights legislation and passed the Taft-Hartley Act over his veto. The reaction of the Republican Congress to Truman's legislative proposals became a major campaign issue in 1948 and is generally credited with contributing to the president's victory. That the "do nothing Congress," as Truman termed it, could become a major issue in a presidential election testifies to how far public expectations of presidential leadership and congressional responses in the legislative arena had been expanded by 1948. Beginning in that year, Truman also started the practice of presenting some of his requests in the form of an annual legislative program. This too has become an expectation which presidents have regularly met with the one exception of Eisenhower's failure in 1954.

While all presidents have proposed legislative programs, they have not placed equal emphasis on the development and enactment of new policy initiatives. In general, Democratic administrations have had their goals more closely tied to innovative legislative proposals than have Republican administrations. Presidents Kennedy and Johnson put social and economic legislation high on their lists of political objectives.

Even before his inauguration, Kennedy and his staff had started planning to extend the frontiers of the New and Fair Deal programs to include legislative initiatives in the areas of civil rights, education, medical aid to the elderly, and national park and seashore preservation. Between 1961 and 1962, the administration submitted most of these new proposals to Congress, where they met considerable opposition and were stymied by a coalition of southern Democrats and Republicans. Some extensions of old programs, initiated by Presidents Roosevelt and Truman, were approved, however. These included an increase in minimum wages, public housing, community health projects, and the traditional public works measures.

It took the tragedy of the Kennedy assassination, the public and congressional support the new president received, the huge Democratic majorities in 1964, and Lyndon Johnson's experience and skill as a legislative leader to win backing for Kennedy's innovative legislation as well as for his own Great Society program. Johnson's remarkable success in the 1964–1966 period clearly established his preeminence as a chief legislator and indicated the scope of the president's power for shaping public policy. In examining the source of legislative initiatives during the period, author James Sundquist saw the president as clearly dominant:

> With the exception of anti-pollution measures, the major legislative impulses of the 1961–66 period came from a single source—the White House. Members of Congress could retard, accelerate, or deflect those impulses, and they could expand, limit or modify the specific proposals initiated from the White House. But they could not set in motion the legislative stream itself. Constitutionally, they had every right to do so. Theoretically, perhaps, they had the opportunity. Practically, they did not.[35]

In fact, by the end of the 1960s it seemed that the legislative power of the presidency had extended beyond the mere suggestion of policy to the declaration of it. Presidents and their staffs helped set the agenda for congressional debate; they developed proposals from inside and outside the executive branch; they had the legislation drafted and presented it to Congress; they monitored congressional deliberations and influenced congressional judgments. Some political scientists went so far as to claim that

presidential and congressional roles had been reversed; that the only effective instrument for Congress to exercise in the legislative process was a veto or a rubber stamp. Samuel Huntington put it this way:

> Congress can defend its autonomy only by refusing to legislate, and it can legislate only by surrendering its autonomy. . . . If Congress legislates, it subordinates itself to the President; if it refuses to legislate, it alienates itself from public opinion. Congress can assert its power or it can pass laws; but it cannot do both.[36]

Huntington's view was not unanimous. Others noted the large number of laws in which the president had taken little or no interest and the number of so-called presidential initiatives that previously had been introduced by members of Congress. In studying the legislative history of 90 bills between 1880 and 1940, Lawrence Chamberlain argued "not that the President is less important than generally supposed but that Congress is more important."[37] Ronald C. Moe and Steven C. Teel reached similar conclusions.[38]

Another political scientist, John R. Johannes, examined a number of case studies since World War II and contended that the president's position was superior for initiating legislation by virtue of the institutional and political resources at his disposal:

> Because of the powers and incentives built into his unique position in the political system, in both legislation and administration, the President, assisted by the executive bureaucracy and his staff, usually leads in defining problems, issues and solutions. Congress is left with the review and oversight function, adding to the technical-political proposals of the President a second round of primarily (though not exclusively) political judgments based on a different, segmented, constituency to test the acceptability of the President's recommendations.[39]

Johannes concluded, however, that Congress retains "a modifying or second guess capability" and that it could and would take the initiative if, for a variety of reasons, the president chose not to do so.[40] In his book, *Congressional Power: Congress and Social Charges,* Gary Orfield has pointed out that Congress constantly remolds programs through its amendments and appropriations. "While single changes may not be dramatic," he writes, "the accumulation of year by year alterations can ultimately be more important than the initial legislative process."[41] Orfield suggests that Congress' contribution is consistently underestimated because of the high visibility given to the president's legislative programs. While the debate over the chief initiator will undoubtedly persist,[42] the president's role as a chief policy maker, a proposer of legislation, and a lobbyist in the legislative process has not been challenged per se.

Richard M. Nixon and Gerald R. Ford also developed, presented, and fought for their own legislative proposals although neither of them displayed the same kinds of enthusiasm for new and innovative domestic social and economic programs that John Kennedy and Lyndon Johnson had. Faced with opposition majorities in both houses throughout their presidencies, Nixon and Ford used their executive powers to counter Congress' legislative priorities. Nixon impounded funds that the Democratic majority had approved. Finding his impoundment authority extremely limited by the Budget and Impoundment Control Act of 1974, Ford utilized the veto extensively to prevent what he considered to be unwise programs and unwarranted spending.

Despite the lower priorities which these presidents attached to new social policy, their administrations' legislative activity continued at approximately the same pace as that of previous administrations. The number of special messages, legislative drafts, department and agency opinions, and testimony did not decline appreciably. The number of White House and executive branch agents engaged in congressional liaison efforts remained roughly the same. The number of presidential vetoes was increased, evidencing the philosophical and partisan differences between these Republican presidents and their Democratic Congresses. The continuance of this relatively high level of activity suggests that the legislative functions and responsibilities of the executive branch and, to some extent, even the president, are relatively independent of the emphasis which a particular administration wishes to place on the achievement of certain legislative goals.

CONCLUSION

The presidency has become heavily involved in the business of legislation despite the constitutional investiture of legislative powers to the Congress. The creation of separate and independent branches of government with designated spheres of authority was presumed to require some institutional interaction, especially between president and Congress during periods of emergencies, but it was certainly not intended to provide inordinate amounts of executive influence. On the contrary, the president's legislative duties and powers were designed to utilize his national perspective, and if need be, to protect his executive authority. The right to recommend and veto, however, provided a lever which political influence was able to expand into powerful legislative weapons. The carefully constructed balance of powers was thus upset partially by the mechanism designed to protect and secure it and partially by the growing needs for legislative initiatives in the domestic sphere.

With the major exceptions of Jefferson, Jackson, and Lincoln, a presidential response to these needs took place in the twentieth century. For most of the first 100 years, Congress jealously guarded its prerogatives and its autonomy. It was not until the Theodore Roosevelt and Woodrow

Wilson era that chief executives became more actively engaged in proposing and influencing the enactment of legislation. A variety of factors contributed to this increased activity: the presidency had become a more visible office thereby enhancing the potential for public support; Roosevelt and Wilson were more personally active and adopted a philosophy inclined toward a more assertive presidential role; the congressional parties were more amenable to strong leadership both from within the Congress and by the president; and economic and social conditions created a need for regulatory legislation to which presidents, by virtue of their national perspective and constituency, could more easily respond.

The legislative initiatives that began to emanate from the presidency had the effect of overcoming the constitutional separation by providing policy direction and by mobilizing political support. Despite the fear that the president had become too powerful, the office never reverted back to its nineteenth-century form. Beginning with Franklin Roosevelt, legislative policy making became an important expectation of the presidency, and influencing the Congress became a necessity if the executive's domestic priorities were to be achieved.

The president's legislative tasks have since become institutionalized. Franklin Roosevelt expanded the budget clearance function to include the coordination of substantive proposals from the departments and agencies. In addition to utilizing the Bureau of the Budget for central policy clearance, Truman presented Congress with an annual legislative program, becoming the first president to do so. Eisenhower continued the ongoing clearance and annual programing functions; he also created the first White House office specifically devoted to congressional liaison.

Presidents Kennedy and Johnson placed a high priority on the fulfillment of these legislative tasks. Seeing innovative policy making as key to the achievement of their social and economic goals, both presidents vigorously tried to assert legislative leadership from the White House. They increased the president's involvement in and with Congress, extending the scope and enlarging the mechanisms of the legislative presidency. While Presidents Nixon and Ford did not further expand Kennedy and Johnson's involvement, they did perform what have come to be regarded as the president's legislative tasks: annual programing, ongoing clearance, and congressional liaison. Additionally, they seemed more concerned with the administration of legislative proposals than their Democratic predecessors.

The president has become a driving force within the legislative system much of the time. This force works to produce policy output, which is why Congress looks to the president for new initiatives and why it tolerates his influence. As an institution Congress realizes benefits from a presidential presence on Capitol Hill. It gains a national perspective, policy leadership, and, in some cases, help in mobilizing partisan support—all important for an institution composed of state and district constituencies, an institution in which power is divided, party is weak, and staff resources are not extensive. Individual members may also get needed publicity, patronage, social amenities, and/or aid in handling their constituency problems.

The executive's legislative involvement has also increased the information and expertise available to both Congress and the presidency for making policy decisions. Within the presidency, new structures and processes have been created to service this expanded executive role. The remainder of the book will examine these structures and processes.

IMPLICATIONS FOR THE FUTURE

The legislative presidency is not likely to shrink. An activist government requires strong legislative leadership. Under our system, the president can provide that leadership probably better than the Congress on many controversial, large-impact issues. Having a national constituency, superior resources, and a more supportive internal structure makes it easier for the president, through the presidency, to solicit, synthesize, and sell national policy objectives to the Congress than for the Congress to do this itself. Moreover, a president's ability to shape public opinion and generate external support, especially for innovative domestic proposals, provides the muscle for coalition building that Congress so often lacks.

The personal incentive for an active legislative role is usually present as well, although this tends to vary with the president's own objectives and personality and the political climate that exists in Congress. In general, a president's popularity, electoral success, and place in history appear to be more closely tied to legislative activism than are the careers of individual members of Congress, even the leaders. Presidents are usually judged on the basis of what they have done. A laundry list of national legislative proposals and enactments contributes to the high evaluation of performance in office. Legislators, however, are judged more by responsiveness to their constituencies. For most, this is evaluated by services their office performs and local impact legislation that they got passed. On a national scale, it is both easier and more important for the president to lead. Perhaps this is what President Carter meant when he said:

> I have great respect for the Congress, but the Congress is not capable of leadership. Our Founding Fathers never felt the Congress would lead this country.[43]

NOTES

1 The 1777 New York constitution provided for a single executive, chosen for a three-year term directly by the electorate with no limits placed on his

reeligibility. In addition to possessing the prerogative of a commander-in-chief and admiral of the navy, the governor had limited authority to summon, prorogue, and dissolve the legislature and to pardon and reprieve citizens. He was obligated to describe the condition of the state at every legislative session, recommend measures that would contribute to its welfare, correspond with the Continental Congress and other states, transact government business with both civil and military officers, faithfully execute the laws, and expedite legislative acts and resolutions. He also served on councils charged with the appointment of officials and revision of laws.

2 By 1787, *The Spirit of the Laws* had become widely known in America. It had been advertised in newspapers in almost all sections of the Union, was available in many circulating libraries, and had been used in some colleges and universities. Paul Spurlin notes that at the outset of the Constitutional Convention, "the ideas of Montesquieu were, and long had been, 'in the air.' They had constituted a part of the general reading matter." Paul Spurlin, *Montesquieu in America, 1760–1801* (Baton Rouge: Louisiana State University Press, 1940), p. 177.

Many prominent statesmen such as John Adams, Samuel Adams, John Dickinson, Benjamin Franklin, Alexander Hamilton, Thomas Jefferson, George Mason, and James Wilson probably had copies of Montesquieu's works in their personal libraries (ibid., pp. 58, 90–91, 145, 195). Madison asserted that he frequently quoted Montesquieu from memory. In fact, he was alleged to have outlined *The Spirit of the Laws* for Washington before the convention (ibid., pp. 90 and 166). Six delegates (Hamilton, Wilson, Madison, Randolph, Butler, and McHenry) cited Montesquieu in the course of the debates.

3 Charles de Montesquieu, *The Spirit of the Laws* (New York: Macmillan [Hafner Press], 1962), chap. I, sec. 2 and 3, pp. 4–5.

4 For an elaboration of the argument that the Montesquieuian model provided the framework in which the constitutional system was cast, see Stephen J. Wayne, "Empowering the Presidency: Precedent and Product" (Ph.D. diss., Columbia University, 1968). Another view of Montesquieu's influence is presented by Louis Fisher in his study, *President and Congress* (New York: The Free Press, 1972), pp. 3–6, 243–251.

5 Wayne, *Empowering the Presidency,* 113–144.

6 That some presidential authority could be used to establish policy initiatives, especially in foreign affairs, was not viewed as inconsistent with the constitutional framework or even potentially dangerous so long as the Congress or a part of it retained sufficient opportunity to participate in policy making and check presidential decisions. Similarly, whatever implementing power was contained in the elastic clause was not seen as a threat to the president's executive authority. On the principal division between powers, the framers were agreed.

7 The fear of a powerful and distant government, reflected in Jefferson's oft-quoted dictum, "That government is best which governs least," reinforced the conviction that accumulated power was unnecessary. A nation of self-reliant farmers, separated and protected by oceans and slow intercontinental transportation, was not thought to need a lot of legislation in the domestic or international spheres.

8   According to Wilfred Binkley, Hamilton considered the position of secretary of the treasury as somewhat analogous to that of the British prime minister. As secretary, he acted accordingly. He saw himself as the principal conduit between Congress and the president. He even went so far as to ask his friends to refer to him as the first lord of the treasury. Wilfred E. Binkley, *President and Congress* (New York: Random House [Vintage Books], 1962), p. 49.

9   Ibid., p. 45.

10   Binkley writes, "He [Gallatin] seems to have been almost as active as Hamilton had been in steering measures through Congress. He shared with the President the management of the party in that body." Ibid., p. 66.

11   James S. Young, *The Washington Community* (New York: Columbia University Press, 1966), p. 167.

12   Ibid., pp. 168–169. President Washington also held dinner parties for members of Congress.

13   Young's thesis is that the constitutional division of powers combined with living and social patterns to effectively separate and to some extent isolate Congress from the presidency during this period. Ibid., pp. 158–159.

14   Ibid., pp. 236–237.

15   In defending Jackson's appointment of political supporters, Senator William Marcy of New York offered the simple justification, "To the victor belongs the spoils." The term "spoils system" has come to be associated with Jackson and the large number of appointments that occurred at the beginning of his presidency.

16   Binkley, *President and Congress*, pp. 109–110.

17   Ibid., p. 126

18   Ibid., p. 145.

19   Writing in 1870, Henry Adams observed: "The success of any executive measure must now be bought by the use of the public patronage in influencing the action of legislators," as quoted in Leonard D. White, *The Republican Era, 1869–1901* (New York: Macmillan, 1958), p. 26.

The failure of the president to make appointments requested by Congress aroused considerable consternation on the Hill which not only adversely affected presidential influence but departmental influence as well. White notes that as the civil service system grew, "the volume of dissatisfaction tended to decrease, but at the turn of the century the improvement was not pronounced." Ibid., p. 27.

20   During his first term alone, President Cleveland vetoed 413 bills and resolutions. While the bulk of these (343) were private pension bills, also negated were laws relating to public lands and buildings, internal improvements, coinage of silver, and immigration. See Carleton Jackson, *Presidential Vetoes, 1792–1945* (Athens: University of Georgia Press, 1967), pp. 149–164.

21   Woodrow Wilson, *Congressional Government* (New York: New American Library [Meridian Books], 1956), p. 170.

22   Ibid., p. 173.

23   Binkley, *President and Congress*, pp. 228–246.

24   Theodore Roosevelt, *Autobiography* (New York: Macmillian, 1913), p. 292.

25   Representative George Norris of Nebraska led a successful "insurrection" against the Speaker, stripping him of his authority to name committee chairmen and standing committee members and denying him the chairmanship of the House Rules Committee which the Speaker had held. As a result of the revolt, the party in Congress became less cohesive, its leadership lost influence, and power was dispersed to the senior members of the majority party.

26   Woodrow Wilson, *Constitutional Government* (New York: Columbia University Press, 1908), pp. 70–71.

27   Ibid., pp. 72–73.

28   Neil MacNeil, *Forge of Democracy* (New York: McKay, 1963), p. 258.

29   A formal procedure had been followed in the first two administrations. After the president had addressed the Congress, each house individually appointed a committee to draft an "Address in Reply" which was delivered to the president by a specially appointed committee. Jefferson stopped the practice of appearing before Congress to deliver the State of the Union Address and the houses, in turn, discontinued their formal reply.

While presidents did address the Congress from time to time, none personally delivered the State of the Union until Wilson resumed the practice in 1913. In this first address, he stated:

> I am very glad indeed to have this opportunity to address the two Houses directly and to verify from myself the impression that the president of the United States is a person, not a mere department of the government hailing Congress from some isolated island of jealous power, sending messages, not speaking naturally and with his own voice—that he is a human being trying to cooperate with other human beings in a common service.

30   This quotation comes from an article in the magazine, *New Republic,* quoted in Edward S. Corwin, *The President: Office and Powers* (New York: New York University Press, 1957), p. 271.

31   Ibid.

32   Franklin D. Roosevelt, "First Inaugural Address," March 4, 1933, as appears in the *Congressional Record,* Seventy-third Congress, Special Session, pp. 5–6.

33   Joseph Kallenbach, *The American Chief Executive* (New York: Harper & Row, 1966), p. 340.

34   Richard E. Neustadt, "Presidency and Legislation: Planning the President's Program," *American Political Science Review* XLIX, no. 4 (December 1955): 1015.

35   James Sundquist, *Politics and Policy* (Washington, D.C.: The Brookings Institution, 1968), p. 489.

36   Samuel P. Huntington, "Congressional Responses to the Twentieth Century," in *The Congress and America's Future,* ed. David B. Truman (Englewood Cliffs, N.J.: Prentice-Hall, 1965), p. 6.

37   He credited the president with responsibility for initiating approximately 20 percent of the legislation he examined and Congress with 40 percent; 30 percent was the product of joint presidential-congressional interaction and the remaining 10 percent the consequence of outside forces. Lawrence H. Chamberlain, *The*

President, Congress and Legislation (New York: Columbia University Press, 1946), p. 454.

38   Ronald C. Moe and Steven C. Teel, "Congress as Policy-Maker: A Necessary Reappraisal," *Political Science Quarterly* LXXXV (September 1970) : 443–470.

39   John R. Johannes, "Congress and the Initiation of Legislation," *Public Policy* XX (1972) : 284.

40   Ibid.

41   Gary Orfield, *Congressional Power: Congress and Social Change* (New York: Harcourt Brace Jovanovich, 1975), p. 54.

42   The contending positions cannot be resolved until there is agreement over what is meant by the word initiation. Is it the origin of an idea, the first time it is introduced in Congress, or the point at which it becomes the center of a public or congressional debate? Clearly, the president has an advantage in getting attention for issues even if the idea did not begin with him or his staff. A presidential position, in and of itself, generates support and often opposition as well.

43   Jimmy Carter, as quoted in *National Journal,* XXII (May 29, 1976): 739.

CHAPTER 2

Structuring a Personal Staff: The Organization and Style of the White House Office

The [Truman] White House staff was staff in
the old-fashioned sense of the word. They were
assistants to and subordinates of the
president. They were in every sense very much
junior to the cabinet officers and the
responsible heads of agencies in the executive
branch. The White House staff was not a
layer between the agencies and departments
and the president . . . if any cabinet member
had called up and asked for a meeting with
the president and been turned off by a staff
member, by God that staff member would have
been fired within 24 hours by Harry Truman.

George Elsey
(Truman administration)

The president's chief function is to lead, not
to administer; it is not to oversee every
detail, but to put the right people in charge,
to provide them with the basic guidance and
direction, and to let them do the job.

Richard M. Nixon,
September 19, 1968

> **Nothing is more frustrating to me . . . than to**
> **have staff jealousies. Nothing gets my**
> **mind off what I want to think about more than**
> **to have little petty jealousies in staff**
> **people. I just can't tolerate it, and it's**
> **more disturbing to me than anything.**
>
> Gerald R. Ford, as quoted in
> John Hersey, "The President," *The*
> *New York Times Magazine,*
> April 20, 1975, p. 76

INTRODUCTION

The president cannot legislate alone. As his institutional responsibilities have grown so have the structure and processes that have been designed to help meet them. Most of this growth has occurred in the twentieth century, much of it since the 1960s. The president and the presidency have become clearly distinguishable.

In the nineteenth and early twentieth centuries, this was not the case. There was no elaborate presidential structure. Presidents depended on only small numbers of aides, many borrowed from other executive agencies, and some clerical help to perform their official duties and carry out their personal and presidential obligations. It was not until 1857 that Congress even appropriated funds for a presidential clerk,[1] and the annual budget for such help as well as other incidental office expenses did not exceed $80,000 until Calvin Coolidge's administration. As a consequence, presidents were forced to perform many routine tasks themselves. Lincoln opened his own mail and took care of his own correspondence. Cleveland wrote many of his letters in longhand and personally answered the phone at the White House. Wilson typed some of his own speeches.[2] The number of personal aides was never large. Grant had a staff of 6, McKinley 27, and Coolidge 46, primarily consisting of messengers, clerks, and typists.[3]

For political and policy advice, presidents did not turn to these personal staffs but rather to their department heads both individually and collectively. As a group, the secretaries comprised the president's cabinet. Throughout most of the nineteenth century, the cabinet functioned as the principal executive advisory body for legislative counsel. Administration positions on controversial proposals were often thrashed out at cabinet meetings. To a large extent, presidents were dependent on their cabinets for political support on Capitol Hill as well.[4]

It was not until the beginning of the twentieth century that this began to change. As the chief executive's influence in Congress increased, the potency of the cabinet secretaries individually and as a group started to decline.[5] The change was not precipitous. Harding and Coolidge were still reliant on their secretaries for legislative advice but Woodrow Wilson and Franklin D. Roosevelt were not. The latter continued to meet with their cabinets, in part because they were expected to do so, but neither of them used the meetings to establish legislative priorities. With the major exception of Eisenhower, subsequent presidents have not done so either although most have sought the opinions and help of individual department heads in policy formulation and legislative liaison.

The cabinet's decline can be attributed to several factors: the growth in the number of officials who regularly attended its meetings, the increasing amount of interest group pressure on the department and agency heads and their responsiveness to that pressure, the need to assert more centralized direction over priority presidential policy making, and the tendency of some administrations to look beyond the bureaucracy for innovative policy proposals.

Beginning in 1939 with the creation of a separate White House office within the newly established Executive Office of the President, chief executives have turned increasingly to their personal aides for assistance in carrying out legislative responsibilities. This reliance on White House staff has had a profound effect on presidential policy making and has contributed significantly to the distinction between the president and the presidency. It has enhanced the president's institutional capacity to make policy, to some extent, independent of the departments and agencies. It has also resulted in a larger structure, one that is not only more powerful but, parenthetically, more difficult even for the president to control. A bureaucracy within a bureaucracy has been created and this, in turn, has magnified the potential for elevating and isolating the president and has increased the status and clout of his personal aides.

This chapter explores these organizational aspects of the presidency by focusing on the evolution of the White House staff system. The discussion is organized chronologically by administrations, commencing with that of Franklin D. Roosevelt. Each section describes the president's staffing objectives and the system instituted to achieve them. It briefly details major structural and functional components that relate to legislative policy making and then examines the relationships between the president and his policy advisors. Particular emphasis is placed on the president's personality and style of decision making in discussing his interaction with the White House staff. After summarizing trends in the development of the White House office, the chapter concludes by suggesting several implications which this development has for the nature of the presidency in general and legislative policy making in particular.

ROOSEVELT:
PERSONALIZING THE WHITE HOUSE OFFICE

Before Congress had provided for a While House office in 1939, Roosevelt had gotten along with only three secretaries, one administrative assistant, and a small number of other aides on the White House payroll. He was forced to borrow people from the departments and agencies and had also turned to outsiders for advice, counsel, and help (see Appendix A). Roosevelt continued to use "detailees" throughout his administration thereby augmenting his official White House.

In operating his staff system, Roosevelt's goals were to maximize his own position, to extend his influence, and enhance his control. He saw his aides as an extension of himself. He wanted them to provide information and ideas; he used them to help settle disputes, perform chores, and maintain contacts.

To achieve these objectives, Roosevelt organized the staff around himself. As his own chief of staff, he gave orders and received reports, rewarding and punishing assistants with praise and access. His assignments tended to be ad hoc. The president wanted to encourage the development of generalists rather than specialists. He did not want to become dependent on any of his staffers nor did he want them to carve out their own niche within the White House. Anonymity, not indispensability, was to be the hallmark of his staff system.[6]

In some cases, fixed areas of responsibility were unavoidable such as with appointments and press relations. But even here, Roosevelt overlapped assignments and interlaced activities in order to minimize the influence of individual staffers. Although it may have served nonpolicy needs as well, introducing competition among his aides also enlarged the perspectives on which the president could base his policy decisions. Alex Lacy states:

> Roosevelt felt a special need, perhaps in part because of his own physical limitations and the restrictions those limitations placed on his activity outside of the White House, to have differing points of view available to him before he made decisions. He frequently gave two or more staff members the same assignment and delighted in their rivalry.[7]

Richard E. Neustadt also suggests that the president "positively encouraged" his staff to jostle: "He evidently got a kick out of bruised egos."[8] Roosevelt's need to dominate can be seen in many aspects of his relations with the White House staff. He enjoyed power.

Decisions and deadlines, not programs and functional divisions, shaped his staff's work. Even relatively fixed assignment areas were oriented toward those actions and decisions the president had to make, such as resolving a political conflict, determining a position on pending legislation, presenting a policy, or nominating a person for a government position. Roosevelt's staff handled concrete and immediate presidential tasks.

Within the staff, Judge Samuel I. Rosenman was the principal domestic advisor. As special counsel to the president, Rosenman handled legislative matters such as message writing, legislative drafting, and making recommendations on acts of Congress awaiting presidential action. His duties, his position, even his title, became closely associated with the institutionalization of the president's legislative responsibilities.

While the Roosevelt presidency shifted power to the White House, the departments and agencies still retained considerable autonomy, especially as it related to their own administrative responsibilities. Not only did they oversee existing programs, but they also introduced and pushed new proposals on the Hill, subject to presidential clearance.

However, Roosevelt was suspicious of the lasting power of the bureaucracy. His development of a White House office was an acknowledgment of and a response to this power. The interests of the departments and agencies and the presidency did not always coincide. It was the job of the White House staff to provide presidential input where necessary and to vigorously enforce the president's priorities.

Roosevelt's highly personalized and keenly synchronized White House provided him with flexibility and thereby maximized his influence. It enabled him to innovate and energize while at the same time offering some protection from criticism and resistance within the government. Throughout his presidency, Roosevelt's aides took much of the heat.

To insiders, the system made sense and worked; to outsiders, however, it appeared disorganized, chaotic, and unsystematized. Richard Neustadt understood the Roosevelt system. In writing on the presidency, he presents the Roosevelt White House as the archetype for extending the president's personal power.[9] Harry S. Truman was not so sure.

TRUMAN: BEGINNING THE TREND TOWARD INSTITUTIONALIZATION

Upon becoming president, Truman initially desired to provide continuity in staffing. His request that Roosevelt's aides and cabinet secretaries remain delayed the inevitable personnel changes that come with any new administration. It was common knowledge that Truman was uninformed about many aspects of the Roosevelt presidency. The staff system was one of them. At the time he became president, he had no staffing plan of his own and only two personal assistants, Matthew Connelly and Harry H. Vaughn. The White House transition took almost two years to accomplish.

Truman desired to eliminate what he believed to be disorder, waste, and duplication of efforts. In reorganizing the executive and especially his personal staff, he wanted to clarify roles and pinpoint responsibilities. In his own words, "I wanted to establish government lines so clearly that I would be able to put my finger on the people directly responsible in every situation." [10] Truman also desired to reshape channels of communication between the White House and other branches of government. In the end, he accomplished much of this. His White House became less of an ad hoc operation than Roosevelt's although it did retain some of the personalized elements of the latter's staff system.

Truman's staff had a small number of assistants who were generalists with broad assignment areas. John R. Steelman had the title of assistant to the president and responsibilities in the areas of economics and interagency conciliation. Clark Clifford was the special counsel. In addition to providing political advice and writing messages and speeches, Clifford also assumed direction of the development and presentation of the president's annual legislative program, a practice started in the Truman period.

Clifford was assisted by a small number of aides.[11] He looked to the executive department and agencies for suggestions for presidential messages to Congress and for concrete legislative proposals.[12] Both the White House staff and the Bureau of the Budget (BOB) coordinated these suggestions and proposals. By using the latter as a critical link between the departments and agencies and the president, the White House was able to meet enlarged responsibilities without increasing its own size or formalizing its own mode of operation. The president's aides saw their staff system as "pretty informal." "We reasoned and argued together pretty much as a team," said one high official.[13]

Having a relatively small staff with only a few principal advisors seemed desirable from Truman's perspective. It was the way he liked to operate. Truman was the kind of person who tended to depend on a few people—those he could and did trust. Clark Clifford describes this aspect of the president's personality:

> If he did not have confidence in an individual, if he did not feel comfortable with him, he didn't see that person very much. That person would have considerable trouble getting his views before Mr. Truman. On the other hand, if he was comfortable with the man and worked well with him and had developed confidence in him, he saw that individual and wanted to continue to see him. This is one reason why the operation around President Truman was limited to a few advisors. He did not want to bring a lot of people in. He did not want to have to expand a whole lot of contacts. He preferred to enlarge the duties of the people on whom he depended.[14]

Writing in his memoirs, Truman stressed the importance of trusting his closest aides:

'The Presidency is so tremendous that it is necessary for a President to delegate authority. To be able to do so safely, however, he must have around him people who can be trusted not to arrogate authority to themselves.

Eventually I succeeded in surrounding myself with assistants and associates who would not overstep the bounds of that delegated authority, and they were people I could trust.[15]

James D. Barber also notes that trust was an important factor in shaping Truman's relations with others. "Truman's loyalties were hard, but also brittle: when they broke they shattered completely." [16]

The intense kind of competition that had been engendered in the Roosevelt White House was absent in his successor's. Truman did not see staff competition as useful for generating the kind of information he wanted. "I need the best advice and information I can get. I believe honest men will arrive at honest decisions if they have the facts," he said.[17]

Truman saw it as his staff's responsibility to provide him with this information. He saw it as his own to make the final decisions. "Every final important decision has to be made right here on the President's desk," he asserted, "and only the President can make it." [18] His penchant for making that final decision, his relish for stopping the buck at his desk, not only indicates his image of the presidency and his view of presidential responsibility, but it also reveals an important psychological insight into his character. Barber puts it this way:

Thrust up into the Presidency and called upon to say yes, no or maybe on questions he lacked training for or experience in, he thought he could base policy on particulars, and he was determined not to drift, not to confirm all those expectations that he would turn out to be inadequate for the job.[19]

Truman's fear of being indecisive may have contributed to his decisiveness.[20] There was no problem in getting him to take the final decision or to actively participate in the decision-making process, but he was also flexible enough to modify or reverse his decisions if they did not appear to be working out well.

Senior staff did not rival cabinet officials. Throughout the Truman period, policy initiative clearly rested with the individual departmental secretaries and agency heads. The cabinet as a group was not frequently used. The White House office helped coordinate and present legislative policy, focusing on recurrent presidential obligations. In the words of one aide:

The White House staff was staff in the old-fashioned sense of the word. They were assistants to and subordinates of the president. They were in every sense very much junior to the cabinet officers and the responsible heads of agencies in the executive branch. The White House staff was not a layer between the agencies and departments and the president . . . if any cabinet member had called up and asked for a meeting with the president and been turned off by a staff member, by God that staff member would have been fired within 24 hours by Harry Truman.[21]

EISENHOWER: FORMALIZING THE INTERNAL STAFF STRUCTURE

The status and role of the Eisenhower staff was similar. They too deferred to departmental secretaries and agency heads for policy development. They too acted to synthesize, coordinate, and help package that policy, although in a more formalized way. Senior aides performed roughly the same functions in both White Houses, and there were many continuities in the manner in which they did them. What was different was the larger size, more differentiated structure, and more elaborate policy-making machinery that was constructed in the Eisenhower period. The operating styles of the two presidents also contrasted sharply.

Eisenhower came to the White House with a definite understanding of the type of staff system he wanted to construct.[22] He desired to establish a hierarchial structure with clear lines of authority, a structure similar to the one he had experienced in the military. For Eisenhower proper organization was an imperative:

> Organization cannot make a genius out of an incompetent; even less can it, of itself, make the decisions which are required to trigger necessary action. On the other hand, disorganization can scarcely fail to result in inefficiency and can easily lead to disaster. Organization makes more efficient the gathering and analysis of facts, and the arranging of the findings of experts in logical fashion. Therefore organization helps the responsible individual make the necessary decision, and helps assure that it is satisfactorily carried out.[23]

Eisenhower did not see it as always his responsibility to make this decision. He was not nearly as concerned as Truman with the buck reaching his desk.

The staff's job was to handle everyday operational problems that came to the White House. The president did not want to get bogged down in details. He did not want to be bothered by every trivial issue, nor did he want to participate in the "welling-up" of decisions. It was up to the staff, as he saw it, to raise problems, state facts, sift alternatives, and make recommendations. Eisenhower desired to come in when this process was completed. He saw his responsibility as providing overall direction and making the final important decisions.

The system established to perform these presidential goals was, on the surface, fairly structured, with specialized functional assignments and relatively clear lines of authority. From 1953 to 1958 former New Hampshire

Governor Sherman Adams headed the White House staff. Holding the title of assistant to the president, Adams gave out assignments, received reports, presided over staff meetings, and settled internal disputes.[24] In theory, everyone worked for Adams and Adams worked for the president. He was the chief of staff. Eisenhower described Adams' role as follows:

> His task was to coordinate all of these sections and their operations, to make certain that every person in them understood the purport and the details of each directive issued, and to keep me informed of appropriate developments on a daily basis. He did not lay down rigid rules to restrict the staff members in their access to me; they worked flexibly, with a voluntary cooperation based on mutual friendships and respect.[25]

As the main conduit to the president, Adams also decided when issues merited presidential attention. He "O.K.'d" all reports that went to the president. He personally presented issues for Eisenhower's resolution.

Adams believed it his responsibility to reduce the president's work. "Eisenhower simply expected me to manage a staff that would boil down, simplify and expedite the urgent business that had to be brought to his personal attention and to keep as much work of secondary importance as possible off his desk," he wrote.[26]

In his capacity as assistant to the president, Adams and his deputy, Major General Wilton B. (Jerry) Persons (Ret.) played a major role in coordinating domestic policy. They were instrumental in the preparation and presentation of the president's legislative program. They also monitored the progress of the administration's initiatives within the executive branch.

When he was forced to resign in 1958,[27] Adams had become a highly visible, almost legendary taskmaster in the Eisenhower White House, known for his "all-business" attitude and demanding work schedule. He exercised what some considered to be more power than the president himself in the domestic affairs of state. Persons succeeded Adams. In contrast, Persons was an easygoing, easy to work for, boss who maintained an open door to his staff [28] and had more of a consensus approach to work.

The functions of the office of special counsel were much more narrowly defined than they had been during the two previous administrations. Primarily concerned with legal matters, especially those having legislative application, the counsel also participated in program development. While he was a senior member of the White House staff, he did not have a preeminent role as had his Democratic predecessors.

Despite the more differentiated functions and formalized staff structure, senior White House aides did not view the lines of authority and areas of jurisdiction as rigid or stultifying. In the words of one White House official, "Standing on formality, standing on protocol was very minimal . . . there were lines but there was no rigidity: no inability to cross those lines where there was a reason to do it." [29] For one thing, senior aides enjoyed considerable discretion in the performance of their own jobs, coming to Adams when they had a problem and usually on their own initiative. For another thing, they had access to the president when they needed it. As a group, the senior staff participated in general policy discussions. According to Persons, "You got into anything you ought to get into, and you brought in anybody that you thought could make a contribution to the particular subject." [30] Cooperation and teamwork characterized the entire staff operation. "We had a very high degree of loyalty," said one aide; "there was very little intrigue and jockeying for position," marveled another. "It was remarkable. I have never seen anything before or since like it," noted H. Roemer McPhee, associate special counsel. [31]

Eisenhower himself deserves much of the credit for fashioning this attitude. His genius lay in getting people to work together. He did not enjoy turmoil or dissent and he was not adept at manipulative skills. Rather, he was content to preside over a well-organized, well-run staff system. His orientation toward consensus encouraged a team approach.

The structure of the Eisenhower White House reflected the president's desire for ordered relationships and systematized processes. He did not desire fluid patterns of interaction. Rather, he was most comfortable in established situations where his role was clear and his alternatives carefully laid out. While he was willing to be decisive, if he could make a reasonable choice between options, he did not like being involved in internal controversy, preferring instead to have his staff work out the problems. [32]

His work style was verbal. He desired oral briefings. In his book Adams comments that Eisenhower "was impatient with the endless paperwork of the presidency and always tried to get his staff to digest long documents into one-page summaries. . . . He seldom exchanged written memoranda with me or with Cabinet members or his staff," Adams wrote. "He preferred talking and reasoning it out." [33]

The staff, with the possible exception of Adams, viewed itself as junior to department and agency heads. The cabinet secretaries were the prime movers in those days, claimed aide Bryce N. Harlow, who added: "They were the principal people, we were staff instead of our being the principal people and they staff." [34] Cabinet members could almost always see the president if they were unhappy with staff decisions and actions. [35]

The cabinet as a body enjoyed a resurgence during the Eisenhower administration. Meetings were held on a regular basis with the president personally presiding. These meetings often featured elaborate presentations of policy proposals by individual department heads and their staffs. Replete with visual aids and supporting materials, these presentations were the prelude to final decisions on the administration's legislative program prior to its presentation to Congress. [36]

While Eisenhower's use of the cabinet differed markedly from that of

Roosevelt and Truman and his White House staff was more hierarchical in form and specialized in function than either of his Democratic predecessors, there were also continuities in staffing patterns between the three administrations. Despite Eisenhower's larger, more differentiated secondary structure, his principal aides remained small in number. No more than six to ten regularly participated in major policy decisions. Despite the more formalized mode of operation during the Eisenhower period, the staff's functions remained basically the same. These included coordinating and synthesizing departmental programs, helping to resolve agency problems and meeting recurrent presidential obligations. Only in the area of congressional liaison was a new function added. Despite the role which Adams assumed, the senior staff still regarded the White House as a small, informal, highly personal place. Changes were to occur in the status, power, and to some extent, role of the White House staff, but these were not very visible during the Eisenhower presidency.

KENNEDY:
GENERATING A WHITE HOUSE ORIENTATION TO POLICY MAKING

President Kennedy wished to abandon the trappings of cabinet government: the formal meetings, standing interdepartmental committees, standardized White House procedures, and fixed areas of staff responsibility. He purposively reverted to the Roosevelt model, but with modifications.[37] Kennedy's political objectives were similar to Roosevelt's: he wanted to extend his influence and maximize his options. To do so, his advisors suggested that he create a flexible staff structure, one that would get "information in his mind and key decisions in his hands reliably enough and soon enough to give him room for maneuver." [38]

Kennedy established a bilateral staff structure with generalists performing action-forcing assignments. In an effort to deinstitutionalize the presidency and to make it a more personal office, he also abolished the staff secretaries and elaborate secondary mechanisms that supported the cabinet and National Security Council during the Eisenhower period. In their place were personal advisors with broad assignment areas that "were distinguishable but not exclusive." [39] These aides were expected to alert the president to potential problems, to answer his questions, and to respond to his needs.[40] "Our role," wrote Theodore C. Sorensen, Kennedy's alter ego and chief domestic policy advisor, "was to enable him to have more time, facts and judgments with which to make them [decisions] himself—to increase his influence, not ours; to preserve his option, not his ego; to make certain that questions were not foreclosed or answers required before he had an opportunity to place his imprint upon them." [41]

Sorensen held the title of special counsel. In this capacity he oversaw the development and presentation of the president's legislative program much as Rosenman, Clifford, and his successor, Charles Murphy had done. Sorensen was assisted by two other lawyers, Myer Feldman and Lee C. White, who handled the more routine work of the office such as executive orders, enrolled bills, pardons, and civil rights matters. Feldman was the principal contact with the legislative arm of the Bureau of the Budget.

Other influential aides in the Kennedy White House included the so-called Irish mafia; Kenneth O'Donnell, Ralph Dungan, and Lawrence F. O'Brien. O'Donnell was appointments secretary; however, his responsibilities were broader than simply planning the president's schedule and guarding the door to his office. He supervised the administration of the White House staff although he was no chief in the Adams' sense of the term. Dungan, a general political troubleshooter, handled jobs and patronage matters and wrote speeches. O'Brien directed Kennedy's congressional liaison activities. While their roles varied with the issues and circumstances, all three participated to some extent in White House policy making.

Kennedy was his own chief of staff. He made the assignments and personally received the reports. He was not prone to call staff meetings, preferring instead to meet with aides individually as Roosevelt had done. While there was some overlap in assignments and some internal competition, this seemed to be more a product of his fluid staff system than the president's need to dominate all aspects of its activities. According to Richard Neustadt, "he [Kennedy] seems to have no taste for ego-baiting and low tolerance for egoism, even perhaps his own." [42]

Coordinating departmental relations was essential to the Kennedy mode of operation. While the president reverted to a Roosevelt-type White House and looked outside the government for new policy proposals, he also recognized the internal needs of the departments and agencies. They were used to having an input into important policy decisions and naturally wanted an opportunity to get presidential support for their pet programs. As a consequence, the Kennedy staff attempted to channel these executive branch activities.[43] They turned to individual departments and agencies for advice, especially in the second and third years of the administration, and paid the usual deferrence to cabinet secretaries.

But the Kennedy White House also began to develop a status and prestige of its own. Senior assistants did not see themselves as superseding department and agency heads. Sorensen writes: "We did not replace the role of Cabinet officers, compete with them for power or publicity, or block their access to the President . . . our role was one of building governmental unity rather than splintering responsibility." [44] Nonetheless, Kennedy aides did assume more initiative, especially, when generating new ideas and programs. The staff had a substantial role in the development of the New Frontier program.

Kennedy's senior aides also exercised considerable decisional authority on his behalf. Many had worked closely with him for some time so they could anticipate his desires. They also enjoyed easy access to the president. Together these factors contributed to the esprit de corps that developed in the White House and clearly distinguished the president's men from the rest of the administration. To many outside the White House, these insiders appeared to flaunt their position and power. They seemed to be both active and aloof, involved and inviolable. This dualism seemed apparent in Kennedy's personality as well. It was reflected in his rhetoric and evidenced in his way of relating to others.

Kennedy was both self-assured and coolly detached. While he preferred to deal with his aides on a one-to-one basis, he let few of them into his personal life. The drive and energy that he brought to the presidency carried over into his running of the White House. He and his staff were constantly on the go: developing new ideas, marshaling bureaucratic support, fashioning public appeals, pushing a legislative program. Innovative policy making, not consensus government, lay at the core of his administration's objectives and fashioned its decisional style.

JOHNSON: CREATING A DOMESTIC POLICY STAFF IN THE WHITE HOUSE

Lyndon B. Johnson had a very different kind of personality. While his basic political goals did not deviate markedly from Kennedy's, his operating style and personal manner did. He too wanted to be at once on top and in the thick of things, informed and influential, active and assertive. The fluidness of the Kennedy staffing system facilitated the achievement of these objectives, but the rapid turnover of presidential aides (including the departure of some of his own original appointees) did not. Like other presidents who had succeeded to the office, Johnson sought to maintain the appearance of continuity.

For him, the retention of Kennedy's top aides was absolutely essential. In reflecting on his feelings during this period, Johnson confessed:

> I constantly had before me the picture that Kennedy had selected me as executor of his will, it was my duty to carry on and this meant his people as well as his programs. They were part of his legacy. I simply couldn't let the country think that I was all alone.[45]

Asking and getting the Kennedy staff to remain [46] helped satisfy Johnson's political and psychological needs but it also delayed the development of his own staff system. The early years in the Johnson White House were marked by considerable uncertainty in roles and responsibilities and a lengthy adjustment for the president in his new position.

While the Kennedy holdovers continued to perform their old duties, the first group of new Johnson aides were given ad hoc assignments conditioned largely by the immediate needs of the president. Their jobs never really evolved into definite functional or specialized issue areas. Of the early appointees, Walter Jenkins, Jack Valenti, and Bill D. Moyers were the most influential. Jenkins handled administrative matters. Positioned next to the door to the Oval Office, he funneled the paper flow into the president. Jack Valenti, another long-time associate, who happened to be with Johnson on the day of the assassination, served him in many personal ways, in addition to working in an editorial capacity on presidential public statements. Bill Moyers initially wrote speeches for Johnson. A close personal relationship developed between the two which one White House aide likened to that of a father and son.[47] The president quickly recognized Moyers' ability to deal with substantive policy issues and enlarged his responsibilities accordingly. Moyers became Johnson's domestic policy coordinator and played a major role in the development of the Great Society program.

It took approximately a year for major staff changes to occur. They were mainly in the domestic area. Douglas Cater joined the administration in May 1964 as a special assistant to the president and became involved in education and health matters. In 1965, Joseph A. Califano, Jr., was brought in from the Defense Department to oversee domestic policy operations and, in effect, replaced Moyers who had been appointed press secretary. Califano, formerly a special assistant to Robert McNamara, sought to systematize legislative programing by developing and coordinating the domestic policy-making process.

Within the White House, Califano established a policy staff. Consisting of a small number of assistants with general responsibilities, this group isolated problem areas, designated task forces and intergovernmental groups to develop proposals, analyzed suggestions for new legislation, and helped to put together the president's legislative program. The Califano group also had an input into special legislative messages and major presidential addresses although the principal speech writing was handled by others.

Shorn of its programing responsibilities, the special counsel's office continued to advise the president on the legal aspects of routine legislative and administrative matters such as executive orders, enrolled bills, and administrative regulations and pardons. Califano, however, was increasingly involved in the more important and controversial legislative issues that reached the president.

The appointment of policy advisors in the White House and their organization into a loosely structured domestic policy staff had important implications for the departments and agencies. It reduced their influence on presidential policy making. Moreover, the administration of pet presidential programs was also subject to greater White House scrutiny than in the past. Johnson even assigned aides to oversee each of the departments.[48]

These developments enhanced the growing status of the White House staff and strengthened its position within the government. The staff's power, Califano writes, resulted from the ability to say, "The president wants. . . ." [49] As policy making became more White House centered and more presidentially directed, domestic policy aides were able to say this more and more. The decline in department and agency influence followed.

From Johnson's perspective, the concentration of power in the White House benefited his own political needs and was consistent with the way he liked to do business. Johnson wanted to maximize his influence, enlarge his information flow and extend his options. A larger, more capable policy-oriented staff in the White House permitted this. It enabled him to check or even bypass the executive departments if he chose. Moreover, it increased his capacity to develop new initiatives rather than be saddled with what the bureaucracy came up with. The departments and agencies had to be responsive to their own clientele. The kind of proposals they would suggest and the positions they would take were affected by what their publics wanted. By distancing himself from the departments and agencies, Johnson also distanced himself from those kinds of influences thereby increasing his flexibility in policy matters.

The greater involvement of the White House staff in policy development served another purpose. It helped satisfy Johnson's almost obsessive need to be informed of details. No issue was too small for him, no decision too premature. Johnson was especially fond of new ideas. James Gaither, a member of Califano's staff, stated:

> Johnson was involved in various stages [of policy making]. Our problem was to prevent him from getting too involved. If he had his wish, he would have been getting a report everyday and the program would have been out the next day. He loved new ideas; he got very excited about them and couldn't hold them.[50]

Johnson was constantly consulting with people inside and outside of the government on policy matters. This presented difficulties for his staff. Their authority was always contingent upon the president's wishes. Theoretically, this is always true for presidential staff, but in practice, Johnson's volatile moods and disposition made staff decision making even more precarious than it had been in the three previous administrations. Myer Feldman describes the difference in his own latitude as a senior aide for Kennedy and Johnson:

> I had to be a lot more careful about minor matters with Johnson than I did with Kennedy. I knew Kennedy well enough so that whatever determination I made, I knew he would support me. All I had to do was meet with him at the end of the day and tell him what positions had been

taken. With Lyndon Johnson, I would give a tentative approval, pending a discussion with the president, rather than a final approval as I could with Kennedy.[51]

"Working for Lyndon Johnson," Harry McPherson writes, "an assistant did not easily forget that he carried his authority on sufferance." [52] George Christian explained, "Johnson was not adverse to delegating authority when he had to, but he left little doubt as to who was to make the important decisions. In brief, he ruled." [53]

Johnson considered his senior staff equal in the sense that most had the same titles and the same salaries. He dealt with them on a one-to-one basis. Senior aides all reported to him and, for the most part, enjoyed relatively easy access.

The problem was not getting to see the president. It was being on call almost continuously. Johnson's workday extended from 7 or 8 o'clock in the morning until 8 to 10 at night (with a two-hour break in the afternoon). Aides were expected to be available at all times. Doris Kearns writes of Johnson:

> He expected a precise account of how each staff member spent his time, whom he talked with, and where he went. Minutes became valuable, holidays a misfortune. Johnson considered it something dangerously close to treason for a staff member to spend Sunday afternoon with his family instead of at the office.[54]

She added, "he never drove an assistant harder than he drove himself." [55]

There are many stories of his "chewing out" aides who were not there when he wanted them.[56] The president had a direct telephone connection to senior White House officials. He expected an immediate response to his calls. Aide Lawrence O'Brien writes that when Califano failed to answer the phone one day being otherwise occupied in an adjoining bathroom, Johnson immediately had an extension placed in the bathroom. "We'll have no more of that," he is said to have "roared" to Califano.[57]

Johnson was a very difficult person for whom to work. He could and did heap excessive praise on individual staffers, rewarding them with the usual perquisites of the presidency: access, intimacy, and power. However, he was also capable of great abuse, often rebuking them in front of others as if to make a psychological point. The practice of dressing down assistants was primarily directed toward those White House aides he appointed, not the Kennedy holdovers. "He knew we wouldn't stand for it and he desperately wanted us to stay on," was one Kennedy staffer's explanation.

Unable to accept criticism, the president monopolized discussions. His administration tolerated little internal criticism. Kearns writes:

> Johnson was ravenous for information when things were going well. Under siege, however, his operational style closed in and insulated him within

the White House, where discussion was confined to those who offered no disagreement.[58]

Johnson demanded complete fidelity from his staff. He had to dominate staff relationships. As his administration progressed, he depended on fewer and fewer people.

Johnson's well-known rigidity in foreign affairs did not carry over into the domestic legislative sphere.[59] Persuading and bargaining characterized his relations with those outside the White House, those whose support he needed; submissiveness and selfless service were demanded from his most loyal aides. It was natural that he would look to the White House, which he could command, rather than to the departments and agencies where he exercised less direct control for developing, and to some extent, overseeing priority programs, programs that he increasingly considered his own.

NIXON: SYSTEMATIZING POLICY MAKING WITHIN THE PRESIDENCY

Richard Nixon may have had similar political and personal needs but he did not acknowledge them in the initial construction of his White House staff. In fact, he expressed quite the opposite intentions both publicly and privately. In a campaign speech on the presidency, Nixon had called for an "open administration" and a chief executive who would "consciously and deliberately place himself at the center." [60] Seeing his role as making the most critical judgments, Nixon argued that the president should not have to make every single decision himself:

> The president's chief function is to lead, not to administer, it is not to oversee every detail, but to put the right people in charge, to provide them with basic guidance and direction and to let them do the job.[61]

The right people for Nixon were to be a strong cabinet charged primarily with policy-making responsibilities and a strong White House charged with operational duties. He was determined that the two groups would not clash. If cabinet members needed access to the president, then it was the job of the White House to encourage, not to inhibit this, Nixon believed.[62] He looked toward Eisenhower's cabinet approach to government as a more acceptable model for his presidency than the pattern that had evolved during the Kennedy-Johnson period.

The initial design for the White House, however, bore less of a resemblance to the Eisenhower system in form than in objective. It was less hierarchial at the top and more differentiated at the bottom, presumably addressing two of Nixon's principal concerns: his fear of personal aides dominating his thinking and his desire not to get overly involved in the day-to-day operational details. The more elaborate secondary staff structure also reflected the growth of presidential duties and responsibilities since the Eisenhower period.

The original plan called for a small number of assistants to the president who were to be given general administrative responsibilities (Bryce N. Harlow, congressional affairs; H. R. Haldeman, White House administration; John D. Ehrlichman, counsel; and Henry A. Kissinger, national security affairs), and a large number of special assistants with more specific functional assignments.

From the perspective of domestic policy formulation, the two most significant appointments made during this early period were those of Arthur F. Burns, counselor to the president, and Daniel A. Moynihan, assistant to the president for urban affairs. Both were expected to be policy initiators and coordinators. Their roles were never clearly defined, however. Burns was originally charged with overseeing the reports of the 14 election task forces which were due in December. Moynihan was brought in to direct the newly created Urban Affairs Council. Having very different political philosophies and very strong personalities, they proceeded to rival one another. For a president who valued a team approach, who wanted effective implementation, who did not enjoy mollifying staff conflict, and, above all, who looked to his aides to present and analyze options systematically in a nonconflictual atmosphere, two competing circles of policy advisors was not satisfactory.

At Haldeman's suggestion, Ehrlichman's role as counsel was expanded. Acting as a kind of policy broker between the Burns and Moynihan groups, Ehrlichman eventually became the president's chief domestic policy advisor.[63] On November 4, 1969, he was given the title of assistant to the president for domestic affairs and was subsequently appointed executive director of the newly created Domestic Council, which was established on July 1, 1970.

Ehrlichman's job on the council was to supervise the interagency groups that developed policy, coordinate their reports and convey them to the president. He also served as administrative head of the Domestic Council staff.

The key to Ehrlichman's position was his contact and rapport with the president. He was one of three White House aides (together with Haldeman and Kissinger) who enjoyed easy and ready access to Nixon. Substantive policy papers from departmental secretaries or the council staff normally had to filter through him before they reached the president. Ehrlichman enjoyed complete discretion in the kinds of matters he brought to Nixon's attention.

Whereas Ehrlichman was concerned with the substance of the domestic policy decisions (what the papers said), Haldeman was concerned with operational details (that they arrived on time and were complete). He ensured that deadlines were met, that the president had all the information he needed, and that his interests were protected and his wishes executed. He managed the White House staff. "He was an abrasive, no-nonsense guy, a crackerjack of an administrator," stated Jerry Jones, a personnel assistant and later staff secretary in the Nixon White House, who added:

> The place had a structure, had a way of doing things, had a flow and follow-up system that was beyond belief. Things happened.[64]

John Dean, counsel to the president from 1970–1973, provides a vivid illustration of the Haldeman system:

> I spent too much time preparing my answers to a few action memoranda, let the due dates slide by, and discovered the consequences. First a secretary in the staff secretary's office called my secretary, asking where the answer was, and when the explanation was found unsatisfactory a very bitchy Larry Higby called to say, "What's the matter, Dean, can't you meet a deadline? Do you think you're someone special?" When I explained I was working on the response, Higby snapped, "Work a little harder." Higby was chewed out by Haldeman when the paper did not flow as the chief of staff wanted, so he leaned on others.[65]

Haldeman was the overseer of the entire operation, much like Sherman Adams had been for Eisenhower. As Haldeman saw it the difference was that he did not usually get as involved in substantive policy decisions as his predecessor had:

> Adams spent little time with the President but a lot of time acting for him. I spend a lot of time with the President. I act at the President's direction. I transmit and coordinate with the President's direction. I don't directly act in policy matters.[66]

By the end of 1970, the lines of authority in the Nixon White House were clear. By 1972, the size of the White House had grown considerably and its organization had tightened with more specific assignment areas and well-established procedures (see Figure II-I). Daily access to the president was limited to Nixon's three principle advisors, his press secretary, his budget director, and one or two others. Haldeman guarded the door to the Oval Office, controlling all appointments and telephone calls. He usually attended meetings that Nixon had, took notes, and made sure that any presidential decisions were executed. Alexander P. Butterfield, an aide to Haldeman, testified before the House Judiciary Committee that Nixon spent over 70 percent of his staff time with Haldeman alone.[67]

Cabinet secretaries had difficulty seeing the president. According to Egil (Bud) Krogh, Jr., a White House aide who also served on the Domestic Council staff, a department or agency head needed a good reason to gain an appointment. "With the exception of John Mitchell," Krogh

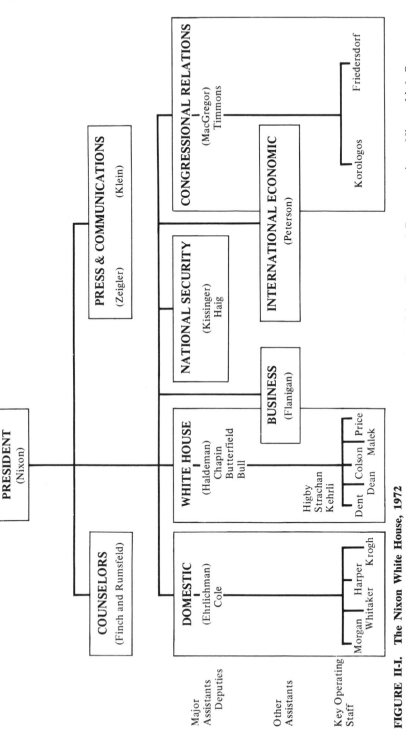

FIGURE II-I. The Nixon White House, 1972

SOURCE: Alexander Butterfield, Hearings Before the Committee on the Judiciary, House of Representatives, Ninety-third Congress, Second Session, July 2, 1974.

noted, "cabinet members had a very serious problem with presidential access." [68] John Ehrlichman quipped: "We only see them at the annual White House Christmas party; they go off and marry the natives." [69]

Complaints by those who were not insiders surfaced with the resignation of the secretary of interior, Walter Hickel, in 1972. Hickel's inability to meet or speak with the president was alleged to be the principal reason for his departure. He had publicly complained that the president was "isolated just sitting around listening to his staff." [70] Reacting to criticism that the administration was insulated from cabinet and congressional views, President Nixon proposed and subsequently implemented on July 1, 1973, a new organization plan that reduced the Domestic Council staff in size and created a counselor system. The supercabinet proposal, as it was called, established three presidential counselors who were also department heads. They were given responsibility for initiating and coordinating policy proposals within broad spheres of authority which extended over departmental lines. Each of the counselors was to be assisted by a small staff with Ehrlichman overseeing the entire operation and acting as the major conduit to the president.

Difficulties in the operation of the system, the growing controversy over Watergate, and the resignation of Ehrlichman and Haldeman in the spring of 1973 placed the plan in jeopardy. When General Alexander Haig took over Haldeman's position as White House chief of staff, he recommended that this system, the last vestige of the Haldeman-Ehrlichman era, be discontinued and Nixon consented.

Haig's role in the Watergate-era White House was similar to the one Haldeman performed. He directed the staff operation, met daily with senior aides, and was the prime channel to the president. Melvin Laird, former defense secretary, came closest to replacing Ehrlichman. While his original task was to coordinate domestic activities, the hostile political climate within the government and the lack of a supporting staff within the White House made policy oversight difficult. Laird stayed for only a few months. Bryce Harlow who left in 1970 returned for a brief period also to aid in the president's public relations, especially with Congress.

The organization of the White House and the way it functioned did not alter appreciably with the new team. Haig attempted to improve presidential access and enlarge the circles of presidential advisors. However, Nixon's increasing preoccupation with Watergate made these changes hard to achieve. The president's style did not permit much flexibility, especially under conditions of stress. As the tapes controversy heightened and impeachment became a real possibility, the White House staff responded accordingly. They brought fewer and fewer matters to the president's attention.

From the perspective of Nixon's character, the structure and operation of the White House from 1970 reflected and magnified his personality needs. Richard Nixon had always been a very private person. Unlike Johnson, he did not enjoy personal interaction and tended to distance himself from his staff. He preferred to work alone and off paper. He read a great deal. Nixon made few verbal policy decisions, lending obvious irony to his taping of presidential conversations in the White House. His decisions were usually transmitted on memos often at the behest of Haldeman. He saw only a few close associates on a regular basis. The president's isolation atop the White House hierarchy was self-imposed.

Richard Nixon was not a spontaneous person in his words, actions, or relations with others. He preferred structured situations in which roles were clearly defined. Good management, a Nixon trademark, was both a personal habit [71] and a practical necessity. What he tried to avoid, at all costs, was letting situations get out of hand. His day was always well organized. He demanded and secured time for reflection. He even had a hideaway office in the Old Executive Office Building where he could escape and work in solitude. But he found it difficult to relax. Butterfield comments:

> There was a lot of leisure time for the President, but he chose not to take it in the form of indulging . . . in recreation. It was my observation that he had no hobbies. The Presidency was his hobby.[72]

Careful preparation characterized Nixon's way of doing things. In public, he rarely spoke off the cuff. He spent considerable time going over his own speeches. He chose his words carefully and made decisions deliberately. He always did his homework. He expected as much from his staff. Their analyses had to be thorough, their recommendations clearly and logically presented, their loyalty never in doubt. Richard T. Johnson, a White House fellow during the Nixon period, writes:

> The President's day, organized into half-hour segments, provided time to read, discuss, and above all, lots of time to think and decide . . . any matter, be it a legislative proposal or an important letter, was meticulously staffed out before it went on the President's desk. Each request for an appointment was put through a fine-mesh screen. The staff prepared a "script" about each visitor to the Oval Office that told who he was and the nature of his business. It even provided suggested subjects for small talk and indicated how long the audience was to last.[73]

Nixon used his staff to avoid uncomfortable situations, especially personal confrontations. He did not like conflicts and he let his aides handle the dirty work. This had the added advantage of allowing scapegoatism. Ehrlichman, Haldeman, and the Office of Management and Budget (OMB) shielded him, taking much of the public and private criticism.

The staff did what the president wanted. The hierarchial organization allowed him to deal with those few who knew him best and whom he knew best. They could be counted on to cater to his style of decision making.

The elaborate mechanism permitted a thorough analysis of policy and an efficient implementation of presidential decisions. The memo approach avoided the vicissitudes of much personal interaction at the presidential level. It provided Nixon with time to think and things to think about— alone if he chose. Moreover, it allowed the presentation of alternatives in a way that did not challenge the president. Together, style and structure created an ordered, harmonious environment for Nixon, one that seemed to enhance and thereby encourage his capacity to control events. The Watergate cover up suggests in a very forceful way how far this control might be extended. It also indicates the extent to which such a White House could hold the president hostage and/or allow him to be both perpetrator and victim at the same time.

FORD:
COMBINING OPENNESS WITH COLLEGIALITY

After Nixon resigned the presidency, Alexander Haig remained in adminis-trative charge of the White House, but the staff system was upset by changes in personnel and eventually, in the structure itself. Initially, President Gerald R. Ford requested most of Nixon's aides to remain to help smooth the transition. Only press secretary Ronald Zeigler and the former president's legal staff were not invited to stay on. President Ford also appointed a number of his own former associates to top White House posts. They included Philip W. Buchen, Robert T. Hartmann, John O. Marsh, Jr., and L. William Seidman. These appointments, combined with the president's open style of decision making, had the effect of blurring areas of responsibility and lines of authority during the early months of the new administration. It was not until the departure of General Haig and the appointment of his replacement, Donald H. Rumsfeld, in October 1974, that the transition between administrations was complete and the Ford White House assumed its own distinctive shape.

After Rumsfeld was appointed, the president announced a major White House reorganization designed to remedy the more obvious staffing problems that had occurred during both the Nixon administration and the transitional period. Ford hoped to increase the amount of information and the variety of viewpoints he received. He also wanted to be more accessible, not only to more people on his own staff, but to others outside the White House, as well. It was the president's wish to give department secretaries and agency heads a greater voice in major administration decisions, a wish that has been ritualistically voiced at the beginning of almost every contemporary Presidency.

Under the new plan, there were nine key staff aides who reported directly to the president and who supervised White House personnel and several others who, while not considered senior staff, also worked closely with Ford. Figure II-II lists the principal positions in the Ford White House.

The major difference in the organization of the Nixon and Ford White Houses was at the top. There were more White House aides who regularly saw President Ford than President Nixon. Moreover, each had a deputy with authority to act in his absence and on his behalf. No one was to be indispensable under the Ford plan although in actual practice senior aides found it difficult to delegate responsibility.

The basic administrative divisions accorded with the previous White House staff structures. Responsibilities were divided along functional lines with the assistant to the president being the key official for coordinating White House activities and overseeing staff operations. Donald Rumsfeld held this position until his appointment as secretary of defense in the winter of 1975 when Richard B. Cheney, his deputy, took over. Together, they regulated the flow of people and papers to and from the president.

Rumsfeld and Cheney's influence stemmed largely from their administrative responsibilities, their knowledge of in-house details and deadlines, and most importantly, from their personal influence and frequent contact with the president. By virtue of their position, they saw the president more often than did other senior aides. As a consequence of their procedural duties, they also became involved in substantive decisions although they tried to avoid becoming advocates for an individual or group on the staff. "It is important that the rest of the troops feel that we will honestly present their position to the president," Cheney remarked.[74]

While Rumsfeld and Cheney had similar duties as assistant to the president, their operating styles were quite different. Rumsfeld, like his predecessors Haldeman and Haig, had the reputation of being a tough administrator, efficient but abrasive. Cheney had a less imposing presence. Aides viewed him as "low-keyed," and "even-keeled." [75] He initially strove to achieve greater coordination by moderating staff tensions and enlarging staff responsibilities.

The administrative responsibilities of the other senior White House aides were divided along familiar lines. The main domestic advising chores continued to be handled by the executive director to the Domestic Council, Kenneth R. Cole, Ehrlichman's deputy and later successor, and following him, James M. Cannon. Cole and Cannon were also given the title assistant to the president for domestic affairs.

In addition to regularly participating in major White House decisions, the senior staff also constituted the core of the presidential advisory system. They met as a group each weekday morning at 8 A.M. to coordinate the day's activities. The assistant to the president chaired these meetings. Decision making in the Ford administration was much more broadly based than it had been during the Nixon presidency. Not only did

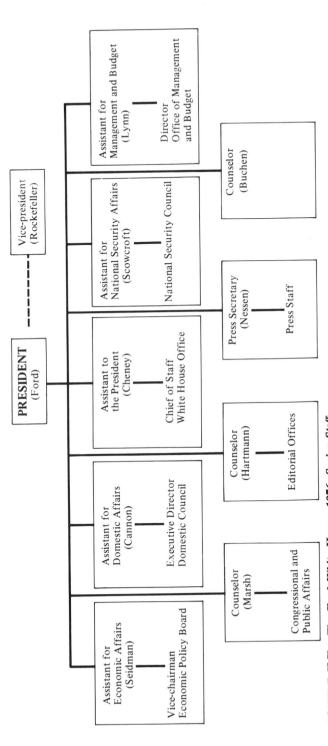

FIGURE II-II. The Ford White House, 1976: Senior Staff

the senior staff enjoy easy access but cabinet members were able to see the president on request. There was a standing rule in the Ford White House that any cabinet official could talk with the president as long as there was time available on the president's schedule. "Nobody ever screens out a cabinet member," Richard Cheney stated. "The president will always be told so and so wants to see him." [76] Members of Congress also encountered much less difficulty than in the previous administration. The congressional leadership conferred with the president on a regular basis.

The increased access to the president resulted in a much wider circle of policy advisors than Nixon had. Ford spent an estimated 50 percent of his time with his White House staff, but only about 10 percent with Cheney alone.[77] No one, with the possible exception of Secretary of State Kissinger, grew to dominate relations with the president. In fact, just the opposite situation occurred. "Ford sees everyone in sight," noted one Nixon holdover. "One of the difficulties we encountered during the transition was that there were so many players." During the 1976 presidential campaign, however, the president began to guard his time a little more closely and saw fewer advisors on a regular basis. Senior aides with the exception of Cheney and General Brent Scowcroft, the national security advisor, did not automatically have a slot on his schedule. They could still get in to see the president but had to be given the appropriate time by Cheney or his aides.

In addition to giving department heads a greater voice in administrative policy making, Ford also revived the cabinet meeting. He was the first president since Eisenhower to appoint a cabinet secretary and regularly preside over cabinet sessions. Meetings were held monthly and served largely as an information exchange among the president, his department secretaries, White House aides, and Executive Office officials. The White House staff still retained a large role in policy matters, but its input was not nearly as exclusive as it had been during the Nixon period.

Ford's collegial approach to policy making encouraged the operation of concentric circles of policy advisors at the senior level, which contrasted sharply with the latter years of the Nixon presidency. Among junior White House aides, the contrast was less marked. Senior aides could normally see the president alone or in groups. Most had direct telephones lines from the president. Juniors might be included in presidential meetings when the subject fell within their areas of responsibility but they did not regularly meet with the president. The staff remained highly differential. A larger secondary staff structure still supported the policy operation and related activities.

The president attempted to reduce the size of the White House but found it difficult. He achieved only a modest overall reduction of professional personnel during his presidency, while some White House staffs such as public liaison and the Domestic Council actually grew in size. In 1976, there were still almost 500 full-time permanent employees in the White House and a handful of persons detailed to it from executive departments and agencies.

The overlap in advisory relationships and differentiation in administrative roles satisfied both the personal needs of the president and the institutional needs of the presidency. Ford desired an open office but he also wanted an ordered one. His propensity to consult with a variety of policy advisors was not only a calculated reaction to the Nixon era and the so-called imperial presidency, but it was also a natural result of his own style of decision making.

Ford liked people and enjoyed interacting with them. In the White House as in Congress, he preferred to assemble his key advisors, hear the issues debated, and then render a judgment. Prior to an important meeting, he would normally study option papers prepared by his staff. One high official described Ford's decision-making style as follows:

> In all the meetings I've had with him, he insists on having written analyses of the issues before he meets and he likes to have a night to read them over. He likes to have the issue presented to him in cogent terms and described analytically and objectively. He likes to have alternatives and know who is for and against each alternative.

Only in the most routine cases was Ford likely to depend on the paper alone as the basis for his decision. "I think I'm a better listener than I am a reader," he told author John Hersey, adding, " I have learned to read fast and to absorb, but there are certain things you can't do quickly, without talking them out—at least I can't." [78]

The contrast with Nixon is striking. Richard Cheney who had also served in the Nixon administration compared the two presidents' decision-making styles as follows:

> Nixon was not one who liked extensive policy debates with large numbers of people. He liked to work off paper. He liked to consult with one or two individuals but never with a group. Most of the group meetings in which I participated with Nixon, like a cabinet or Cost of Living Council session, were almost like a public meeting. It was not a place where you'd seriously discuss policy. Under President Ford, it is a very different situation. When there is a major decision to make, he likes to get everyone in the room so you may end up with 15 or 20 people sitting around the cabinet table. Sometimes he'll disagree with a majority of his advisors. There is no such thing as democracy rule in there. [79]

Ford seemed to derive considerable satisfaction from making decisions in this manner. Having contending points of view presented and argued, in a structured and nonthreatening way, enabled him to make reasoned judgments and to be decisive.

As president, Ford displayed little outward emotion in public or private. "To a considerable degree he is what you see," commented counselor Robert T. Hartmann." He has very little pretense and is a perfectly lousy actor. If he's not being genuine, it's pretty clear." [80] Hartmann described Ford's temper as "well disciplined" and "controlled" while another aide used the words "patience and tolerance." Hartmann added:

> I have very rarely seem him chew anybody out publicly. His general practice is to call someone in privately if he is annoyed. You can tell he's upset the minute you walk into the room but he doesn't rant and rave. Rather, his attitude is a sort of set to the jaw.[81]

Relying more on intuition and careful consideration, Ford consciously tried to downplay his own emotions in making decisions. In speaking with Hersey, he recalled his mother's advice:

> She taught me that you don't respond in a wild, uncontrolled way. You just better sit back and take a hard look and try to make the best decision without letting emotions be the controlling factors.[82]

As important as taking a hard look and making as rational a judgment as possible was decisiveness. For a person who thrives on challenges, decision making can be character building. It was for Ford. Throughout his life, he always found competition invigorating and challenges rewarding.

> I always have enjoyed facing up to problems; it's always been a sort of way of life with me and you certainly have them here. I really enjoy getting up every morning, looking at the schedule, seeing what the problems are. I don't long for the end of the day.[83]

The satisfaction that problem solving brought to Ford, combined with the initial uncertainties and insecurities he felt in the job, helps explain the self-imposed paradox of not liking conflict but insisting on it, of struggling with decisions but then tenaciously adhering to them. Ford was a man who had to prove to himself that he could do it. Being president and making decisions provided much of that proof.

While personally thriving on challenges, the president did not derive similar satisfaction from the contests and conquests of others, most notably, those of his staff. From his own aides, he wanted "competence, loyalty and hard work." [84] In talking with Hersey, he noted:

> Nothing is more frustrating to me . . . than to have staff jealousies. Nothing gets my mind off what I want to think about more than to have little petty jealousies in staff people. I just can't tolerate it, and its more disturbing to me than anything.[85]

While the need to avoid internal conflict, except within the context of a policy debate, and to achieve a unified team effort appeared to have been a major consideration in Ford's dismissal of his secretary of defense,

James R. Schlesinger, and his elevation of Richard Cheney to chief of staff,[86] the president's patience and tolerance seemed to get in the way of making other personnel changes. Ford's loyalty to old and trusted friends kept senior aides in top positions even though it was clear to many in the White House (perhaps including the president) that they should not have been retained. One experienced presidential aide stated, "Ford was such a nice guy that he refused to demand quality work." He added, "thank God for Rumsfeld and Cheney. They were the class of people that Ford brought with him. They were able to pull together a reasonably quality back-up staff."

Within the White House a subterranean advisory system evolved by the last year of the administration and was particularly active during the 1976 campaign. A separate speech-writing capability was established under the direction of David Gergen, a former Nixon aide, and a second track for developing some policy issues of particular complexity or importance to the president was set up. Certain individuals, usually designated by Cheney, were given special tasks that cut across traditional areas of responsibility, especially in the domestic and economic sectors. The projects generally involved decisions and actions that had significant political consequences for the president. Cheney's inner circle became the core decisional unit for the White House during the Ford campaign.

The establishment of back channels to the president had the effect of circumventing some senior advisors. "What tended to happen," stated a White House official, "was that all the good guys seemed to come to the top and pushed aside the people who couldn't cut it. It was a long process. The frustrations were legion." Another more junior staffer commented to the same effect:

> The people who were good got engaged in what was going on. Once they were engaged, they were busy all the time. Other people had titles and offices and wondered what the hell was going on. They had more time to play tennis, to have guests in from the press, to give speeches around the country and things like that.

While the development of a separate speech writing capability was perhaps Cheney's most flagrant challenge to a senior staffer, it was not the only one. There were other conflicts which generated considerable infighting. Press leaks by department and White House officials anxious to maintain their own positions, rally supporters, and head off certain decisions of the insiders became more common than during the first year. Who went to what meetings, who signed-off on what issues, and who could speak to the president last, were sources of contention. In the words of one official who performed frequent assignments for Cheney:

> There was a lot of back stabbing. They [cabinet heads and senior staff] would snipe at me through the press. They would try to keep me away from meetings or schedule them when I wasn't aware of them. But none of

that stuff worked. The plants always got back to me. I usually knew who did it. I didn't care about a decision or a meeting until it got to the president. And I was plugged in there.

White House staffing problems were, of course, not unique to the Ford presidency nor was Ford the first president to have loyalty impair his judgment. Staff has often functioned as a vital support mechanism for presidents, especially for those who have felt particularly challenged or beleaguered. Johnson during Vietnam and Nixon during Watergate provide obvious illustrations of presidents under attack who turned to their staffs for help, although both also demonstrated a great need for staff loyalty and support during less trying times. Truman too demanded fidelity as a condition for delegating authority and establishing close advisory relationships. The parallel between Truman and Ford is striking.

Neither sought to be president but neither shirked the duties and the decisional responsibilities of the office. Both brought a tremendous amount of energy to their job. Both placed a high priority on staff work and easily interacted with trusted subordinates. Neither had much patience with internal rivalries. Emphasizing the need to be reasonable and to use common sense, both seemed to derive positive reinforcement from making decisions. Their confidence appeared to increase as their presidency progressed. They enjoyed being president and campaigning for their first elective term as president.

It is thus not surprising that Ford recalled the Truman experience at the beginning of his administration in 1974. His favorable evaluation of Truman as president obviously had more to do with latter's style of decision making than with the substance of the decisions themselves. The President Truman model represented a realistic aspiration for Ford as president. When Ford hung Truman's picture in the cabinet room in the early days of his presidency, it was as if he were hanging his own portrait.

The Ford-Truman personality parallels do not extend very far into the structure and operation of their White Houses, however. By 1974, the White House was no longer the small, informal, highly personal office it had been in the late 1940s and early 1950s. The tremendous growth of presidential responsibilities combined with the institutionalization of presidential functions required a much larger and more specialized staff operation, especially at the secondary level. Procedures had become more formalized and lines of authority more distinct than in Truman's day. Despite Ford's desire to reverse the flow of personnel and power to the White House, he soon found that there was no turning back. In terms of size, structure, and administrative procedures, his White House was much more like Nixon's than Truman's.

In terms of style of decision making and mode of operation, however, it was very different from that of Nixon. From a management perspective, the Nixon White House functioned more efficiently than did Ford's. Jerry Jones, who served in both administrations, compared their operating styles as follows:

> Nixon was not necessarily a good manager but he was an activist president. He knew what he wanted done and brought in Haldeman and other very able management types to do it. Nixon really generated a lot of work. . . . It was sort of a top down motivational system.
>
> Ford didn't really want a structure that was a very aggressive, activist organization and took up steps to insure that it didn't become that. . . . He rarely said, "Hey, I want a program to do this or that." Things floated to him; he considered them, decided them and they went back down.[87]

Jones added that while the Nixon managerial style seemed to be more efficient, Ford's decisional style was probably more conducive to making better decisions:

> Nixon's psyche and biases frequently got in his way. He was overly concerned with political matters. Ford was able to say, "I'm not really interested in my political problems on this one. Let's do the right thing." And he was willing to bring people in long, endless, rambling meetings which would wind up maybe with a better solution in the end than would have been reached in the cut and dry five options on a piece of paper approach.[88]

In short, Ford's decisional structure permitted a more thorough airing of views, at least within the ideological and political framework of the advisors who regularly participated, but it also produced more internal bickering over jurisdictions and raised serious questions about the most efficacious use of the president's time.

CONCLUSION

The growth of presidential policy making has encouraged the development of a large, specialized and highly structured White House, one that has become capable of assisting the president in more of his duties but one that also has become less amenable to his direct, personal control. Initially, the White House had been viewed as the president's own office, a very personal place, designed primarily to help him with unavoidably presidential decisions and actions. Franklin Roosevelt used his staff in this way. He appointed a small number of aides, gave them action-forcing assignments and used their information for his own political as well as presidential ends. Truman and Eisenhower did so as well although more formal procedures and institutionalized arrangements for handling recurrent presidential obligations were established during their administrations.

Kennedy reverted to the Roosevelt model in purpose and form. He could not revert to it in size. His revitalization of the president's policy-making role, especially in the domestic area, created a need for greater White House involvement in the development and coordination of new policy proposals, and this, in turn, required a large presidential office. During the Johnson, Nixon, and Ford administrations, the staffs expanded considerably to handle these policy-making tasks as well as their subsidiary merchandising functions (see Table II-I).

In the process of expansion, the White House aggregated considerable power. By the 1970s, it had clearly become more than the president's personal office. It served the disparate needs of the presidency as well.

Along with the growth of the White House has come greater specialization in its function, formalization of its structure, and routinization of its procedures. Roosevelt appointed generalists and established bilateral relationships with overlapping assignments. While Truman too had a small number of principal assistants who enjoyed broad spheres of authority and easy interaction with him, he also turned to the institutional structures in his Executive Office such as the National Security Council and the Council of Economic Advisers which Eisenhower also used. Additionally, Eisenhower created secretaries, appointed special staff assistants, and more carefully differentiated roles, especially at the junior level.

Kennedy's return to Roosevelt's style deemphasized some of the func-

TABLE II-I.   The Size and Cost of the Contemporary White House

	Size		Cost (in thousands)	
FY	Estimated (in previous year's budget)	Actual	Estimated (in previous year's budget)	Actual
1971	533	533	9,568	9,568
1972	540	540	9,882	9,342
1973	510	510	9,767	10,825
1974	510	505	11,885	13,092
1975	540	533	14,053	15,398
1976	500	500	16,763	15,832
1977	485		17,162	
1978	460		17,580	

SOURCE: United States Budget, fiscal years 1970-1978.

tional divisions between aides and provided for a more horizontal staff organization. He looked outside the White House for new ideas, a practice that Johnson continued. Frequent interaction between Presidents Kennedy and Johnson and their White House aides tended to blur lines of authority at the more senior staff levels. It also had the effect of accentuating policy differences between the White House and the departments and agencies. With the emphasis on new presidential initiatives in the 1960s, the number of White House aides who were regularly involved in legislative policy making increased.

The creation of a loosely structured policy staff reflected the trend toward formalization and specialization in the organization of the White House. Until the middle of the 1960s, the special counsel handled most of the president's domestic legislative needs. Assisted by a few lawyers, the counsel was generally charged with coordinating legislative suggestions, drafting administration bills, writing special messages, and advising the president whether to sign or veto acts passed by Congress. With the establishment of the Cater and Califano operations during the Johnson presidency, the special counsel's role in domestic policy formulation was reduced. White House aides acquired increasing skills in dealing with policy matters.

The Nixon Domestic Council staff system was a natural consequence of these institutional developments. Its large, highly differentiated structure organized along subject-matter lines enabled the president to look within the White House for most of the advice and information he needed. This had the effect of distancing the departments and agencies from the critical points of decision. Reinforced by Nixon's "private" decision-making style, the structure elevated and isolated the president even within the presidency. While Ford's more open and candid manner encouraged greater participation from outside the White House and permitted final department and agency appeals, it did not change the basic position of the White House or its central role in the policy-making process. By the 1970s, the White House had acquired an identity and autonomy of its own.

The effect of the president's personality on the size, structure, and shape of the office has been muted somewhat by the staff's growth in numbers and responsibilities. When the White House was small and more informal and when there were fewer recurring presidential obligations, personality was a more important influence on staffing arrangements and operations. In Franklin Roosevelt's White House, the president's personality shaped the objectives, conditioned the organization, and affected the performance of his staff. But as the office has evolved, the impact of the president himself became less. Today, personality no longer dictates the entire staffing arrangement; rather, it shapes the relationship between the president and his senior aides, as to whom he consults on major issues, at what point he involves himself in the decisional process, whether he encourages his aides to present and argue different points of view or reach a consensus, and how much discretion he gives them. For the rest of the staff, there is a filtration effect.

All presidents have desired staff support but the degree to which they required loyalty and could tolerate dissent has varied considerably. Johnson and Nixon were notorious for their "thin-skins" and "we-they" attitudes. For Johnson, this translated into a need to dominate relations, to brook no dissent, and to be deeply involved in many administrative matters. In advisory relationships, he encouraged unanimity; in administrative relations, he discouraged independence. Nixon reacted in a very different manner. Instead of personally dominating these relationships, he avoided them and hid behind more formal structural arrangements. Instead of getting involved in details, he delegated supervisory authority to a few trusted aides. While he did not seek the concurrence of his advisors, he also did not have patience with disorganized dissent. The use of option papers provided him with alternatives without threatening his position as final and ultimate decision maker. By examining alternatives on paper and making his judgments alone, Nixon further insulated himself from the rancors of debate, avoided potential challenges to his decisions, and oriented staff expectations toward an advocacy role once the decision had been made.

Roosevelt, Truman, Kennedy, and Ford were more comfortable with staff debate. Roosevelt positively enjoyed it; Kennedy felt stimulated by it; Truman and Ford tolerated it, believing it necessary for the making of sound judgments. All, however, carefully drew the line between critical discussion and insubordination. Roosevelt and Kennedy seemed to have little difficulty in generating fierce loyalty on the part of their aides. Truman and Ford had more trouble, especially at the beginning of their administrations. The way each became president probably increased their need and concern for loyalty, most particularly from the holdover members of the previous administration.

In all likelihood, succeeding rather than being elected to the office also affected their own confidence. Believing a president should be assertive and decisive, they built up their own confidence by trying extra hard to be both. Neither they, Roosevelt, nor Kennedy avoided or were compulsively involved in details. All four interacted easily and frequently with their staffs.

Eisenhower was more distant. His preference for a well-organized White House, formalized procedures, and full-dress meetings reflected his military training, coincided with his organizing skills, and was consistent with his personal desire to oversee rather than manipulate, to preside rather than prevail.

IMPLICATIONS FOR THE FUTURE

A large, specialized White House staff is not necessarily inevitable, but it does seem likely so long as expectations and demands on the presidency remain as diversified and extensive as they presently are. Barring a massive public reeducation campaign or massive and persistent public disenchantment with presidential leadership, these demands and expectations are likely to persist. As a consequence, the president will continue to need help; he will continue to require an agency whose perspective is shaped by his priorities, whose schedule is set by his deadlines, and whose tasks are conditioned by his responsibilities. The White House office obviously fulfills all of these criteria while other executive agencies meet only some of them some of the time.

To a large extent, the growth of a White House staff structure has to come at the expense of the departments and agencies. By reducing the president's dependence on other units in the executive branch for information and advice, the president's staff enhances its own position. White House expertise naturally competes with that of the departments and agencies. The danger is where the competition is eliminated and the White House voice is the only voice.

The increased size and structural differentiation of the White House does not have to result in a closed presidency but it can contribute to it by its aggregation of power, position, and professionalism. Presidential aides operating under the strain of deadlines and the pressures of far-reaching, sometimes irreversible decisions, frequently find the bargaining and negotiations within the presidency sufficiently taxing not to want to extend it outside the White House, much less to the rest of the executive branch and the Congress. The size and pace of the presidency discourages touching all bases and conveying the views of all interested parties.

If such a White House is to be an integral part of the contemporary presidency, it has to be efficiently run. It is all well and good to desire flexibility and promote ad hoc arrangements so long as the policy-making machinery is properly coordinated, divergent views solicited and presented, and deadlines met; that is, so long as the president's decisional needs are adequately serviced. To accomplish this, a chief of staff or a small number of senior aides are probably needed. Additionally, there should be a close correspondence between staff rank, competence, and accessibility to the president. To allow staffing patterns and positions to develop through a process of natural selection, where the cream eventually comes to the top, wastes time and magnifies tensions. The Ford experience testifies to this.

In fact, the desire to create a pleasing and supportive environment for the president has often been incentive to limit the circle of policy advisors. Presidents have become isolated and it can happen again.

Presidents will have to agree to have disagreement in order to avoid the political pitfalls of isolation. In 1960, Richard Neustadt wrote that a president must consciously weigh his power stakes in order to make the right choice. By the mid-1970s, it was clear that the key to the power stakes was knowing all the choices. So long as the president was made aware of his options, including those he was not inclined to take, the power stakes were weighed in favor of him and his staff.

Allowing debate and disagreement serves another purpose. While it may not, in and of itself, change policy outputs, especially for a president who has a strong ideological commitment and applies it consistently, it is likely to improve his image and thereby enhance his capacity to govern. People want to be able to express their views and be heard by their president. They want him to listen.

The concentration of power within the White House has increased the potential for presidential clout. It has also made the presidency a more dangerous institution, a much bigger and more potent place than it was two or even one decade ago. Priority policy making is now centered in it. This makes an open presidency absolutely essential if responsive government is to be achieved. Presidents cannot ensure this type of government themselves but they can certainly encourage it by their personal inclinations and operating styles.

How to facilitate executive and congressional input into policy making without disorienting presidential objectives is the critical issue which every president and his staff must face. History offers some guidelines. The next chapter explores executive influence on policy making by examining the development of the central clearance and enrolled bill processes.

NOTES

1   President Washington had to pay his two personal assistants himself. Thomas E. Cronin, *The State of the Presidency* (Boston: Little, Brown, 1975), p. 118.
2   Ibid.
3   Joseph Kallenbach, *The American Chief Executive* (New York: Harper & Row, 1966), pp. 440–441.
4   The personal relationships between the individual secretaries and members of Congress often put the cabinet officials in a better position than the president to influence Congress. At the very least, they could usually sabotage presidential requests. This alone gave department secretaries considerable leverage in helping to design administration proposals. Their administrative autonomy also contributed to their presidential influence.
5   They lost their privileged position between president and Congress with the consequence that the support of the department secretaries became less important than it had been to the president's success in the legislature.
6   A commission, headed by Louis Brownlow, had urged that the president's

aides have a passion for anonymity. Richard E. Neustadt suggests that this caused considerable amusement in Washington at the time, adding that Roosevelt himself did not find it particularly humorous. Richard E. Neustadt, "Approaches to Staffing the Presidency," *American Political Science Review* LVII, no. 4 (December 1963): 857.

7   Alex B. Lacy, Jr., "The Development of the White House Office, 1939–1967," (Paper presented at the Annual Meeting of the American Political Science Association, Chicago, 1967), p. 15.

8   Neustadt, "Approaches to Staffing the Presidency," p. 857.

9   Richard E. Neustadt, *Presidential Power* (New York: Wiley, 1960).

10   Harry S. Truman, *1945 Year of Decisions* (New York: New American Library [Signet], 1955), p. 253.

11   The staff included Charles S. Murphy, administrative assistant to the president and later Clifford's successor; George M. Elsey; David Bell; Richard E. Neustadt; and David D. Lloyd. Bell, Neustadt, and Lloyd had all worked in the Bureau of the Budget (BOB) and this helped facilitate the close working relationship that characterized White House-BOB relations during the Truman period. In general, Clifford and Murphy were concerned with program coordination while Steelman and his group dealt with ongoing programatic operations. There was overlap, especially in the economic area, but, on the whole, Steelman tended to be less directly involved in generating legislation and more involved in overseeing its administration.

12   In his memoirs, Truman writes, "It was my intention to delegate responsibility to the properly designated heads of departments and agencies, but I wished to be in a position to see to it that they carried on along the lines of my policy." Truman, *1945 Year of Decisions,* p. 253.

13   George M. Elsey, interview.

14   Clark Clifford, interview.

15   Truman, *1945 Year of Decisions,* p. 255.

16   James D. Barber, *The Presidential Character* (Englewood Cliffs, N.J.: Prentice-Hall, 1972), p. 263.

17   Harry S. Truman as quoted in William Hellman, *Mr. President* (New York: Farrar, Straus & Giroux, 1952), p. 10.

18   Ibid.

19   Barber, *Presidential Character,* p. 271.

20   Barber phrases it as "the habit of nearly impulsive assertion of definite answers." Ibid., p. 261.

21   Elsey, interview.

22   He had initially discussed the problem of staffing with his brother, Milton. As a consequence of these discussions, he established an Advisory Committee on Government Organization chaired by Nelson Rockefeller. The resulting staff structure was based on the recommendation of this committee, the general guidelines of the Hoover Commission, and the specific suggestions of a private study conducted by a team from Temple University.

23   Dwight D. Eisenhower, *Mandate for Change, 1953–1956* (Garden City, N.Y.: Doubleday, 1963), p. 114.

24   According to Adams, Eisenhower "never specifically defined my responsibilities or outlined their limits. He never gave me, nor did I ever seek, a delegation of presidential power and authority, as so many Capital correspondents and politicians have assumed." Sherman Adams, *First-Hand Report: The Story of the Eisenhower Administration* (New York: Harper & Row, 1961), p. 50.

25   Eisenhower, *Mandate for Change,* p. 118.

26   Adams, *First-Hand Report,* p. 50.

27   Adams was accused of bringing pressure on two regulatory commissions, the Federal Trade Commission and the Securities and Exhange Commission, on behalf of a close friend, Boston industrialist Bernard Goldfine. In one case the action against Goldfine was dropped; in another a settlement that was originally proposed was accepted. Adams admitted to being indiscreet but claimed he did nothing wrong. When it came out that Goldfine had paid $3000 of Adam's hotel bills from 1953 to 1958 and had given him and his wife an expensive oriental rug and a vicuna coat, political sparks began to fly. Republican leaders asked Eisenhower to get rid of Adams. He finally yielded and on September 22, 1958, Adams submitted his resignation.

28   Persons stated, "Anybody on the staff could come into my office any time they wanted to see me. The door was open. There were very rare cases where the visitor asked that the door be closed. It was on those occasions. But other than that, the door was always opened." Wilton B. Persons, interview.

29   H. Roemer McPhee, interview.

30   Persons, interview.

31   McPhee, interview.

32   Barber suggests that Eisenhower was primarily an interpersonal coordinator but had "a propensity for withdrawal, for moving away from conflict and detail." He argues that this is characteristic of what he terms a passive-negative personality—"the man does as little as he can of what he does not like to do." Barber, *Presidential Character,* p. 172. Erwin Hargrove offers a different interpretation. Hargrove contends that Eisenhower was self-confident and had an inner strength. His style was an appeal to unity which he used to maximize support and minimize conflict within his administration. Getting his aides to work together enabled Eisenhower to delegate authority. Hargrove characterizes his personality as "active-positive." Erwin C. Hargrove, *The Power of the Modern Presidency* (New York: Knopf, 1974), pp. 58–64, 323.

33   Adams, *First-Hand Report,* pp. 72–73.

34   Bryce Harlow, interview.

35   In his book Adams states, "Whenever members of Congress requested appointments, Persons and I arranged them unless we knew of good reasons not to do so." Adams, *First-Hand Report,* p. 51.

36   Richard E. Neustadt, "Presidency and Legislation: Planning the President's Program," *American Political Science Review* XLIX, no. 4 (December 1955): 987–996.

37   Clark Clifford and Richard Neustadt had each prepared reports for Kennedy on the problems of transition and the creation of a new staff system. The Brookings Institution had also made a comprehensive study which Kennedy

examined right after the election. Together, these three reports provided the president-elect with detailed analyses as well as concrete recommendations.

38   The quotation attributed to Richard Neustadt in the background paper on staffing he prepared for Kennedy appears in Theodore C. Sorensen, *Kennedy* (New York: Harper & Row, 1965), p. 259.

39   Ibid., p. 262.

40   Arthur M. Schlesinger, Jr., *A Thousand Days: John F. Kennedy in the White House.* (Boston: Houghton Mifflin, 1965), p. 687.

41   Sorensen, *Kennedy,* p. 259.

42   Neustadt, "Approaches to Staffing the Presidency," p. 861.

43   According to Sorensen, Kennedy wanted his personal assistants to represent him and his interests. The staff's role was "to summarize and analyze those [departmental] products and proposals for him, to refine the conflicting views of various agencies, to define the issues which he had to decide, to help place his personal imprint upon them, to make certain that practical political facts were never overlooked, and to enable him to make his decisions on the full range of his considerations and constituencies, which no Cabinet member shared." Sorensen, *Kennedy,* p. 258.

44   Ibid.

45   Lyndon B. Johnson as quoted in Doris Kearns, *Lyndon Johnson and the American Dream* (New York: Harper & Row, 1976), pp. 174–175.

46   At another point Johnson told Kearns: "I needed that White House staff. Without them I would have lost my link to John Kennedy; and without that I would have had absolutely no chance of gaining the support of the media or the Easteners or the intellectuals. And without that support I would have absolutely no chance of governing the country." Ibid., pp. 177–178.

47   Joseph A. Califano, Jr., *A Presidential Nation* (New York: Norton, 1975), p. 39.

48   Devier Pearson, interview.

49   Califano, *A Presidential Nation,* p. 37.

50   James Gaither, interview.

51   Myer Feldman, interview.

52   Harry McPherson, *A Political Education* (Boston: Little, Brown, 1972), p. 285.

53   George Christian, *The President Steps Down* (New York: Macmillian, 1970), p. 19.

54   Kearns, *Lyndon Johnson and the American Dream,* p. 241.

55   Ibid.

56   One such story tells of aide Jack Valenti catching a late plane to New York City one evening to join his wife for the last act of a Broadway play. Johnson had announced that he was going to bed early. That night, the president came down with the flu and was hospitalized. Eric Goldman commented that the next few days were not happy ones for Valenti. Eric Goldman, *The Tragedy of Lyndon Johnson* (New York: Knopf, 1969), p. 108.

57   Lawrence F. O'Brien, *No Final Victories* (Garden City, N.Y.: Doubleday, 1974), p. 182.

58   Kearns, *Lyndon Johnson and the American Dream,* p. 319.

59   Frequently, the animosities displayed toward individual Vietnam critics did not carry over as well. Joseph A. Califano provides a vivid illustration in the case of Senator Wayne Morse, an early and vociferous critic of Johnson's policy in Southeast Asia, who had called for the president's impeachment:

> At lunch, one day with Harvard professor Richard Neustadt and me, during the early stages of the 1966 airline strike, Johnson concluded that we would have to stop the strike and set up an emergency labor board. He picked up the phone under the dining room table and asked the operator to get him Wayne Morse. When Morse got on the line, Johnson said, "Wayne, I know why you are always calling for my impeachment and why you want Bobby Kennedy to be president. It's because of all those tough jobs I ask you to do on our education bills and labor problems. Well, I've got another one." By the time the conversation had ended, Morse had agreed to chair the emergency board, which Johnson considered critical to the maintenance of the wage-price guideposts, a significant line of defense against inflation. (Califano, *A Presidential Nation,* pp. 209–210.)

60   Richard M. Nixon, from an untitled speech given on the NBC and CBS radio networks on September 19, 1968.

61   In an obvious reference to the Johnson presidency, Nixon complained, "its functions have become cluttered, the president's time drained away in trivia, the channels of authority confused." Ibid.

62   Robert Semple, Jr., "Nixon Rules Out Agency Control by Staff Aides," *The New York Times,* November 14, 1968, p. 1.

63   Burns left the White House in January 1970, to become chairman of the Federal Reserve Board. Moynihan was "elevated" to counselor to the president late in 1969 and left the administration in the summer of 1970 to return to Harvard. He later returned to the Nixon administration as ambassador to India.

64   Jerry Jones, interview.

65   John W. Dean, *Blind Ambition: The White House Years* (New York: Simon & Schuster, 1976), p. 65.

66   H. R. Haldeman as quoted in Dom Bonafede, "Men Behind Nixon/ Haldeman Directs Staff as Nixon's Alter-Ego," *National Journal Reports* III, no. 10 (March 6, 1971): 513.

67   Butterfield, "Testimony Before the Committee on the Judiciary," House of Representatives, Ninety-third Congress, Second Session, July 2, 1974, Book I, pp. 32 and 40.

68   Egil Krogh, Jr., interview.

69   John Ehrlichman as quoted in Richard P. Nathan, *The Plot that Failed: Nixon and the Administrative Presidency* (New York: Wiley, 1975), p. 40.

70   Ibid., p. 46.

71   Butterfield described Nixon as a clean desk man. Other than a clock and an out box, the only thing he would usually have on his desk were briefing papers which were stacked in order of the president's meetings. "Testimony Before the Committee on the Judiciary," p. 29.

72   Ibid., p. 65.

73   Richard T. Johnson, *Managing the White House* (New York: Harper & Row, 1974), p. 217.

74   Richard B. Cheney, interview.

75 Dom Bonafede, "People in Washington," *The Washingtonian* XI, no. 5 (February 1976): 47.

76 Cheney, interview.

77 Foster Chanock, interview.

78 Gerald R. Ford as quoted in John Hersey, "The President," *The New York Times Magazine,* April 20, 1975, p. 110.

79 Cheney, interview.

80 Robert T. Hartmann, interview.

81 Ibid.

82 Ford, in Hersey, "The President," p. 76.

83 Ibid., p. 40.

84 Ibid., p. 76.

85 Ibid.

86 In reflecting on these personnel changes, the president stated: "for me to do the job as well as I possibly can, I need a feeling of comfort within an organization, no tension, complete cohesion. There was a growing tension, and I felt very strongly that I needed to have a comfortable feeling even though people might disagree." Ford, Statement made on "Meet the Press," NBC television, November 9, 1975.

87 Jones, interview.

88 Ibid.

CHAPTER 3

Providing Legislative Clearance and Coordination: White House-OMB Interaction

White House assistant: "You're out of your Goddamn mind if you think you can go and tell the president that he is supposed to veto a bill that would give benefits to blind veterans."

Bureau of the Budget official: "Listen, you big policy guys can make that decision. What I am saying is that we recommend a veto. There are precedents in this case that could give us great fits."

> As recalled by Harry C.
> McPherson (Johnson administration)

> You've got in the OMB hierarchy some people who
> understand political considerations. The
> concept that OMB is filled with objective
> bureaucrats who don't pay attention to politics
> is mythology.

> Glenn R. Schleede (Nixon and
> Ford administrations)

> The Domestic Council and OMB have a unique relationship.
> We come at the same problem with different
> disciplines. Their discipline is that, first
> and foremost, they have to have the dollar in mind.
> Our discipline is, first and foremost, to find out

what are the real policy alternatives. But once
you get below that initial discipline, there is an
overlapping and interlocking concern with the
problem.

Arthur F. Quern
(Ford administration)

INTRODUCTION *

The need to coordinate executive machinery in its formulation of policy
decisions has been closely associated with the expansion of that machinery
and the growth and complexity of those decisions. So long as policy
demands on the president were limited and his primary domestic responsibilities were administrative in character, coordination seemed less of a
problem than coping with the vast number of executive decisions, many
of which routinely found their way to the president's desk. Having few
personal assistants of his own, the chief executive was forced to delegate
considerable authority to his department and agency heads.

Budget deficits at the end of the nineteenth century and the beginning
of the twentieth made economy in government as important an objective
as administrative efficiency. In 1921, Congress made it a presidential
responsibility with its passage of the Budget and Accounting Act. This law
required the president to submit annual budget estimates on behalf of the
departments and agencies. Cabinet secretaries and agency heads were
prohibited from making their own financial requests to Congress unless
specifically asked to do so by either House.

The Budget and Accounting Act created a Budget Bureau in the
Department of the Treasury to provide staff support. A directive, issued
by the first director of this office, General Charles Dawes, stipulated that
any department or agency request for legislation that would expend funds
from the Treasury had to be approved prior to its submission to Congress.[1]
The Budget Bureau was to act as the President's surrogate in these matters.

Beginning in the 1930s this centralized clearance process was extended to include all executive branch requests for legislation, regardless
of whether or not money would be expended. In each case, the budget

* The discussion in the early part of this chapter is based largely on Richard E.
Neustadt's Ph.D. dissertation, "Presidential Clearance of Legislation" (Harvard University, June 1950). Readers who are interested in a more detailed treatment of the
subject matter for the Roosevelt and Truman period should examine this work.

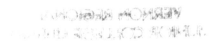

officials had to decide whether the proposal was in accord with the president's legislative program. If it was not, then it could not be submitted to Congress by executive departments and agencies.

At the end of the legislative process, after bills had passed both houses of Congress and were awaiting presidential action, a second coordinating process was instituted. Known as the enrolled bill process, it too was run by budget officials for the president. The procedure was to send copies of the newly enacted legislation to all departments and agencies that had been involved in its formulation, would be involved in its execution, or might have a legitimate interest in its substance or wording.[2] The departments and agencies were given 48 hours in which to advise the president whether he should approve or disapprove the legislation. Recommendations to disapprove were expected to list the objections in the form of a veto statement.[3] The Budget Bureau, which had been moved from the treasury department into the newly created Executive Office of the President in 1939, then collected and summarized these recommendations, added one of its own, and sent the entire file to the White House for the president.

This chapter will discuss the institutionalization of these two executive branch centralized coordinating processes. Particular emphasis will be placed on the interaction of the Office of Management and Budget (before 1970, the Bureau of the Budget) and the White House. The chapter is organized into the three parts. The first describes the structural and procedural arrangements for clearing legislation and for coordinating recommendations on enrolled bills during the Truman and Eisenhower administrations. The second and third parts examine these processes during the Kennedy-Johnson and Nixon-Ford administrations. The focus in these two sections will turn from the more formal clearance mechanisms to informal patterns of influence. While the formal procedures continued, they became less illustrative of key decisional responsibilities within the domestic presidency.

Beginning in the 1960s, the growth of the White House and, later, the politicization of OMB, not only affected the way in which clearance and enrolled bill decisions were made, but who made them. In examining these trends, this chapter will focus on two key questions: How did the size, experience, and, to some extent, shape of the White House staff influence the role and position of the OMB and how did the reorganization and reorientation of the OMB in the 1970s affect its influence in and with the White House?

The clearance and enrolled bill processes are discussed separately. While it is useful to conceptually distinguish between clearing proposed legislation and recommending action on enacted legislation, the two processes are, of course, interrelated. They are the beginning and end points of the legislative process within the executive, run by the same officials for the president. They lie at the core of the legislative presidency.

THE INSTITUTIONALIZATION OF PROCEDURES AND STRUCTURES: TRUMAN AND EISENHOWER

The administrative structure and operating procedures for the central clearance and enrolled bill processes were developed during the Roosevelt presidency and only slightly modified during the Truman and Eisenhower periods. Primary responsibility for clearing legislation and circulating enrolled bills was given to the Legislative Reference Division of the Bureau of the Budget. Since its creation in the mid-1940s, Legislative Reference has always been a small division, composed entirely of civil servants and headed by an official at the rank of assistant budget director (for legislative reference). Clearance and enrolled bill matters that required White House consideration during this period were handled by the president's special counsel's office. Between the two staffs, less than a half-dozen people usually were involved.

Clearance decision making was largely an internal Budget Bureau affair. The Legislative Reference Division itself made the initial judgment whether the proposal was in accord with the president's program. Only in very important and controversial decisions was the budget director normally involved. In determining the content of the program of the president, Legislative Reference analysts used campaign statements, major addresses and reports, and special messages to Congress. "From there on," stated Roger Jones, head of the division during much of the Truman and Eisenhower periods, "it was just a question of common sense." [4]

If there was a major issue in which the Budget Bureau was uncertain how the president's program applied or what that program actually was, the president's special counsel would be consulted. This was rare and it was often not so much for guidance as for support. "If an agency got obstreperous and started accusing us of trying to bite them with the president's teeth, why I would go to the White House," Jones stated.[5]

Throughout, Legislative Reference tried to avoid political judgments in making its decisions. Its job was to apply the program, not to determine what the program should be. In the words of Jones's successor, Phillip S. Hughes, "I never regarded Legislative Reference or me personally as kind of policy setters. I regarded us as agents of the presidency in matters of program establishment or development." [6]

The division's advice was usually final. While departments and agencies could appeal to the White House, this practice was not encouraged and was rarely successful. Jones had the ear of the president. Besides, both Truman and Eisenhower wanted the clearance mechanism to work. The number of agency end-runs to Congress, attempts to short-circuit the BOB's decision by encouraging a congressional appeal, were also surprisingly few and did not become a major problem for either administration.[7]

In fact, Congress itself found the clearance function useful. Beginning in 1947, standing committees of both houses started requesting the president's position on pending legislation that did not originate in the executive departments and agencies.[8] This was part of the Republican majority's attempt to obtain and maintain a more institutionalized and less personalized relationship with the president. The practice has continued.

Several important purposes were served by the clearance process. In addition to helping the president monitor department and agency legislative initiatives, it provided a mechanism for imprinting the presidential seal on those proposals that the president supported and withholding it from those he opposed. It also made the departments and agencies more aware of each other's views. As a matter of course, Legislative Reference distributed drafts of executive-initiated legislation to all departments and agencies that might have an interest in it. In coordinating their views, the division emerged as an administration problem solver and consensus builder. One of its most important functions was the resolution of conflict. Rather than provide negative advice and kill a proposal, the Budget Bureau would try to have the objectionable parts removed and mediate differences between agencies.[9] (See Appendix B for the types of clearance advice.)

From the departments' perspective, however, the clearance requirement was seen as a constraint and the Bureau of the Budget—the enforcing agency—as the people who said "no." The White House viewed it very differently. "The Bureau of the Budget for clearance was indispensable," stated Gerald Morgan, special counsel to President Eisenhower from 1954 to 1958. "They did a superb job of coordinating the government," he added.[10]

The volume of clearance requests and agency submissions was staggering. By the end of the Eisenhower period, over 13,000 separate congressional requests, agency reports, legislative drafts, and private bills were being regularly processed through the clearance mechanism during each Congress, with roughly twice as many items coming in the first session than the second. Since many of these reports and drafts were not of the routine variety, they required considerable time to examine. In order to cope with this tremendous volume of material, Legislative Reference's staff of approximately a dozen professionals had to depend heavily on the assistance of the budget examiners who were assigned to various departments and agencies. The examiners performed program-oriented work, providing Legislative Reference with substantive analysis and input.

Regularizing the Enrolled Bill Operation

The administration's dependence on the BOB's coordination and advice carried over into the enrolled bill phase of the process. Here too, Legislative

Reference exercised considerable autonomy in its own decision-making sphere and exerted much influence on the president. Clark Clifford, Truman's special counsel, put it simply: "We were not equipped to do that job ourselves, Budget did it and did it effectively." [11] During the Eisenhower period, enrolled bills averaged over 600 during the first session and over 1000 during the second. Moreover, the tendency of Presidents Truman and Eisenhower to use the veto frequently enhanced the potential effect which this process had on presidential decision making. It did influence the president's judgment. Truman vetoed 250 bills and Eisenhower, 181.

The procedures for considering enrolled bills followed a pattern that had been established in the Roosevelt administration. After the legislation had been passed by both houses of Congress, the Bureau of the Budget circulated copies to departments and agencies, received their responses, collated and summarized these views, appended its own recommendation, and sent the entire file to the White House. There it went to the special counsel's office where it was reviewed again before being sent to the president.

For both Truman and Eisenhower, the special counsel's office was the critical link between them and the BOB on these matters. It was up to the counsel to decide whether other presidential aides need be consulted, to alert the president to any particular problem, and to advise him when the BOB recommendation should not be followed. In the vast majority of cases, the file would be examined and then forwarded to the president. Routine legislation or bills that had unanimous or near unanimous recommendations required little additional scrutiny beyond what the Bureau of the Budget had done. Only if the bill were controversial or if it was an issue of major importance would the special counsel attach a covering memorandum with recommendations or even call a White House conference to consider the legislation.

The Legislative Reference Division was expected to base its advice on the merits of the legislation. It was not supposed to take partisan considerations into account. This was left to the White House. Throughout the Truman and Eisenhower periods, White House aides who dealt regularly with the Budget Bureau did not see it overstepping its legitimate bounds and making political judgments. They valued BOB's objective, analytical advice.

Presidents Truman and Eisenhower differed in the way they handled enrolled bills and made their decisions. Consistent with the way he did business, Truman took an active interest in enrolled enactments. He scrutinized them closely and even got involved in the actual drafting of the veto messages and signing statements. Eisenhower was not as interested in all kinds of measures and tended to deal with enrolled enactments quickly and without detailed personal review. President Eisenhower did take an interest in particular issues, however, such as a private relief bill that would have paid money to a military officer for an invention he made while on active duty. According to one aide who was with Eisenhower at the time he considered this bill:

> The president did not think anybody in the military had spare time in service to the United States. He reminded us how he, as a young officer in Washington, had served General Pershing, working until two or three in the morning, "none of which was spare time." He got quite exercised as he was making his decision but he signed the bill anyway, almost putting the nib of the pen through the bill paper.[12]

The working styles of the two presidents were also different. Truman preferred working from the written memoranda, although on important bills his special counsel would be present when he considered what to do. Eisenhower liked his staff to give him an oral briefing. While the assistant director for Legislative Reference participated in some of these briefings with the president, the BOB's major influence was in the compendium it prepared for each enrolled bill. In many cases, its file constituted the only information at the president's disposal and its advice was generally given the greatest weight since the BOB was the only agency, other than the White House, that spoke directly for the president. Also, its recommendation was the last one to be added before the bill reached the White House. It was confidential even to the agencies and thus not easily subject to appeal. This, of course, contributed to the mystique of the Budget Bureau and its clout with the president.

An examination of the BOB's recommendations and presidential actions for the Eisenhower period, 1953–1960, reveals a very high level of agreement between what the Budget Bureau advised and what the president did (see Table III-I).

That presidents tended to agree more with their Budget Bureau's recommendation to approve rather than veto legislation is not sur-

TABLE III-I. BOB Recommendations and Presidential Actions on Enrolled Bills, 1953–1960

	BOB Recommendation	Presidential Action	Percent Agreement
Approve the legislation	6659	6654	99
Disapprove the legislation	228	174	76

SOURCE: Legislative Reference Division, Office of Management and Budget.

prising. For most enrolled bills, there is a presumption in favor of the legislation; Congress has passed it and many of the same forces operating in the legislature are felt in the executive as well. On the other hand, the BOB is more insulated from these pressures than are the departments and agencies. Moreover, its recommendation is not supposed to be based primarily on those partisan factors, which may ultimately influence the president to approve the legislation.

Relying on the Bureau of the Budget

The White House and the Bureau of the Budget interacted smoothly during this period. To some extent, the small number of presidential aides in the special counsel's office had little choice but to depend on Legislative Reference for staff support in handling the large volume of legislative activity within the executive branch. Personal relationships also worked to cement the institutional arrangements. Major structural adjustments that could have been expected when the White House changed hands, when each White House staff gained in experience and expertise, or when a new assistant director of Legislative Reference was appointed, did not occur. This undoubtedly reflected the high evaluation of the BOB's performance held by Presidents Truman and Eisenhower and their respective aides.[13] It also indicated the self-generating nature of the processes themselves.

Roger Jones, the assistant director of Legislative Reference from 1949–1957, was universally praised by White House aides. One aide who joined midway through the Eisenhower administration commented that Jones had been introduced to him by a senior White House official as "the most valuable man in the U.S. government." "In retrospect, this turned out to be true," he added. Jones saw the president on frequent occasions. He commented:

> For reasons best known to himself, Ike would sometimes stop and talk to me when he saw me around the White House. Several times he took me out in the backyard when he was getting ready to hit golf balls.[14]

Jones's personal contacts with the president were heaviest in the 1953–1956 period. Phillip (Sam) Hughes, head of the division from 1958 to 1965, had less contact with Eisenhower but had a good working relationship with the president's staff. James F. C. Hyde, Jr., who worked with both Jones and Hughes as a legislative analyst said:

> Both men were able to establish close relationships and gain high respect from key White House people. . . . Roger Jones was a very dominant figure. He was very much involved in policy making; he had no notion that a career person should be difficult. Sam Hughes was also very much that way.[15]

Jones and Hughes praised their accessibility to the Truman and Eisenhower White Houses. There was no difficulty in knowing whom to consult on what types of issues. Jones noted:

> We knew exactly where each peg fitted in the picture and if there was a question of a veto coming down the pike, you knew who was the White House man with whom you were going to have to work on that veto message; it wasn't always the same person: it depended on various and sundry things.[16]

In addition to the influence of personalities, the processes also worked toward their own perpetuation. Departmental initiatives, encouraged by the White House, soon became an expectation not only of the departments but of their congressional and interest group clientele. The growing number of these policy proposals required and, at the same time, engulfed the structure that was designed to coordinate them. Policy positions were expected to reflect department and agency views. If distinctions were to be made between presidential and nonpresidential interests, then a central clearance mechanism, controlled either directly or indirectly by the president, had to be established. Ironically, it was the successful operation of this mechanism that relieved departments and agencies of much of their responsibility for making this distinction themselves. Budget became the initial judge and the White House and, ultimately, the president, the final arbiter.

During the Truman and Eisenhower presidencies, when the departments and agencies were the primary sources for new policy proposals, clearance served the very important goal of highlighting those executive branch proposals that the administration wished to claim as its own. It also was employed to help in the internal coordination of other executive initiated proposals within the bureaucracy. Once the primary sources for new domestic policy began to shift from the departments and agencies in the 1960s, however, the function of the clearance process began to change as well. It evolved into a presidential mechanism for saying no, for preventing legislation which the administration viewed as undesirable. This more negative use of the clearance system plus the routine character and tremendous volume of legislation to be cleared, made the process of less value to the president for creating a legislative record but perhaps of greater value in keeping the bureaucracy in line.

THE GROWTH OF WHITE HOUSE CLEARANCE: KENNEDY AND JOHNSON

During the Kennedy-Johnson period, with its emphasis on new presidential initiatives, centralized clearance procedures continued to be required; however, the White House began to play a larger role in the decisions on priority items, especially as they concerned program development. This had the effect of expanding the Legislative Reference Division's workload but diminishing its influence.

The relatively small White Houses of the Kennedy and early Johnson years were dependent on the BOB for staff support. Sorensen stated:

> We had to rely on the Bureau of the Budget to do the legislative work, to be the extra eyes, ears, arms and legs. That made the bureau's legislative function particularly important.[17]

Lee White, a member of Sorensen's staff, noted simply, "There was just too damn much to do without that type of assistance." [18]

The Budget Bureau's memory was especially critical for new White House staffers at the very beginning of their administration. Aide Myer Feldman recalled an incident right after Kennedy's inauguration in which the BOB provided him with a quick lesson in standard operating procedures.

> My swearing in was deferred while Kennedy asked me to draft his first executive order. It was an order to provide surplus food for poor people. He had made that a campaign commitment in West Virginia. I went up to my office, wrote it and typed it out myself, brought it downstairs, cleared it with the president, and released it to the press. I then got a call from the Bureau of the Budget which went something like this:
>
> BOB: What's this all about?
> *Feldman:*   We just issued an executive order.
> BOB: Don't you know you're supposed to go through a regular procedure? You have to clear it with all government agencies involved.
> *Feldman:*   No, but we will in the future.

"And we did," he added.[19]

During the 1960s, the number of clearance submissions remained relatively constant but the complexity of the legislation increased. There was a greater overlapping of jurisdiction among agencies with the result that more time had to be spent on the coordination of their legislative activities. Legislative Reference also assumed a larger role in message drafting. Analysts in the division helped in the wording of the legislation, the writing of the special messages, and the drafting of signing and veto statements.

While the fluidity of Kennedy's initial staff structure created some early problems of coordination, interaction between the White House and Bureau of the Budget developed to the point where it was lauded as "maybe the best relationship there ever was between the two institutions" by one of Johnson's special counsels and as "very flexible, easy but not undemanding" by the head of Legislative Reference during this period.

As time wore on, however, the White House became more involved in the clearance decisions. Items of greater presidential interest were distinguished from the more routine department and agency requests. A two-track system began to emerge with White House aides handling the more important matters.[20] Budget participated in these decisions but it was not to the same extent nor at the same administrative level as during the Truman and Eisenhower periods. The increased involvement of the president and his staff weakened the Budget Bureau's role in clearance decision making. In some cases, it encouraged department and agency heads to short-circuit the process by coming directly to the White House; in others, it made appeals to the president more likely.

Stylizing the Veto Process

The extension of White House involvement in legislative policy making is less evident with respect to the disposition of enrolled bills. Democratic control of Congress produced less disagreement between executive and legislative branches. There was a significant decrease in the number of vetoes. Kennedy vetoed only 21 bills and Johnson, 30. Congress did not override any of these vetoes.

The basic structure of the enrolled bill process did not change materially. Legislative Reference introduced minor alterations in the format of its covering memo (see Appendix B) and also reorganized its own internal operation.

Within the White House, there were also some changes but they were mainly stylistic. The special counsel's office still continued to be the focal point for all enrolled bills, although, in the last few years of the Johnson presidency, others, especially domestic policy advisor Joseph Califano, participated in making recommendations to the president and in helping to prepare the enrolled bill message. There was also input from the president's congressional relations aides when vetoes were contemplated. For most bills, however, only the counsel's office and frequently only a single person in that office saw the file before it went to the president.[21]

For the president's counsel, scrutinizing all the bills with a small staff and limited time available proved difficult. Dependence on the BOB continued, especially for legislation which was initially judged routine and noncontroversial—the large majority of all legislation. In making recommendations to the president, the Budget Bureau frequently took a harder line than the departments and agencies, applying cost factors, the president's program, and precedent as reasons for its recommendations. As in the past, the departments and agencies tended to recommend approval more often, largely to placate their clientele and congressional friends.

Sometimes these political interests rendered the BOB recommendation unrealistic. Harry McPherson recalled the following conversation on a BOB recommendation to veto a bill to benefit blind veterans:

White House assistant: You're out of your Goddamn mind if you think you can go and tell the president that he is supposed to veto a bill that would give benefits to blind veterans.

Bureau of the Budget official: Listen, you big policy guys can make that decision. What I am saying is that we recommend a veto. There are precedents in this case that could give us great fits.[22]

After the special counsel considered the legislation, he sent his recommendation along with the others to the president. Kennedy used the enrolled bill file exclusively in acting on noncontroversial bills where there were no differences among the recommendations. In important bills where there were differences, he would talk the matter over and occasionally supplement these discussions with a call directly to someone whose opinion he particularly wanted, such as Larry O'Brien. Johnson liked to consult with a variety of individuals before making his decision. He left few stones unturned although in the end, he too, looked to his own staff for guidance.

The pattern of presidents accepting their Budget Bureau's recommendations to approve legislation continued. Only once during the entire eight-year period was the BOB's approval advice rejected. However, its negative recommendations were not followed as frequently in the Johnson administration as they were in the two previous administrations. Between 1965 and 1968, the president approved 27 bills out of a total of 62 that the BOB recommended be vetoed. The larger role of the White House staff, the declining influence of the Legislative Reference Division, and the president's own sensitivity to political influences contributed to his disagreement with the Budget Bureau's veto recommendations.

Centralizing Decision Making in the White House

The alterations that were taking place in White House-BOB relations did not become evident until the end of the Johnson period. They were the result of structural and personality changes: the growth in the size and organization of the president's domestic policy advisors under the leadership of Joseph A. Califano, Jr., the establishment of a new position of assistant director for human resources programs in the Budget Bureau, and the resignation of Phillip S. Hughes as assistant director of the Legislative Reference Division in 1966 and his replacement by Wilfred H. Rommel. Together, these developments signaled the beginning of a more highly specialized and politicized relationship between the White House and the Bureau of the Budget.

The centralization of White House decision making and the systematization of the policy process were part of Califano's original design. He had intended to organize the domestic side of the White House, making it into a more coherent and systematic operation. While his assistants tended to be generalists by training, they soon developed specialized areas of responsibility. This too was intentional. Califano states:

> Over a period of three or four months, I brought in about five or six people to work for me. They were divided functionally as distinguished from the departments and agencies. In other words, if someone handled manpower and employment problems, he would handle them regardless of the government agency in which they jurisdictionally fell. And he would handle the legislative affairs program in those areas.[23]

This carried over into the clearance process. Referrals to the White House took into account these individual staff responsibilities.

In addition to a more differentiated staff structure, the White House began taking a greater interest in departmental coordination, especially as it related to the Great Society programs. Califano estimated that in his first two years he spent 20 percent of his time on the departments and 80 percent on legislative and economic policy. "In the last two years, the bulk of my time was spent on trying to get my departments to work together," he added.[24] This had the effect of involving the White House more in ongoing clearance decisions.

Items in which the White House had an interest were regularly referred to the president's aides for determination. Departments and agencies took to clearing congressional testimony directly with the president. Johnson wanted to oversee and coach the administration line. As a consequence, the civil servants in the Legislative Reference Division were left with the more routine legislative matters. They also became distanced from critical points of decision. The establishment in the Bureau of the Budget of an assistant director for human resources programs further extended this trend. By dealing directly with the White House on a number of policy problems, this Budget Bureau office broke the near-monopoly which Jones and Hughes had created in channeling the flow of legislative items to the White House. Wilfred H. Rommel, the new assistant director of the Legislative Reference Division did not challenge these developments. Differing from his predecessors, Jones and Hughes, in style, temperament, and philosophy, Rommel believed that policy positions should be taken by the political appointees of the president and not civil servants in the bureau. He saw his division's role in ministerial terms and his own contributions as more technical than policy oriented. His perspective both augured and hastened the declining influence of senior civil servants in the Bureau of the Budget.

POLITICIZATION AND DIFFERENTIATION: NIXON AND FORD

The transition between the Democratic and Republican administrations was made difficult initially by the proliferation of staff around competing circles of domestic policy advisors in the Nixon White House. For BOB officials, sensitized to White House clue giving, this was particularly frustrating. One senior official in the Legislative Reference Division stated:

> There were times when I damn near went off my rocker because of short deadlines, and complex problems. They hadn't yet come up to the point of being able to handle it in the decision-making process. They just weren't ready for it.

The problem of not having a mechanism in the White House capable of responding to clearance decisions was partially resolved by a temporary arrangement in which Legislative Reference officials met each day with a group of White House aides. The meetings provided a basis for establishing administration policy. In addition, they enabled new political appointees in the White House to evaluate the work and the loyalties of BOB careerists.

To new and relatively inexperienced presidential aides, who may have felt at the mercy of a hostile bureaucracy, asking the right questions and getting factual information from an institution that could be trusted filled an immediate and pressing need.

Throughout the Nixon and Ford presidencies, the White House depended on the BOB's successor, the Office of Management and Budget (OMB), to coordinate policy, to maintain a consistent administration position, and to referee minor disputes. "Without that function there would have been chaos," said one Nixon assistant, concluding, "It was an absolutely irreplaceable function. The White House lacked the staff, the experience and the time to assume legislative oversight on a continuing basis." [25]

The principal points of contact on clearance matters were between Legislative Reference and the appropriate member of Ehrlichman's staff once he had emerged as the president's main domestic policy advisor. The subsequent reorganization of his aides into a Domestic Council staff had little effect on these channels of communication. Throughout the Nixon presidency, the Domestic Council staff was practically indistinguishable from the White House staff. [26]

Operating a Specialized Staff Structure

Clearance decisions were handled in much the same manner during the Nixon and Ford presidencies. Budget officials consulted with the staff member of the Domestic Council who had subject-matter jurisdiction over the proposed legislation or congressional testimony. Whether this staff member made the policy decision or deferred to his superiors on the council staff depended on the gravity of the issue and the time available. A 24-hour or even 48-hour response obviously did not permit the same kind of consultation that a longer period allowed.

There was greater control and centralized decision making during Ehrlichman's tenure as executive director than during that of his successors, Kenneth R. Cole or James M. Cannon. As the Ford period developed, associate directors of the Domestic Council staff enjoyed considerable autonomy within their respective spheres. Stated Richard D. Parsons, a Ford associate director, "I have the authority to clear what I need under the circumstances. It is really my call if I want to go higher." [27]

In general, it was up to the OMB to use its judgment when to involve Domestic Council staff on clearance questions. There was an ebb and flow in decision making during much of this period, reflecting shifts in the nexus of power between the White House and OMB.

The enrolled bill process was more formal and more internalized within the respective presidential offices. Instead of joint decisions, there tended to be separate recommendations. Within the White House, the procedures for handling enrolled bills were more elaborate and systematic than they had been in previous administrations. When copies of legislation, including department and agency reports and OMB recommendations, reached the White House, they were sent to appropriate members of the Domestic Council staff, the congressional relations staff, and any other White House aides who had a particular interest in the legislation. The executive director of the council exercised overall supervision.

If the bill was not controversial and there were no objections to it, the file would be sent pro forma to the executive director of the council for final approval before being forwarded through the staff secretary and the assistant to the president to the chief executive for his action. If the bill was controversial, it was the job of the Domestic Council staff members to prepare a covering memo, pinpointing the controversy and summarizing White House opinion as well as that of the OMB and, in some cases, the major departments or agencies. This memo, in effect, became an option paper for the president.

The lack of time to properly consider the enrolled bill was a persistent problem for busy White House aides charged with making recommendations to the president. As a consequence, they continued to depend on the arguments and positions of the departments and agencies, most notably, the OMB. In effect, the Domestic Council memo usually summarized the OMB memo which synthesized the opinions and recommendations of the departments and agencies. The president's aides thus appeared to exercise more of an independent judgment than they were actually able to do most of the time.

In general, President Ford was more interested in enrolled legislation than was President Nixon and used the veto more as a strategy in dealing with Congress. The decision-making styles of the two presidents were also different. Nixon preferred to work from the written enrolled bill report, focusing his attention on those bills on which opinion was divided. Ford wanted controversial issues not only presented on paper but also in meetings. Moreover, he requested that his aides specify whether their opinion was based primarily on substantive or political considerations so he could be certain that he understood the basis for their judgments.

Exercising the Veto

In arriving at their decisions, both presidents, like their predecessors, continued to be influenced by the OMB and by the principal department or agency into whose jurisdiction the bill fell. An OMB recommendation to approve the bill was almost always followed. As the agency that says "no" most often, its advice to the president to sign the legislation seemed to be regarded as an all-clear signal by the White House.[28] Rarely did either president disregard this opportunity to approve legislation.

Ford tended to go along more with the OMB's veto advice than did Nixon. In the two and one-half years of his administration, the OMB offered more negative advice and President Ford responded in kind. He vetoed 66 bills compared to Nixon's 43 in five and one-half years. Table III-II indicates the number of OMB veto recommendations and presidential actions on controversial legislation during most of this period. Controversial legislation in this table is considered to be any bill or resolution in which there was at least one recommendation to veto. Three other factors seem to have contributed to Nixon's greater inclination to approve legislation than Ford: the larger size of his domestic policy staff, the greater disagreement among executive branch agencies during his administration, and the natural aging of the Republican presidency from 1968 to 1976.

The White House is the place that political pressures, especially those emanating from the Congress, are most likely to be conveyed to the president. Once the Congress has passed the legislation, these pressures are normally for the president to approve. The relatively large number of domestic policy aides during the 1970–1972 period had the effect of extending the White House's political antennas and making it more sensitive to these pressures. President Nixon, very conscious of the political implications of his decisions, tended to be persuaded by these political considerations much of the time.

TABLE III-II. OMB Recommendations and Presidential Actions on Controversial Enrolled Bills, 1969–1976 (June 30)

		OMB Recommendation		
		Approve	*Disapprove*	*Total*
N I X O N	Approve	52	43	95 (73.1%)
	Disapprove	2	33	35 (26.9%)
	TOTAL	54 (41.5%)	76 (58.5%)	130 (100%)

		OMB Recommendation		
		Approve	*Disapprove*	*Total*
F O R D	Approve	23	30	53 (56.4%)
	Disapprove	2	39	41 (43.6%)
	TOTAL	25 (26.6%)	69 (73.4%)	94 (100%)

SOURCE: Stephen J. Wayne, Richard L. Cole, and James F. C. Hyde Jr., "Advising the President on Legislation: Patterns of Executive Branch Influence," (Paper delivered at the Annual Meeting of the American Political Science Association, Washington, D.C., September 1–4, 1977).

Greater executive branch disagreement over whether the president should approve or disapprove legislation during the Nixon presidency also decreased the likelihood of his vetoing bills. Presidents are reluctant to negate acts of Congress unless they receive strong opposition to the legislation from within the executive. They are primarily concerned with the recommendations of the OMB and the lead agency, the one that would be principally charged with administering the bill. There were more splits between the lead agency in President Nixon's first term than during President Ford's administration. Most of these splits saw the lead agency support the legislation and the OMB oppose it. This is the typical pattern. Many of the same clientele pressures that are exerted on the Congress are also exerted on the departments and agencies. The OMB tends to be more resistant to these pressures because it is a presidential agency. President Nixon reacted to these differences of opinion between the lead agency and the OMB by giving the legislation the benefit of doubt and approving it. President Ford, receiving more unified advice to disapprove enrolled bills, found it easier to exercise his veto.

Finally, the age and partisanship of an administration and a Congress are also related to the number of presidential vetoes. If Nixon and Ford are any indication, Republican presidents appear to be more willing to go along with Democratic legislatures at the beginning of their presidencies when the hopes of achieving their legislative goals are greatest. As the time to the next election nears, however, they naturally try to distinguish their policy positions from those of a Democratic Congress in order to campaign against that Congress. Nixon and Ford both increased their vetoing as their administrations progressed. Ford's larger number of vetoes may be explained in part by his succession to the presidency in August preceding the November congressional election and then, by his own quest for the presidency two years later.

Reorienting and Reorganizing the OMB

In the same 1970 reorganization that created the Domestic Council, the Office of Management and Budget was created from the Bureau of the Budget and given additional management responsibilities and political staff. Its new internal structure divided budget, management, and legislative responsibilities among four assistant—later associate—directors, whose positions were classified as political not civil service. They were charged with national security and international affairs, human and community affairs, economics and government, and natural resources, energy, and science respectively. Figure III-I charts this organization. Designed to parallel the counselor system that went into effect at the same time—January 1973—it also paralleled to some extent, the divisions within the White House's domestic policy-making staff.

Within the OMB, the associate directors were placed in the critical policy positions. Since they had supervisory authority over the operating divisions in which the examiners were assigned, they became key decision makers on major budgetary, managerial, and legislative questions within their respective subject-matter spheres. While the head of Legislative Reference could appeal these decisions to the OMB director, in practice he did not often do so. As a consequence, clearance decisions tended more and more to reflect the associate director's view rather than that of the civil servants in the Legislative Reference Division.[29]

The OMB's channels of communication with the White House were also affected by the change. The major contact occurred between the associate directors of the Domestic Council and the Office of Management and Budget. They were both housed in close proximity to one another in

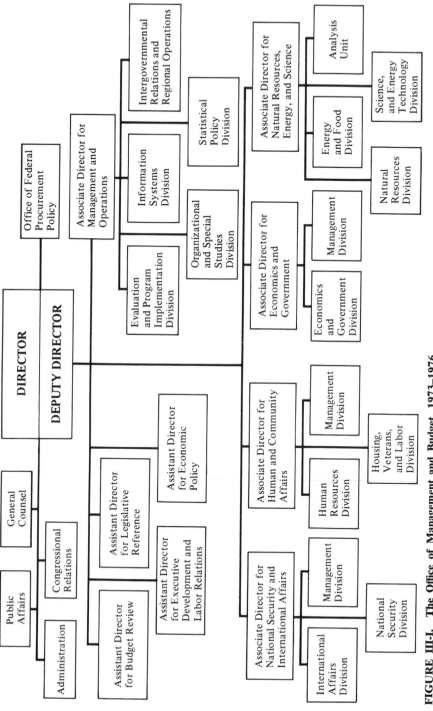

FIGURE III-I. The Office of Management and Budget, 1973–1976

the Old Executive Office Building across from the west wing of the White House. They jointly participated in the morning staff meetings in the Nixon and early Ford periods.[30] And they frequently communicated with each other throughout the day on budgetary as well as legislative matters.

The shift in decisional authority from civil servants to political appointees within the OMB was apparent in enrolled bill decisions as well. On the sensitive issues, especially those in which the departments and agencies disagreed on recommendations, bills would be referred by Legislative Reference to the appropriate OMB associate director for a decision. In general, if the administration did not have a clearly articulated position, the associate director would be called on to determine one. If there was a position, Legislative Reference would simply use it as a yardstick in rendering a recommendation to the president.

These developments within the OMB placed the departments and agencies at a disadvantage. The associate directors of the OMB had more authority than the director of the Legislative Reference Division had. Their functional responsibilities cut across budget, management, and legislative lines. They were also more politically responsive to the president on policy matters. As a result, they tended to be less amenable to negotiations and compromises pushed up by civil servants within the departments and more insistent on bringing the bureaucracy into line with the administration's position. Instead of ideas welling up, initiatives were sent down, especially during the first term of the Nixon presidency. This accelerated the centripetal tendencies that had been at work in the executive branch since the early 1960s.

Shifting White House-OMB Relationships

The politicization of the OMB also contributed to that agency's own position vis-à-vis the White House, at least in the short run. As the second term of the Nixon administration began, the OMB's policy-making role expanded and its influence equaled that of the Domestic Council. In fact, in the aftermath of Watergate, the OMB became the dominant voice in coordinating and developing policy initiatives to the extent that they were developed at all. Possessing a larger staff, greater information resources, more technical skills, stronger leadership, and more extensive operational influence over department and agency activities, the OMB filled the vacuum which was created by the reduction in size of the Domestic Council, the departure of Ehrlichman, and the demise of the counselor system. As one OMB official saw it by the end of 1975:

> The center of decision-making power tended to shift from White House staff to these associate directors, checking with the White House staff but maintaining really in their hands the basic initiative. They had the

big staff that could work the problem. And more and more, as time went on, they sort of took over.

By the summer of 1974, OMB's associate directors were checking very infrequently with the Domestic Council.

During the 1972–1974 period when the OMB began to assert its institutional muscle, relations with the Domestic Council became very tense. According to one OMB official, "each side viewed the other as fierce competitors. It was very rough and nasty in those days." Kenneth Cole, executive director of the council at the time, also confirmed the competition, suggesting that it created some harsh feelings. However, he regarded a degree of competitiveness as a natural consequence of the institutional relationship between these two presidential agencies.[31]

By 1976, however, a more equitable balance had been restored. Improved morale under a new president, new personnel, and a slightly larger size revitalized the Domestic Council staff operation. While the OMB still retained superior resources, the council staff strengthened its position and gained at least equal access to the president. Relations also began to improve and tensions started to ease, with collegiality rather than competition characterizing the institutional interaction. Together, changes in personnel, the emphasis on holding down domestic spending, and the Ford style of policy making seemed to move the OMB and the Domestic Council back onto the same political wavelengths.

Far from being threatened, the president's domestic policy aides seemed to welcome the OMB's budget perspective and its political sensitivities. Arthur F. Quern, a deputy director of the Domestic Council staff during the Ford administration put it this way:

> We come at the same problems with different disciplines. Their discipline is that first and foremost, they have to have the dollar in mind. Our discipline is, first and foremost, to find out what are the real policy alternatives. But once you get below that initial discipline, there is an overlapping and interlocking concern with the problem.[32]

Obviously, the political agreement between senior Domestic Council and OMB officials helped cement these "overlapping and interlocking" concerns. Glenn Schleede, a Domestic Council associate director who had previously worked in the OMB, put the matter simply and directly:

> You've got in the OMB hierarchy some people who understand political considerations. The concept that OMB is filled with objective bureaucrats who don't pay attention to politics is mythology.[33]

Whether this political agreement, however, provided the president with adequate nonpolitical advice was another issue, one on which there was considerable disagreement.[34]

CONCLUSION

The objective of legislative clearance has always been to coordinate executive policy making from a presidential perspective. Developed at the time policy initiatives were rapidly becoming an expectation of the modern presidency, the clearance mechanism has served to facilitate oversight, direction, and if need be, control for the chief executive. The OMB has played the pivotal role in this process. As the major coordinating and policing agency, it has performed legislative functions in a somewhat analogous manner to its budget duties. Helped by institutional resources that have exceeded those of the White House, the OMB has provided the process with muscle and stability.

From the perspective of the departments and agencies, the changes in the formal procedures have been minimal. Legislative views, testimony, and proposals emanating from the executive branch still require presidential clearance. The OMB's advice is still binding on executive branch action. Positions on enrolled bills continue to be sent to the OMB where they are coordinated and summarized before being forwarded to the White House.

What has changed has been the decision-making structure within the presidency and most notably, the White House-OMB relationship. Largely as a consequence of the growth and differentiation of the presidential staff structure, the clearance mechanism has become larger and more complex. It has also increasingly reflected the tendency of recent presidents to depend more on political appointees for their policy recommendations.

Until the mid-1960s, legislative relations between the Bureau of the Budget and the White House involved only a few individuals. Civil servants in the Legislative Reference Division of the BOB did the bulk of the coordination and made most of the clearance decisions and enrolled bill recommendations without significant interaction and interference from the budget director or the White House. In fact, contacts tended to go in the other direction with the assistant director of the Legislative Reference Division initiating requests for comments and recommendations of senior White House and budget officials when he felt it necessary. Controversial questions were referred to the president's special counsel with the head of Legislative Reference participating more or less on a regular basis in meetings where major policy decisions were made. Figure III-II diagrams the principal points of interchange.

The small size of the White House, the relatively short tenure of presidential aides, their lack of specialized knowledge and their unfamiliarity with executive procedures, and the growing number of policy demands indicate some of the reasons that early presidential staffs had little choice but to depend on the BOB. Its pivotal position and its technical skills, both

CENTRAL CLEARANCE   **ENROLLED BILLS**

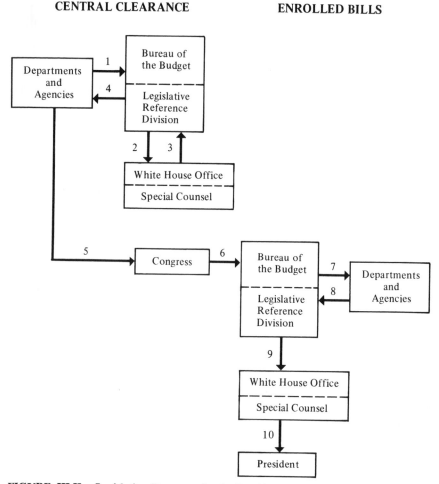

FIGURE III-II.   Legislative Processes in the Presidency, 1945–1965

generated by the budgetary process, made the Bureau of the Budget the most appropriate unit within the executive branch to coordinate the bureaucracy's legislative positions and policy initiatives for the president.

The success of the White House-BOB relationship was closely tied to two other factors: the generally high evaluation of BOB's legislative work by presidential staffers and presidents themselves, and the department and agency orientation of presidential policy making. Beginning in the Kennedy administration, this orientation began to change with the president depending more on the White House and less on the bureaucracy for formulating new legislation.

The number of presidential aides increased which, in turn, permitted greater White House involvement in clearance and enrolled bill decisions. This had the temporary effect of reducing the bureau's role in general and the influence of its Legislative Reference Division in particular. While the division still performed most of the leg work, its clout declined both within the BOB and with the White House. One apparent consequence of these developments was that the bureau's negative recommendations on enrolled bills were not as frequently followed, especially during the Johnson and Nixon presidencies.

In subsequent years, the shift in decisional responsibility to political appointees improved the budget agency's position with the president and his domestic policy staff, making it more responsive to the same kinds of considerations that the White House staff would normally take into account in recommending presidential action. These changes, a larger White House role, greater involvement of the BOB's top officials, and the declining influence of the bureau's civil servants marked a transition in White House-BOB relations, and augured the trend toward specialization and politicization that accelerated during the Nixon and Ford period.

In the 1970s, the clearance and enrolled bill processes continued to serve the same purposes for the president, but decision making within the presidency became compartmentalized and decentralized, especially during the Ford administration. With the formal establishment of the Domestic Council in the White House and the reorganization of the program divisions in the OMB, the most important clearance decisions became the responsibility of the respective associate directors or their superiors. Similarly, most critical and controversial enrolled bill recommendations were also funneled through these directors. The new pattern of enrolled bill decision making is illustrated in Figure III-III. Clearance decisions followed similar channels.

The reduction in the size of the Domestic Council staff at the end of 1972, combined with the Watergate controversy and the resignation of John Ehrlichman, adversely affected the White House's decision-making capabilities. In the short run, the Domestic Council-OMB partnership became unequal with the OMB's associate directors assuming greater policy-making responsibility. However, with the succession of a new president, new personnel on the council, and the development of new patterns of decision making a more equitable balance was restored. Other presidential aides also began to participate on a more or less regular basis in clearance and enrolled bill matters.

IMPLICATIONS FOR THE FUTURE

Legislative clearance has become more routine. While its procedures have remained intact and its objectives much the same, department and agency

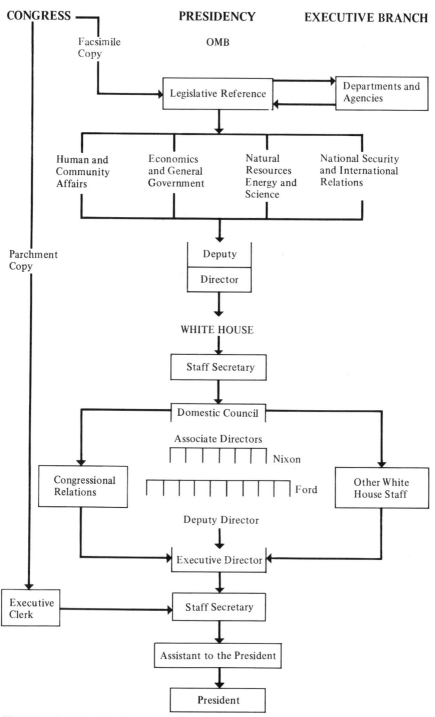

FIGURE III-III. The Enrolled Bill Process, 1971–1976

initiatives and positions seem less important to the president, at least as far as his legislative priority setting is concerned. There are now two congressional tracks, one that processes presidential goals and one that deals with departmental aims. Clearance concerns the latter most of the time. Occasionally, these tracks intersect; usually they are separate. So long as presidents and their staffs see a difference between the two, clearance is likely to remain more of an oversight mechanism and less of an instrument for developing presidential policy.

It is also likely to remain more subject to the institutional influence of the presidency than the personal influence of the president. By satisfying recurrent presidential obligations rather than fulfilling the president's personal and/or political aspirations, the clearance and enrolled bill processes do not encourage the president's active involvement nor are they particularly sensitive to his own style of decision making except perhaps at the end points of the processes.

Clearance is a staff operation. The process has acquired a stability of its own. While personalities have, of course, affected the character of White House-OMB interaction, contributing to the influence of the Budget Bureau's civil servants in the early period and detracting from this influence in the later period, structure and roles seem to have shaped the institutional relationship even more. Structural variables include size, experience, and organization; role includes objectives, function, and orientation. In general, the less the time for decisions and the greater the volume and complexity of legislation, the greater the need for OMB staff support; the more controversial the issue, the more likely the White House involvement; the larger and more expert the number of presidential aides, presumably the less their dependence on the OMB. The implication for the future is clear. The degree of specialization and the amount of savvy in the White House's policy staff has tended to be inversely related to the OMB's influence and the scope of its policy role. A large differentiated White House staff develops a capacity of its own, becomes more autonomous in its operation, and may be less impervious to outside influence. Such a staff could, of course, enlarge and extend the powers of the presidency. But it could also have the effect of elevating and isolating the president, a danger particularly evident in the Johnson and Nixon presidencies.

The recent sharing of roles between the Domestic Council staff and the OMB may also portend a similar problem in the long run. That the OMB has become more politicized and the White House policy staff more specialized has tended to blur the distinction between merit and political considerations in rendering presidential advice. The danger is that substantive or, in exceptional cases, even political factors may not receive sufficient weight causing presidents to make poor decisions. Presidential advisors have a tendency to incline toward the president's inclinations, telling him what they think he wants to hear.

The OMB's advice on the merits has traditionally been a hedge against this kind of inclination. Even if White House advisors were more sensitive to political matters, the OMB could have been expected to provide its solid analytic advice colored by its budget orientation. But during the Nixon-Ford administrations, it was also colored by the president's political orientation.

Gerald Ford was particularly conscious of this potential problem. He requested that his policy aides specify the basis for their recommendations and also encouraged a diversity of opinion within the administration on most major issues. While these practices enlarged the scope of the president's policy advice, they did not totally overcome the potential hazards of OMB's politicization.

In the aftermath of the Nixon presidency, Ford also emphasized his own accessibility. While retaining the procedures of the clearance and enrolled bill processes, he permitted departmental appeals. His collegial approach to decision making also facilitated departmental input into presidential policy, but not without adverse effects to the planning of his programing efforts. The next chapter will examine these efforts and those effects within the context of the development of the president's annual legislative program.

NOTES

1   In actual practice, the new clearance procedure was not rigidly enforced, at least not at first. Within the executive branch, it engendered considerable consternation and some confusion. As a consequence, some agencies conformed in whole or part while a few disregarded the order entirely. Neither Dawes nor Harding pressed the issue. The president let it be known that department officers could discuss major policy directly with him on an informal basis without going through the intermediate step of budget clearance. For its part, the Budget Bureau handled the more routine matters.

Compliance improved, however, under Coolidge. By 1926, budget clearance became standard for all financial requests. Coolidge personally reviewed many of the Budget Bureau's recommendations himself. The ones he examined were almost always those requesting additional funds. A stickler for obtaining a balanced budget with the lowest governmental expenditures, Coolidge normally denied or reduced these requests.

Hoover adopted much the same stance, using budget clearance as a negative check against excessive spending. He even went to the extreme of examining practically all Budget Bureau recommendations himself, affixing his initials to the individual clearance report. In many cases, this required his reading the entire file since the bureau did not provide a summary of its contents. Toward the end of his administration and perhaps as a result of the tremendous amount of work, Hoover allowed negative reports on pending public bills and all reports on private relief measures to be submitted to Congress directly without his or the Budget Bureau's approval. Negative positions, of course, presented no threat to his budget.

See Donald A. Hansen, "Legislative Clearance by the Bureau of the Budget," staff monograph, Bureau of the Budget, 1940, and Richard E. Neustadt, "Presidential Clearance of Legislation" (Ph.D. diss., Harvard University, 1950).

2   Presidents, of course, always had the opportunity to consult with their advisors when deciding whether to sign or veto legislation. Washington in his first veto of an appointment bill for the House of Representatives turned to his cabinet only to find their opinions divided. Subsequent presidents also queried their departmental secretaries. On two occasions, President Grant even asked Congress to return bills he had vetoed on the grounds that he had misapprehended the facts.

Beginning with the McKinley period, the executive clerk, the chief administrative officer in the White House, had the function of soliciting departmental opinion. He received the legislation at the White House, and at his discretion, circulated it to those departments and agencies that he deemed appropriate. Since the actual parchment of the legislation was used, the circulation process tended to be slow and potentially risky. A messenger had to hand carry the legislation from department to department. Recommendations to the president were affixed as memos to the enactment and usually accompanied the bill to the president's desk. The executive clerk had to make sure that the president received it within the specified time frame.

When the Budget Bureau took over, it expedited the process by using facsimile copies instead of the actual parchment. This permitted more agencies to be consulted and a more rigid schedule to be met. Department opinions had to be submitted within 48 hours. Budget gave itself a maximum of five days to collect, process, and summarize executive branch views. Appending a recommendation of its own when it returned the completed file to the executive clerk, the Budget Bureau's summary and advice had an important influence on presidential decisions.

William Hopkins, executive clerk from 1948–1971, recalled at least two different instances during the Roosevelt and Truman administrations when enrolled bills were misplaced and the president had to send a special messenger to Congress requesting another parchment of the legislation.

3   The Constitution allows ten days not including Sunday for the president to act. If he signs the bill within this period, it becomes law. If he fails to sign it and sends it back to the house of its origin with his objection, he has vetoed the bill. Overturning a veto requires a two-thirds vote of each house of Congress. The president has a third option—not to do anything. If he fails to act within the time period and the Congress is still in session, the bill becomes law without his signature. If Congress has adjourned, the bill dies. This is known as a pocket veto. However, if the Congress has recessed, the bill may still become law even if the president has not signed it within the prescribed period. In 1970, President Nixon failed to return a bill to Congress which was in a short recess at the time the ten-day period elapsed. Nixon considered the

bill dead, but Senator Edward Kennedy challenged the administration's view that the president had, in effect, pocket vetoed the bill. A 1974 District of Columbia Court of Appeals decision supported the senator's position. Only a *sine die* adjournment of Congress at the end of each session presents an obvious pocket veto situation.

4   Roger Jones, interview.

5   Ibid.

6   Phillip S. Hughes, interview. Davis and Ripley found a similar attitude in their interviews of Bureau of the Budget officials. James W. Davis and Randall B. Ripley, "The Bureau of the Budget and Executive Branch Agencies: Notes on Their Interaction," *Journal of Politics* XXIX, no. 4 (1967): 763.

7   Wilton B. Persons who became assistant to the president at the end of the Eisenhower period attributed this to the high degree of loyalty to Eisenhower personally and the access he permitted cabinet officials. Persons added, "if any agency felt that it was not getting across what they were entitled to, . . . all they'd have to do is pick up the telephone and call Tom Stephens to get an appointment with the president." Major General Wilton B. Persons, interview.

8   Richard E. Neustadt, "Presidency and Legislation: The Growth of Central Clearance," *American Political Science Review* XLVIII, no. 3 (September, 1954): 661.

9   If a problem could not be worked out with an agency-initiated proposal, then the BOB would, more often than not, list the reasons it could not give positive advice and conclude with a statement to the effect: "For these reasons, we plan to take no further action on your draft bill." This meant that the proposal was filed and the agency was prohibited from submitting it or supporting it in Congress. Negative advice would be more frequently given on pending legislation on which congressional committees had requested the BOB's advice. However, this advice was advisory only since members of Congress were not bound by BOB recommendations in the way that executive departments and agencies were.

In any year, there were always a sizable number of items, usually of minor significance, that the departments and agencies wanted and the administration did not object to, but at the same time, did not want considered as part of its legislative program. Private bills fell into this category. For such legislation, the BOB might state that it had no objection to the draft or report but made no determination with respect to the President's program. Most clearances were of this kind. Theoretically, a no-objection clearance allowed the departments and agencies to submit their proposal without committing the administration to it. In practice, however, the lack of presidential support might be sufficient, in and of itself, to kill the proposal, especially if the president's party was in control of Congress.

10   Gerald Morgan, interview.

11   Clark Clifford, interview.

12   H. Roemer McPhee, interview.

13   White House aides of both administrations praised Legislative Reference highly for its "professionalism," its "analytic capabilities," and "its capacity to provide vital staff work." They did not suspect the loyalties nor question the

dedication of BOB careerists. For the Truman administration, this was not surprising since the Budget Bureau had become a proving ground for White House staff; for the Eisenhower period, however, it is more noteworthy since the same personnel who had helped coordinate Democratic policy did so for the Republicans as well.

14   Jones, interview.

15   James F. C. Hyde, Jr., interview.

16   Jones, interview.

17   Theodore Sorensen, interview.

18   Lee C. White, interview.

19   Myer Feldman, interview.

20   The importance of presidential support to the departments combined with the administration's desire to separate presidential and departmental priorities led the Bureau of the Budget to develop a third kind of clearance advice. The advice that a legislative draft or report was "consistent or inconsistent with the administration's objectives" was given to those items that agencies felt were important but the BOB felt were not significant enough to be a major part of the president's program. This third kind of clearance advice was referred to as a "poor man's in accord" by legislative analysts in the bureau (See Appendix B).

21   In the Kennedy administration, this person was Myer Feldman, assistant special counsel; in the Johnson period, the chore was handled at one time or another by Feldman, Lee White, Harry McPherson, and DeVier Pearson. If others were to be alerted or consulted, it was up to the counsel to do so. This happened much more frequently during the Johnson presidency. Throughout the eight years, White House consideration of enrolled bills remained an informal operation.

22   Harry McPherson, interview.

23   Joseph A. Califano, Jr., interview.

24   Ibid.

25   Richard Fairbanks, interview.

26   One OMB official recalled that he had worked closely with a member of the Ehrlichman staff before the Domestic Council was created. "I worked with him almost daily. It was six or eight months after the Domestic Council was created before I found out that he was working on the Domestic Council not on the so-called White House staff." A Domestic Council staff member of both the Nixon and Ford periods also had trouble with the White House staff-Domestic Council staff distinction:

> We are called Domestic Council staff and theoretically we work for the whole Domestic Council with the president as chairman. The fact is that we spend most of our time in day to day operational type fire fighting activities, serve as White House staff to the president, in part as if we didn't work for this Domestic Council.

During the 1976 presidential campaign a careful distinction was made for the purposes of applying the Hatch Act. Most of the Domestic Council staff were deemed to be subject to the regulations of the act while the White House staff were not. The executive director and one of his deputies who held the titles of assistant and deputy assistant to the president for domestic affairs were considered White House staff and were paid from the White House payroll. They helped in the campaign.

27   Richard Parsons, interview.

28   Stephen J. Wayne, Richard L. Cole, and James F. C. Hyde Jr., "Advising the President on Legislation: Patterns of Executive Branch Influence," (Paper delivered at the Annual Meeting of the American Political Science Association, Washington, D.C., September 1-4, 1977).

Much of the discussion that follows in this section is based on the conclusions of this paper.

29   Paul O'Neill, deputy budget director, justified the change as follows:

> I think with the volume of legislative activity, it was probably inevitable that it couldn't be handled through one head. The level of authority we've had in the last five years in my area alone [human and community affairs] coupled with any other part of OMB's legislative responsibilities would probably undo anybody who tried to deal with it at the level of detail that the head of LRD [Legislative Reference Division] did.

Paul O'Neill, interview

A high Legislative Reference official, however, saw it very differently:

> The PADs [program associate directors], for the most part, are people who come and leave within a year and a half or two years. The good ones get an institutional feel for things; most of them don't. Therefore, they tend to see issues on a case-by-case basis, almost a personal basis. They are impatient with the history of an issue, the lessons that have been learned and so on.

He went on to describe his work under the new system as "frustrating and sometimes enraging."

30   The director of the Legislative Reference Division was not invited to these meetings. Initially, all the associate directors of the Domestic Council and OMB participated in addition to the senior congressional liaison officials. In 1975, with the expansion of the Domestic Council to eight associate directors and two deputy directors, the large meetings were ended in favor of smaller legislative strategy sessions attended by the executive director of the Domestic Council, his two deputies, the deputy director of OMB, and the senior liaison aides for the House and the Senate held on an average of three days a week.

31   Kenneth R. Cole, interview.

32   Arthur F. Quern, interview.

33   Glenn R. Schleede, interview.

34   For a discussion of this problem, see Hugh Heclo, "OMB and the Presidency—the Problem of 'Neutral Competence,' " *The Public Interest,* no. 38 (Winter 1975): 80–98; James F. C. Hyde, Jr., and Stephen J. Wayne, "Partners in Presidential Policy-Making: White House—OMB Legislative Relationships" (Paper delivered at the Annual Meeting of the Southern Political Science Association, Nashville, Tenn., November 6–8, 1975).

CHAPTER 4

Creating a Legislative Package: The Programing Process

Our view was the Eisenhower administration was extremely phlegmatic in terms of its legislative initiatives. It was almost as though they had been constipated and the inaugural was a bit of a laxative for new ideas that had been generating both outside and inside the government.

Lee C. White (Kennedy and Johnson administrations)

I had watched this [programing] process for years, and I was convinced that it did not encourage enough fresh or creative ideas. The bureaucracy of the government is too preoccupied with day to day operations, and there is strong bureaucratic inertia dedicated to preserving the status quo. As a result, only the most powerful ideas can survive. Moreover, the cumbersome organization of government is simply not equipped to solve complex problems that cut across departmental jurisdictions.

Lyndon B. Johnson
The Vantage Point
(New York: Holt, Rinehart and Winston, 1971), pp. 326–327

> **When it came to perquisites, clearly the cabinet**
> **secretary was the dominant figure. When it came**
> **to policy development, I think that the Domestic**
> **Council staff, if not the equivalent, was**
> **clearly the principal developer of policy.**
>
> Egil Krogh, Jr.
> (Nixon administration)

INTRODUCTION

The practice of providing Congress with a comprehensive legislative program did not begin until the Truman era. Previous presidents had, of course, recommended "necessary and expedient legislation," but none, including Franklin Roosevelt, presented Congress with an annual bill of particulars. President Truman started the tradition in 1948, using his three required messages to Congress, the State of the Union Address, budget message, and economic report, to convey his legislative intent. Thereafter, annual programing became an expectation of the modern presidency. Today, Congress anticipates it, the public assumes it, departments and agencies demand it, and presidents have provided it, usually announcing parts of their program even before taking office. Government is now geared to an annual presidential effort.

Presenting Congress with a legislative program has done more than simply shift domestic policy initiatives to the executive. It has enlarged and, at the same time, encased the presidency, adding new structures to develop and coordinate programing activities and new procedures to regularize and standardize them. Whether the mechanisms and processes designed to distinguish presidential interest and facilitate presidential influence have actually increased the president's power or merely enhanced the difficulties of exercising it is unclear. What is clear, however, is that programing has been both a cause and effect of the institutionalization of the office. It has contributed to the need for a presidential bureaucracy which, then, has encouraged the persistence of policy demands. This, in turn, has resulted in further bureaucratization of the presidency.

This chapter will explore that cycle by examining those structures and procedures that have been most closely associated with the development of annual presidential programing. It will look at the roles of individuals and institutional entities in the process: the interest and involvement of the president, the functions and discretionary authority of his principal White House aides, the technical and political contributions of departments and agencies, and the input from groups outside the executive. In describing the evolution of the programing process from its inception in the Truman period, the chapter will contrast the way in which different administrations have gone about generating, synchronizing, and presenting their legislative proposals.

How annual programing formally evolved out of the legislative clearance process will be the focus of the next section. How it became increasingly distinguished from department and agency legislative proposals will then be examined in subsequent sections. The search for new policy initiatives outside the government during the Kennedy and Johnson years, for more centralized White House control during the Nixon period, and for a more open and decentralized approach during the Ford presidency will be discussed within the context of evolving executive relationships. The conclusion of the chapter discusses the relationship between presidential policy objectives and structural and procedural change.

THE DEVELOPMENT OF AN ANNUAL PROCESS: THE DEPARTMENTAL APPROACH

The first coordinated programing effort began in 1948. It was developed by President Truman and his advisors who wanted a legislative record on which to campaign. Creating such a record had been made difficult by the slow turnover in White House staff, Truman's own unpreparedness upon taking office, his rather traditional views of the president's legislative responsibilities,[1] and difficulties that his aides encountered in working with the Bureau of the Budget. The poor, almost nonexistent, staff relations that existed between the White House and the Budget Bureau during the 1945–1946 period were particularly damaging to the administration's handling of legislative matters since the president had come to depend on the Budget Bureau for ministerial support in clearing legislative and budgetary requests. It was not until a new budget director was appointed and changes in White House personnel occurred that relationships improved sufficiently to permit comprehensive legislative planning.[2] The 1948 campaign provided the urgency for and later direction of such planning.

Establishing Programing Procedures: Truman

In the fall of 1946, various units in the Executive Office of the President, each charged with helping prepare the president's three messages to Congress, individually requested ideas from the departments and agencies. In 1947, an effort was made to coordinate these requests. Following the BOB's annual call for budget estimates for the next fiscal year, President Truman sent a letter to all departments and agencies formally asking for their suggestions for his State of the Union Address, budget message, and economic report.

The following year, the BOB sought to expand and refine the process by requesting departments and agencies to indicate any legislation they were proposing "which should be taken account of in preparing the budget message or in arriving at budget totals." [3] After the president's election victory, he, too, requested legislative proposals for the next session of Congress. The Budget Bureau's memo followed by the president's letter became, with some scheduling modifications, the standard operating procedure for generating ideas for legislative messages and programs. It has continued through each subsequent administration.

The departments and agencies adjusted quickly to what became an annual effort. Anxious to make their claims on the president's program, their responses, beginning in 1948, tended to provide fairly comprehensive inventories of their legislative goals. In the initial period, an attempt was made by department secretaries and agency heads to establish internal priorities and to highlight the new features in their proposals. Eventually, as the Truman period progressed, and the Korean War began to preoccupy the administration, routine requests pushed up by the agencies tended to constitute a larger and larger portion of the total package.[4] This lessened the value of executive branch suggestions to the president but, at the same time, it increased it for the bureaucracy.

From the White House perspective, tapping a wide range of ideas and goals proved useful. It increased administration options. In the words of Clark Clifford, who as special counsel initially directed the White House's programing operations:

> The purpose of obtaining this information was to have the background of the needs and also the opinions of the departments and agencies of government so that we would be able to extract from that voluminous source of information a legislative program. While much of it was self-serving, at least we felt that we had tapped knowledgeable and experienced people in government. Sometimes in that general request a real pearl would appear. It is like a diver swimming around and all of a sudden there would appear a pearl as large as a hen's egg. In my opinion, that alone would justify the effort.[5]

The White House worked closely with the Bureau of the Budget in processing and integrating these ideas for legislation. The president's letter to departments and agencies specifically directed that message suggestions for the State of the Union be sent to the White House and proposals for legislative programs go to the Bureau of the Budget. In the White House, message preparation was coordinated by the president's special counsel. The Legislative Reference Division of the BOB examined requests for legislation, synthesized proposals, and coordinated them with the preparation of the budget.

For the most part, the president's annual messages to Congress served as the vehicle for packaging the entire program. Special messages were used to highlight individual policies. President Truman was involved in the making of policy decisions as well as the actual writing of his speeches and messages. He believed message preparation to be an important presidential responsibility. In his memoirs, Truman wrote:

> All Presidential messages must begin with the President himself. He must decide what he wants to say and how he wants to say it. Many drafts are usually drawn up, and this fact leads to the assumption that Presidential speeches are ghosted. The final version, however, is the final word of the President himself, expressing his own convictions and his policy.[6]

The departments and agencies were expected to do most of the substantive work on the legislation once it had been designated to be part of the president's program. They drafted the bill, prepared testimony, and monitored its progress on Capitol Hill. While outside views were occasionally sought, the process was essentially department-oriented.

President Truman believed it the prerogative of the president-elect to present the 1953 legislative program. In his last State of the Union Address delivered 13 days before Eisenhower was inaugurated, Truman stated that he did not want to usurp his successor's right and responsibility to chart a future course. Consequently, he did not propose a legislative program of his own.

Continuing the Executive Branch Orientation: Eisenhower

President Eisenhower, however, was not prepared to present Congress with a program in 1953. His failure to provide one may be explained by his constitutional philosophy coupled with the usual problems of transition. Eisenhower had a fairly traditional view of presidential-congressional responsibilities. According to Bernard Shanley, Eisenhower's special counsel and later his personal secretary, "he [Eisenhower] felt very strongly from his school book days . . . that there were three branches of government and that he had no right to interfere with the legislative branch." [7] Some of his staff had similar reservations. They also needed time to get adjusted and learn the ropes. Since presidential programing had become a four- to six-month process beginning in the fall of the year, it was difficult for a newly elected president and his staff to bring the process to fruition at the very beginning of his first term. Within a few months, however, pressures from several quarters forced the administration to alter its nonlegislative posture and become more actively involved in legislative matters.

The procedure adopted for developing a program was based on the institutional practices that had been established during the Truman period. The annual call for budget estimates continued to be used as a vehicle for soliciting legislative proposals and ideas for the president's messages to

Congress. White House consideration, however, was more formal than it had been in Truman's day. Ideas were thrashed out at senior level staff meetings, usually chaired by Governor Adams (and after his departure by General Persons), and involving anywhere from six to ten presidential aides. A representative from the Budget Bureau, usually Roger Jones, also participated in these meetings. While Jones's role was to provide technical advice, his personal influence with the staff and the president gave him more than simply a technical input.

Department secretaries and agency heads would present their proposals to the senior staff, often using elaborate visual aids. The president's assistants saw their function as shaking down the proposals and making the necessary compromises. Only after the proposal had been properly staffed was the president involved, either alone or in conjunction with the cabinet.

Major proposals were presented to the cabinet with the same kind of elaborate staging as they had been to the staff. The cabinet functioned as the final arbiter on major domestic policy questions. Its approval represented the last major in-house hurdle before presentation of the program in late December to the Republican congressional leadership.

The sessions with legislative leaders were designed both to inform them of the president's program and to stylize the package to accommodate their suggestions.[8] Eisenhower's staff quickly realized that giving the leadership an input into the legislation often contributed to their enthusiasm for it later on. In most administrations, congressional previews have become part of the annual programing process.

On a whole, President Eisenhower was less directly involved in the determination of the president's program than his predecessor had been. Truman was "in the thick and thin of it," but Eisenhower tended to participate at the end of the process, after his staff had made the issues and alternatives relatively clear. "The president didn't want to sit at the top and make the decision before he had input from all the appropriate members of his staff and from appropriate departments and agencies," Persons stated.[9] Occasionally, however, the president would offer some suggestion or push a particular proposal. "I am absolutely certain," Roger Jones stated, "that we would not have a health benefits bill for federal civilian employees if the president hadn't grabbed this himself and said, 'My God, we do it for the military, why shouldn't we do it for the civilians?' Similarly, the support he gave to the Government Employees Training Act was tremendous." [10]

While formal procedures for developing a legislative program continued throughout the Eisenhower presidency, there was considerably less fanfare and considerably less new programing as the administration grew older. The pattern of departments and agencies reintroducing their pet projects repeated in the later years as it had during the end of the Truman administration. According to one BOB official:

We went through that call for legislation and we got that stuff in, but most of that was pretty routine. It wasn't president's program stuff. It was the crap that had been coming up for eight years that agencies still wanted to get enacted. We reviewed, massaged it, and coordinated it, and so on.

The incoming White House seemed to be very much aware of the department orientation of Eisenhower's program and the problems it caused for creating innovative presidential policy. "Our view was that the Eisenhower administration was extremely phlegmatic in terms of its legislative initiatives," stated Lee White, who added, "It was almost as though they had been constipated and the inaugural was a bit of a laxative for new ideas that had been generating both outside and inside the government." [11]

THE EXTERNALIZATION OF PRESIDENTIAL PROGRAMING: THE TASK FORCE APPROACH

Searching for New Ideas: Kennedy

The Kennedy administration began with a burst of energy and a flood of activity. Desiring to take advantage of the momentum which the election victory generated, rather than lose a year as Eisenhower had done in 1953, the Kennedy staff began planning for its first legislative program in the period after the election and before the inauguration. During the campaign, Kennedy had appointed a number of advisory committees to report on some of the issues that his administration would face. These ranged from civil rights matters to the possible reorganization of the Defense Department and a host of national security and foreign policy issues. After the election he set up several more of these task forces. Their reports provided ideas for Kennedy's New Frontier programs.

Also during the transition period, the Legislative Reference Division was asked to compile a list of platform statements and campaign promises made by the president-elect which ultimately would require presidential and/or congressional action.[12] There was considerable overlap between the task force assignments and the campaign list. "I simply cannot afford to have just one set of advisers," Kennedy asserted.[13]

Proposals for legislation were then discussed by Kennedy and his aides in December. From these discussions, the outlines of the president's first messages to Congress were sketched and a rough schedule of when they should be sent and what they should contain was mapped out.

Kennedy's penchant for developing new ideas and approaches to domestic and foreign problems continued throughout his administration. However, outside task forces were not used after the first year. The president and his staff turned instead to cabinet secretaries. The annual call for legislation was used to generate new legislation in much the same manner as previous administrations had done.

In addition to this formal input into legislative policy making, cabinet secretaries were also encouraged to make less formal suggestions. The secretaries participated with White House staff in brainstorming sessions with no other department personnel present. This enabled them to go off the record. The sessions served a number of purposes. From the White House perspective, they encouraged a free flow of ideas and, at the same time, provided opportunities for trial ballooning. They also put the president's staff in a unique, influential position in program development. From the department's perspective, they allowed secretaries to get a feel for administration priorities, what might be accepted in a department program, and what was out of the question, at least in the short run.[14]

The proposals from these meetings, as well as those that came through the more formal channels, were then compiled into a single book that designated the purpose of the legislation, its cost, and its effect on existing laws. Sorensen's staff discussed each proposal with the president in late December. Cabinet secretaries would normally participate in the discussion when their programs were being examined. Meeting at the end of the year enabled the staff to tie decisions on the president's program to the final stages of the budgetary process.

Once the priorities and general shape of the program were determined, the departments and agencies were charged with drawing up the actual legislation, and even writing an initial draft of the message that was to accompany it. The special counsel's office coordinated the preparation of presidential speeches and special messages. The draft of the message would always be checked out with the congressional liaison people and the president before being sent to the Hill.[15]

Sorensen was in charge of the entire process. "He was the guy whom the president looked to," said Lee White adding, "Ted really was on top of that operation. It was a very small cadre and Ted really did most of the major assembling." [16] When Kennedy's advice was sought, Sorensen did most of the seeking.

Kennedy was both accessible to his staff and interested in programing. He tried to stay on top of developments by requesting that Sorensen keep him informed of legislative proposals in the executive pipeline. The December meetings gave the president a final say on the general shape and content of the program before it was marketed on the Hill.

Department secretaries could always see the president. In addition to making formal proposals in the fall and informal suggestions in the White House "skull" sessions, they could also make final appeals at the end of the year meetings. But between these times, during the critical stages of development, initiative and decision making remained pretty much in the White House and the president's aides guarded these prerogatives jealously.

Budget's role continued to be vital. The emphasis placed on new policy initiatives tended to reemphasize Legislative Reference's function as a technical support staff. The division's usefulness to the White House stemmed primarily from its filtering of bureaucratic suggestions and its analysis of policy alternatives on their merits. To the extent that the routine proposals that came up from the departments were not priority items in the president's overall program, however, Legislative Reference had a less important role. Its decline in influence augured shifts in the nexus of presidential power that became more evident during the later years of the Johnson presidency.

Maintaining the Policy Initiative: Johnson

The first six months of the Johnson administration can best be described as a continuation of the Kennedy processes and product with minor stylistic modifications. The slow turnover in White House personnel, the need for uniformities in policy, the logjam of presidential proposals on the Hill, and the time it took Johnson to get adjusted, all contributed to the "let us continue" attitude of the new administration.

The first State of the Union Address that President Johnson delivered, as well as his budget and other early legislative messages, had all been in preparation during the fall of 1963. For his part, Johnson seemed more concerned with building a consensus behind the proposals of his predecessor than with creating a whole new set of legislative goals. One holdover from the Kennedy administration commented: "Johnson wasn't an initiator. He didn't initiate programs—he got them from other people and he pushed them."

The president's operating style was also different from Kennedy's. He was more actively involved in day-to-day discussions. He consulted with more people both on his staff and outside the White House. In contrasting the two presidents' programing styles, Myer Feldman stated:

> Basically, the difference between the Kennedy and Johnson administrations was that in the Kennedy administration when we got a draft back from the Bureau [of the Budget] after the bureau had taken care of circulating it properly and had its input, we didn't have very many people to consult with. . . . In the case of Johnson, he had a lot more people involved at the White House level. He used to get the message from the bureau and only then would a committee that we'd suggest get started working it over and making changes in it using his own language.[17]

Gradually, the new administration began to develop its own legislative proposals and programing style. In the spring of 1964, several top aides from the White House, the Council of Economic Advisers, and the Bureau of the Budget suggested to the president that he establish task forces in several issue areas, mainly within the domestic sphere, for the purpose of identifying issues, analyzing problems, and recommending solutions. The task forces were commissioned in June 1964 and told to report by the middle of November. In all, 15 separate groups were established. Their membership and charge was secret so as to permit them and the president maximum flexibility. Their final report was also secret.[18]

The departments were not represented on these task forces since one of their main purposes was to bypass the bureaucracy. Writing in *The Vantage Point,* Johnson expressed his reservations about policy that emanated from the executive branch.

> I had watched this [programing] process for years, and I was convinced that it did not encourage enough fresh or creative ideas. The bureaucracy of the government is too preoccupied with day to day operations, and there is strong bureaucratic inertia dedicated to preserving the status quo. As a result, only the most powerful ideas can survive. Moreover, the cumbersome organization of government is simply not equipped to solve complex problems that cut across departmental jurisdictions.[19]

Illustrating the process by which new ideas get refined by the system, Johnson wrote:

> The ideas would have to go through a rather tortuous process of study within a department or agency. It would have to be checked with all of the interested groups and constituencies and the various jurisdictions within a given department and elsewhere in the government. As it moved up the line, it would be reviewed by more and more people, people who already had their own ideas and were either fighting to get them heard or, if they had been adopted, to see them preserved. More often than not, the new idea, if it ever emerged, was adulterated by internal bureaucratic considerations and the pressures of the Congress and client interest groups. The general theme was not to rock the boat, not to step on anyone's toes, not to interfere with anyone's jurisdiction, but to make some improvements, often remedial, at times incremental, but seldom innovative. The end product was a compromise. Then these same ideas would be pressed forward by the particular agency or department year after year, hoping for ultimate adoption by the administration.[20]

Bill Moyers, who emerged as the president's principal assistant in the domestic policy area, had the job of coordinating the task force reports. He, in turn, organized several intragovernmental groups that went over the recommendations with an eye toward establishing priorities, determining feasibility, and evaluating costs. Policies that survived this analysis were then refined and presented to the president in December. The basic structure and substance of the Great Society program (including the Elementary and Secondary Education Act of 1965, the Higher Education Act, and the Clean Air Act) emerged from these reports.

The use of task forces to suggest new legislative policy continued throughout the Johnson period. In fact, the number of the task forces was substantially increased. They were asked to investigate a wide range of social issues. Composed of academic, business, labor, and community leaders, they were instructed by the president's staff to present their findings without regard to political consideration or cost. "Their job," stated James Gaither, "was to tell the president what ought to be done, not what could be done within the constraints of the political scene." [21]

The larger number of task forces required that there be an efficient coordinating mechanism. Beginning in the summer of 1965, a separate White House staff was developed to handle these reports. Headed by Joseph Califano, Jr., who had succeeded Moyers as the president's major domestic advisor, the staff proceeded to systematize and cycle the entire programing operation.

Under Califano's direction, planning for the president's legislative program began early in the spring soon after the bulk of his special messages had been sent to Congress. [22] In April and May, Califano and his staff would meet with BOB and other government officials in brainstorming sessions. The purpose of these meetings was to examine legislation that was coming up for renewal, items that had been deferred from the previous year, and new proposals that had filtered in from departments and agencies, from previous task forces, and from outside the government. Trips to 10 to 15 universities were also made in the spring of the year to collect new ideas. Within a framework of 15 to 20 general topics, the proposals were then reviewed by Califano's staff and other senior aides and briefing books were prepared for the president.

After Johnson had an opportunity to evaluate each proposal, Califano and his staff would then work on those the president felt were most promising. In some cases, a new outside task force would be created or an interdepartmental group formed. [23] Occasionally, departments and agencies would be consulted directly. Legislative Reference continued its traditional job of coordinating and integrating proposals within the executive branch. As a final step, the White House congressional liaison aides were consulted. Their job was to consider relevant political factors.

Johnson was extremely sensitive to congressional opinion. He normally included influential senators and representatives in the various stages of the programing process. Occasionally, members of both houses would even sit on the task forces themselves. Since the composition of the groups and their reports were secret, having legislators participate in presidential policy making could be accomplished without political embarrassment, providing, of course, that there were no leaks. During White House consideration of proposals, members of Congress were also involved behind the scenes. "The trick was . . . to crack the wall of separation enough to give the Congress a feeling of participation in creating my bills without exposing my plans at the same time to advance congressional opposition before they even saw the light of day," Johnson said.[24] To prevent premature leakage of the proposals, the Johnson aide who communicated with the congressman would normally preface his conversation with the comment, "The President hasn't decided to do this, but if he did, how would you respond?" [25]

From the president's perspective, the advantages of involving Congress in the policy formulation were twofold: it provided an indication of the program's chances of passage and it gave the president an opportunity to make adjustments to improve those chances. According to Doris Kearns, "these early checks gave the White House an opportunity to redraft its bills so they would be assigned to different and more favorable committees." [26]

By the end of November, a matrix of several hundred proposals had been readied for the president. Once Johnson made his decisions in December and the budget, then in the final stages of preparation, was revised, Califano's staff would orchestrate the formal presentation of the legislation to Congress. Figure IV-I indicates the stages of program development during the post-1965 Johnson presidency.

The actual writing of the legislation usually was fairly routine. Most of the time, the departments produced the initial draft which the Legislative Reference Division would then go over and clear according to regular clearance procedures. Once cleared, the legislation would go to the White House for final presidential approval.[27] Preparation of the special messages and the president's reports to Congress were done by the speech writers and reviewed by Califano and his staff.

The president personally examined the drafts of all legislative messages and directed the presentation of the proposals to Congress. Johnson demanded a head count of Democrats and occasionally, Republicans on the committees and subcommittees that would consider the legislation,

Idea gathering; visits to universities; contracts with outside experts and "idea men" in government	Internal discussions of ideas gathered	Appointment of task forces	Receipt and review of task force reports Agency submissions	White House meetings Final presidential decisions on the program	Preparation of messages Introduction of bills
April/May/June	July	August	September/ October/ November	December	January/ February/ March

FIGURE IV-I. Sequence of Events in Preparing the Johnson Legislative Program
SOURCE: Norman C. Thomas and Harold L. Wolman, "The Presidency and Policy Formulation: The Task Force Device," *Public Administration Review* XXIX, No. 5 (September/October 1969): 463.

an agreement from the chairmen of those committees when they would hold hearings and when the hearings would end, and, if possible, a date when the bill or some modification of it would be reported out. The night before the message was to go to Capitol Hill, Johnson invited the congressional leadership, the chairmen of the appropriate committees, and other key legislators to the White House usually for dinner. They were briefed by Califano, cabinet officers, and their staffs. Johnson considered these briefings extremely important. The president insisted that the legislation be introduced in Congress the day after the message was received.

These procedures were designed to maximize presidential influence. The presentation of the entire package within the first few months of the session corresponded with the congressional agenda. Informing the relevant members prior to public announcement was a courtesy that did not jeopardize the president's headlines, while the promise of hearings and the survey of members provided Johnson and his staff with the knowledge they needed to lobby effectively.[28] Johnson believed that a president's relations with Congress had to be continuous and immediate if they were to be successful:

> If it's really going to work, the relationship between the President and the Congress has got to be almost incestuous. He's got to know them even better than they know themselves. And then, on the basis of this knowledge, he's got to build a system that stretches from the cradle to the grave, from the moment it is officially enrolled as the law of the land.[29]

Within the executive, presidential influence was also enhanced by the programing procedures. Johnson's options were extended by his solicitation of outside views and his budgetary discretion was enhanced by the simultaneous cycling of budgeting and programing processes. In fact, the use of the Bureau of the Budget throughout to coordinate and evaluate proposals served to deflect agency criticism from the president when pet projects were cut or eliminated. The structure of the process and the positioning of Califano's staff at the heart of it kept the departments at a distance, while it stretched presidential control not only over the substance of the program but over the way in which technical and political support could be mustered. The conscious attempt to reduce the department's role in policy initiation had another effect. It freed programing, at least at the outset, from some of the bureaucratic constraints that inevitably characterized a "welling-up" process. For an administration bent on developing new policy initiatives, innovation, or at least the appearance of it, was important, more so than the endearment of the departments, agencies, and their support groups. There was little the departments could do beyond the usual end-runs to Congress and some internal backbiting. The next administration reduced department and agency influence still further, although initially President Nixon had proposed a larger role for cabinet secretaries in domestic policy formulation.

THE INTERNALIZATION OF THE PROCESS: THE DOMESTIC COUNCIL APPROACH

The Nixon administration was slow to build on the formalized structure and procedures of the Johnson presidency. Nixon's initial desire to revert to an Eisenhower-type system that reemphasized departmental responsibilities, combined with his creation of a large and diversified White House staff structure, made concentrated and systematic programing difficult to achieve during the first year. There was to be no Califano operation in fact or form. The president did not want the access of cabinet members impeded by members of his White House staff.

During the campaign, Nixon had established 14 task forces. Economist Arthur Burns was given overall responsibility for coordinating their reports. Unlike the Johnson task forces, no representative of the president-elect was assigned to each of the groups. Neither the composition nor the recommendation of these early Nixon task forces was to be kept secret.

While some early policy proposals of the new administration stemmed from these reports, most emanated from Burns himself, who had also been appointed counselor to the president, and from Daniel P. Moynihan, assistant to the president for domestic affairs. While both Burns and Moynihan conceived of their presidential advisory roles in a similar fashion, their very different political orientations resulted in internal policy debate. The creation of an adversary system in the White House did not serve President Nixon's purposes nor meet his needs. It did not produce a suitable presidential perspective and it did not provide an efficient mechanism for coordinating and evaluating proposals.

Exerting Centralized Direction: Nixon

After approximately six months, John Ehrlichman, counsel to the president, began to assemble a small staff and became involved in domestic policy matters. Almost immediately, according to a White House official, "Ehrlichman found himself a conciliator, compromiser and problem solver as these two gladiators [Burns and Moynihan] had at it." Functioning largely as an impartial broker between two factions, Ehrlichman proceeded to consolidate his middle position and develop a specialized staff, even before the creation of the Domestic Council enlarged and formalized his operation.

The Domestic Council, which grew out of the Ash Council's recommendations, was formally established in 1970 as part of the executive reorganization that redesignated and restructured the Bureau of the Budget as the Office of Management and Budget. The original purpose of the Domestic Council was to isolate problems of presidential interest in the programing area and to carefully and systematically provide alternative solutions for the president.

It was initially contemplated that the council, which consisted of the president's principal domestic policy advisors (ten department secretaries, White House counselors, chairman of the Council of Economic Advisers, and the director and deputy director of OMB), would be a coordinating body dealing with social policy at the macro level in much the same manner as the National Security Council coordinated foreign and defense policy. President Nixon did not view the creation of the council as inconsistent with his cabinet approach. On the contrary, he envisioned that the reorganization would "not only improve the staff resources available to the President, but . . . also strengthen the advisory roles of those members of the Cabinet principally concerned with domestic affairs." [30]

The council was to have its own staff structure. The staff quickly grew to dominate the council's operation and the president's domestic policy-making process. In the words of Kenneth Cole, assistant to Ehrlichman and later executive director of the council:

> We tried to see if we could not put together a system where the council staff could move so we could get fresh ideas and also keep our people from getting stale. It just never worked out that way. They got very locked into what they were doing. More confusion than creativity would have resulted from moving people around. We needed to maintain the experience we had developed. [31]

As it eventually evolved, the staff became organized into six broad groups, each headed by an assistant—later, associate—director [32] and assisted by anywhere from two to five staffers. "They divided up the government between them," said an OMB official. Associate directors tended to work with relative independence within their respective spheres of authority. They had only limited interaction with other staff members. Principal lines of communication were between the associate director, deputy director, and the executive director. According to John Ehrlichman:

> Each Assistant Director was virtually autonomous. I didn't hire their people, they did. Their job was staff support. It was up to each Assistant Director how he programmed his people. Occasionally, I would requisition one of those guys with the approval of Cole and the Assistant Director involved, but ordinarily they worked up through the Assistant Director.
> Nixon didn't like a lot of buttons on his telephone. He would have liked to call me for all domestic stuff, but he knew he couldn't. He still wanted one guy on each issue. Our structure followed this. [33]

The staff organization under Ehrlichman is presented in Figure IV-II.

As executive director from 1971–1973, Ehrlichman supervised the council's work. He helped prepare the agenda for council meetings, directed the work of its committees, oversaw the preparation of its reports, and acted as the principal contact with the president. He exercised a tight rein over staff operations, meeting daily at 7:30 A.M. with his top aides. Egil Krogh,

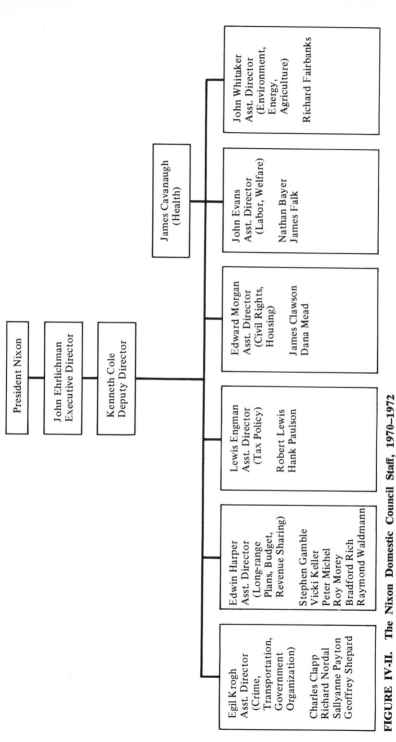

FIGURE IV-II. The Nixon Domestic Council Staff, 1970–1972

SOURCE: John Kessel, *The Domestic Presidency* (North Scituate, Mass., Duxbury Press, 1975), p. 14

Jr., an associate director of the Domestic Council during this period, described Ehrlichman's impact on policy formulation as "direct, immediate and profound," adding, "I don't think anything was developed that he did not have an involvement in." [34]

The council members did not usually meet as a group. When there were formal meetings, it was more for general discussion than for policy development. As one associate director put it, "If there is a problem broad enough to attract the attention of all the members of the Domestic Council, the chances are it also involved the secretary of defense and secretary of state and then you have a cabinet meeting instead."

Work was done primarily by committees of the council organized on the basis of projects or missions. The committees, usually appointed at the behest of the appropriate associate director, consisted of either secretaries or assistant secretaries from the departments, an OMB official, and the associate director who coordinated and directed their activities. Charged with examining issues, conducting studies, and preparing working papers for the president, the committees functioned as intragovernmental task forces.

Only once did the council and its staff turn in any systematic way to people outside the government for policy ideas. In the spring of 1971, several members of the Domestic Council staff went around the country to meet with various community leaders. From the staff's viewpoint the results were very disappointing. "We came back with only 50 or so ideas of which maybe 5 had merit," said one associate director. None of these suggestions were incorporated into the administration's program and the practice was quickly abandoned.

The papers which were developed by the interdepartmental groups provided background on the issues, summarized political opinions, and listed various alternatives, their costs and consequences. Included was an assessment of the legislation's chances on the Hill. Once the papers were completed, they were sent through the appropriate associate director to Cole to Ehrlichman who normally affixed covering memoranda that summarized major issues and options in a checklist fashion.

Ehrlichman's influence was pervasive. In reflecting on his own interaction with the Domestic Council staff in its development of policy papers, he stated:

> On most of them, I didn't see anything until the working group was finished with their recommendations unless there was a problem. Then I would come in and crack heads and play the heavy at the Assistant Director's request.
>
> A great many of these groups were set up on open questions and it was the Assistant Director's job to get what there was from the people at the meetings. But there were times when Nixon wanted to go in some directions and I ramrodded these. Most of the Assistant Directors could

ramrod in that situation as well. Most of them had a keen political sense which was indispensible.[35]

President Nixon generally examined the reports alone. His comments frequently appeared in the form of marginal notes. The president did not usually spend much time on the details of translating the program into legislation. This was considered to be the job of the staff and/or the project group. After the president evaluated the Domestic Council paper, the project group normally reconvened for the purpose of implementing his suggestions. The staff had the prime responsibility for overseeing the preparation of the legislation and approving the accompanying messages to Congress. The actual drafting was usually done by the departments with the OMB providing technical assistance and eventually, central clearance. Important legislation was also checked by the Office of Legal Counsel in the Department of Justice. The messages that accompanied the legislation were written primarily by the president's speech writers with the project group and/or council staff having the final say on substance.

While the Domestic Council operation went on throughout the year, annual programing was cycled to the budgetary process. In the spring, OMB would preview the forthcoming budget for the Domestic Council and its staff. Members of the council were also surveyed individually for their legislative ideas. After initial policy and budgetary decisions were made by the president, council committees were formed to work on priority projects. By August, most of the major budget and program issues had been decided. The fall of the year saw the project, as approved by the president, translated into legislation for the new session of Congress. The State of the Union Address incorporated the policy goals of the administration while special messages detailed the purpose and content of the legislation. After these messages were presented, the Domestic Council staff focused most of its spring work on the congressional debate. A record was kept of how well the administration was doing on each piece of legislation. By June, the cycle for the next year's program had begun.

The growth in both the size and importance of the Domestic Council in the first Nixon administration was gained largely at the expense of departments and agencies. From the White House perspective, the kinds of reforms that the administration desired such as executive reorganization and revenue sharing would never have been proposed, much less accomplished, if left to the departments alone. Without a strong, centralized staff in the White House, it was argued, the president's policy could not be adequately developed and presented. One Domestic Council staffer put it this way:

> If departments and agencies are primary policy initiators, what you'll probably get back is a brief for the status quo. If you want to break some new ground, want something fresh and different, you either have to

create your own staff to do it or get outside groups to bring that information to you or both.

The need to distinguish between presidential and departmental interests was particularly evident in the programing process. There were two paths which legislative initiatives took, depending on who initiated them and how critical they were to the administration. Priority legislation was designed by the White House, developed principally by council staff, and sent to Capitol Hill with much public fanfare and presidential backing; less important legislation was usually introduced by the departments, sent to OMB for clearance, and then submitted to Congress. In addition to obtaining clearance, departments and agencies tried to secure active presidential support. They were hampered by difficulties of access. Ehrlichman, not Nixon, was the final arbiter and judge most of the time and the associate director on the council staff was the principal point of contact for most department officials including the secretary. The need for senior department heads and agency officials to make their case before the more junior, less politically experienced associate directors was itself a source of considerable irritation. In describing his staff's relationship to the cabinet, Ehrlichman stated:

> My guys met with Cabinet officers regularly. That was their job. Cabinet officers had no chance unless and until it was cleared through us to the President. They didn't like meeting with these guys—or with me. They bitched continuously because Nixon wouldn't see them. And Nixon would be the one who'd enforce it. I'd say I was having trouble with Secretary X; he'd pick up the phone and chew him out.[36]

Associate Director Egil Krogh, Jr., presents a similar perspective:

> When it came to perquisites, clearly the cabinet secretary was the dominant figure. When it came to policy development, I think that the Domestic Council staff if not the equivalent was clearly the principal developer of policy.[37]

The pivotal position of the White House/Domestic Council staff between the departments and the president created considerable consternation within the executive branch [38] and was one of the factors that precipitated a change to presumably a more department-oriented system at the beginning of President Nixon's second term.

Creating More Decentralization: The Nixon-Ford Transition

The new system was ostensibly designed to return priority programing responsibilities to the departments and reduce the operational functions of the Domestic Council staff. Created were three super cabinet secretaries with broad area of responsibilities in human resources, natural resources, and community development respectively. These jurisdictions paralleled the president's proposals for cabinet reorganization, the subject matter divisions in the OMB, and, to some extent, the Domestic Council staff structure. The plan called for each counselor to be chairman of a Domestic Council committee consisting of other departmental and agency officials concerned with that area.

Aided by a small staff and housed in a separate office, the counselors were expected to develop policy and resolve interdepartmental disputes. They were to report directly to Ehrlichman who was relieved of his day-to-day duties and charged with overall coordination of the new system. As part of the reorganization, the Domestic Council staff was reduced in size, with principal aides farmed out to the departments as assistant and under secretaries to provide, in the words of one presidential aide, "people who understood what life was like in the White House." Critics immediately saw this as an attempt to infiltrate the departments.

The counselor system did not work well and was aborted after six months. Tensions between the counselors and other department secretaries precluded the type of executive cooperation on which the plan was predicated. The counselors themselves had difficulty wearing two hats, being advocates for their departments and coordinators for the president. Watergate and Ehrlichman's resignation also made coordinated planning difficult. When the system was dismantled, there was little to take its place. The Domestic Council staff operation had been reduced to fire fighting. Its short-range focus was the result of its projected role within a counselor system. Its staff size had been cut substantially. From the 70 or so professionals and supporting personnel of the pre-1972 Ehrlichman council, the staff was reduced by about one-half.

The change in leadership also affected the staff's operation and its clout. Kenneth Cole did not provide the same kind of direction and policy guidance as had John Ehrlichman. "Under Ehrlichman there was a lot of dreaming; under Cole the maximum plan was one year ahead," stated one survivor of the transition.[39] Nor did Cole enjoy the same close relationship with the president or the same influence within the council that Ehrlichman had. In the opinion of at least one staffer who served before, during, and after the change, "Ehrlichman always had the ear of the president; Cole did not. Ehrlichman's recommendations carried more weight with the council; Cole's was one voice among many." Cole conceded that he did not have the same kind of relationship to Nixon, but maintained that he was able to get to the president when necessary:

> John [Ehrlichman] did have a privileged position and I didn't. There are no two ways about it. To the extent that John's privileged position allowed him greater power in terms of making things happen, that was a differ-

ence we had. I still feel, notwithstanding his privileged position and my lack of one, that it didn't seriously affect our work. . . . We had four years of a strong man so to speak. To an extent, a continuation of that when I took over would probably have inhibited the progress we were able to make.[40]

Watergate had its effect as well. It demoralized the staff and isolated the president. It created in the words of one aide, "a bunker mentality." In addition to Ehrlichman, two other former council aides were convicted of crimes.[41] The difficulties in which the administration found itself made planning for an uncertain political future precarious at best. The growing scandal also reduced the president's personal influence with Congress and the rest of the executive branch.

Under Roy Ash's direction, the OMB moved into the programing vacuum. Supported by large institutional resources that included a network of examiners and management associates, by budgetary, clearance, and management processes, and by a structure that accumulated power in the hands of four associate directors at the very time that the White House was dispersing it to cabinet secretaries, the associate directors of the OMB began making the key policy decisions, in many cases without even checking with the Domestic Council staff.

The natural aging of the Nixon presidency also contributed to the OMB's greater influence. Even at the beginning of the second term, the president seemed to place less emphasis on developing new policy initiatives and greater stress on achieving his long-standing legislative requests and managing existing programs. "He was much less compromising on legislation in the last one and one-half years than in his first term," stated a principal staff member of the council, who added, "That made our job more difficult."

The Domestic Council staff attempted to some extent to counter the OMB's influence by aligning itself with the departments, playing on their traditional distrust of the OMB. An attempt was also made to allow cabinet members to take their cases directly to the president. The staff had only limited success in both respects. Nixon's decision-making style, especially under siege, and his built-in fears of losing control to the bureaucracy precluded a more open presidency. His resignation and Ford's succession basically undercut the privileged position that the council had had with the president.[42]

Initially, Ford tended to rely more on his long-time friends and staff aides whom he brought into the White House rather than the Nixon holdovers on the council staff. The new president's more open and verbal way of doing business also presented difficulties for a council used to operating on paper in a fairly formal system.

During the transition and its aftermath, the staff's attention was directed toward the Ford administration's immediate needs such as briefing the president on the wide range of policy issues before Congress and handling the heavy volume of congressional clearances, enrolled bill recommendations, presidential position papers, and cabinet correspondence.[43] These everyday problems had a tendency to drive out long-range planning with the result that preparing a legislative program became a short-range operation. In 1974, most of the projects which the Nixon Domestic Council had been working on were jettisoned in favor of policy initiatives in the economic and energy areas.

Recasting the Domestic Council: Ford

The council's preoccupation with day-to-day problems was itself viewed as a problem and one that was never satisfactorily resolved during the Ford presidency. There were attempts to create a longer-range planning capability. In the spring of 1975, Vice President Nelson A. Rockefeller assumed operational control of the council after an internal struggle for power. Two of his principal aides, James M. Cannon and Richard L. Dunham, were appointed to the top staff positions of director and deputy director for planning and policy respectively and other Rockefeller associates were brought in at the associate director level.[44] The council's official tasks were even redesigned.[45]

Rockefeller, who had headed a committee on critical choices after resigning as governor of New York, was expected to provide leadership and direction for the establishment of social goals. Almost immediately, the vice-president, along with Cannon and Dunham, held meetings with cabinet secretaries to determine what they considered to be the major policy issues facing the administration. While these sessions were largely ceremonial, they established Rockefeller's position as chief policy co-ordinator and set the stage for a legislative programing effort keyed toward the State of the Union in January 1976. Planning actually began during the summer, when the council staff started identifying problems and communicating in an informal way with people inside and outside the government. Sessions were held with individual cabinet members and their staffs in the fall of the year. Six public forums were also conducted from October to December. Although these forums did not have a direct impact on the form of the program and content of the 1976 State of the Union Address, they did produce a public platform, created the appearance of a concerned administration and stressed issues for further study.[46]

However, by late 1975, Rockefeller had announced his decision not to seek reelection and had asked to be relieved of day-to-day operational responsibilities, Dunham had resigned to accept appointment as chairman of the Federal Power Commission, and Cannon was left with a relatively small staff that had undergone a major change in personnel. "It took quite a while to settle down and get into the normal run of things," said one associate director, who added, "there was a hangover of concern and distrust."

While the council staff did participate in the actual preparation of the 1976 State of the Union Address, it did not do so in a very systematic way. One associate director described the putting together of the speech as "a hit or miss operation."

> We were all asked to submit our ideas. At some point in time, these ideas were literally pulled together in a mass of paper. A committee of ten edited it. They threw out three of every four pages to get it down to a usable text size.

Robert Hartmann, counselor to the president, was primarily responsible for drafting the address and James Cannon, director of the council, was nominally in charge of coordinating it.

A second attempt was made in the spring of 1976 to develop a longer-range programing effort. The plan was to relieve some staff of operational responsibilities so they could devote more time to policy studies of potential presidential concern. A special unit was established under the direction of Arthur Quern, deputy director for planning and policy. Staffed with only a few full-time assistants and several paid consultants, the operation never really got off the ground.

The campaign intervened, creating a need for presidential policy proposals but ironically, preventing most of the policy staff from helping to develop them. Anxious to maintain the distinction between political and nonpolitical officials in the light of Watergate, the Ford administration concluded that staff paid from the Domestic Council budget could not participate in the campaign effort under the provisions of the Hatch Act.[47] This left the formulation of campaign policy to the writers and presidential aides who were officially on the White House, not the council, payroll.

By the fall of 1976, the Domestic Council had all but stopped work on annual legislative programing. The extent of the staff's participation in the preparation of President Ford's last State of the Union Address in 1977 was to request department and agency heads to list their accomplishments during the two years of the Ford presidency and the unfinished items on their agenda. From this inventory an outline was prepared for the senior advisors who were working on the address.

The main reason that the staff of the Ford Domestic Council was not able to program far ahead was that the bulk of its time was consumed by the many tasks in the domestic area that required immediate presidential attention. This ranged from answering presidential mail to the preparation of option memos on major policy issues. In the legislative sphere principal duties included congressional clearances, enrolled bill recommendations, drafts of presidential statements, and the staffing of cabinet correspondence. Associate directors of the council were also expected to help explain the president's program on the Hill. Some of them had considerable contact with members of Congress, their offices, and committee staffs.

To better enable the council to perform these diverse functions in the light of its comparatively small size, Cannon restructured the organization to further compartmentalize subject matter areas. In addition to the director and the deputy director for policy and planning, there was a deputy director for operations and ten associate directors. While the increased special-ization of the associate directors helped compensate for their shortage of time and lack of expertise and staff support, it also made coordinated planning difficult.

Each associate director operated with a great deal of discretion in exercising responsibilities, often under severe time constraints. While there was some overlap in areas of responsibility and some informal interchange between associate directors, their jurisdictions were, for the most part, discrete. Figure IV-III illustrates the primary areas. While the staff met once a week, it did not operate as a group in setting priorities and develop-ing policy options. The associate directors did not move in a presidential direction together. They tended to work alone.[48]

Associate directors had their principal contact with their counterparts in the OMB and the departments and agencies but not at the secretarial level as in the previous administration. They had little direct interaction with the president except through their staffing of decision memos for him.

As director of the council, Cannon saw Ford an average of two to four times a week. He regularly participated in the senior staff meetings and coordinated relations with the congressional liaison office. But he was not cut from the Ehrlichman mold and did not exercise strong, aggressive leadership. One associate director put it bluntly:

> We had no leadership. Cannon is a sweet, very nice man who as far as I know never ran a staff; he didn't know how to use any of us. We didn't operate at all as an effective arm. We were entirely free operators.

Functioning within a highly decentralized policy-making system with a highly decentralized structure of its own had serious implications not only for how the staff worked but for whom they interacted with and what influence they were able to exert on domestic policy making. A White House official commented matter-of-factly:

> Once it's clear that when the guy who runs the Domestic Council doesn't have the clout or doesn't know how to use it, it filters down. Everybody understands it. So decisions get made and associate directors of the Domestic Council are not consulted; meetings are set up and they're not included.

An associate director stated his own problem simply, "It became apparent to everyone that people at my level weren't reporting to anyone. Therefore, why deal with us?"

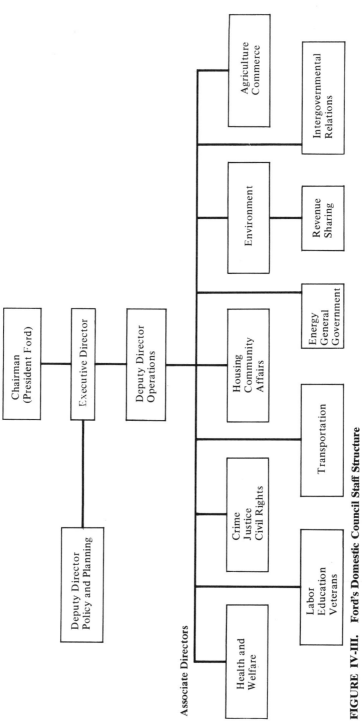

Associate Directors

FIGURE IV-III. Ford's Domestic Council Staff Structure

A variety of other factors contributed to the problems which the Ford Domestic Council faced. The high turnover of council personnel adversely affected the staff's capacity to plan far ahead or even make hard policy decisions, especially in the face of department or agency opposition. In contrasting the Nixon and Ford Domestic Councils, one individual who served on both staffs remarked in 1976:

> We don't have in depth knowledge of federal programs and institutional memory we had in the prior group [Nixon council staff] and we don't have the knowledge of the way the White House works and the personal relationships with other parts of the White House structure and OMB that we used to have. Those things come with time. People gaining confidence in one another—we've lost that. . . . I think it probably has made the Domestic Council staff somewhat less effective than it was before.

The relatively small size of the staff, approximately one-half the number of the Ehrlichman group, obviously limited what it could do. Lacking the institutional resources of the OMB and the departments and agencies, the council staff had to depend on others for information, expertise, and staff support. Requests to significantly enlarge the staff structure met with stiff congressional opposition. The Ford administration had to content itself with only a modest growth in size. The president's desire to limit budget expenditures, the large Democratic majority in Congress, and the conservative criticism within the Republican party during the 1976 campaign for the presidential nomination also did not provide much incentive for developing new domestic programs.

Finally, the establishment of a coordinating unit for economic policy impinged on the council's jurisdiction and the influence of several of its associate directors. Beginning in the fall of 1974, an Economic Policy Board (EPB) exercised major responsibility for economic policy making. The board, a successor to the Council on Economic Policy that existed during the Nixon administration, consisted of all departmental secretaries (except defense and justice) and other advisors from the Executive Office of the President. The key members of this group were the eight officials who comprised its Executive Committee.[49] Chaired by the secretary of the Treasury and, in his absence, by the president's assistant for economic affairs, this committee met daily at 8:30 A.M. in the White House. It operated according to a formal agenda prepared the week before and was staffed with background papers distributed at least 24 hours in advance.

The principal task of the Executive Committee was to coordinate interagency activity and develop policy options for the president. In keeping with Ford's decision-making style, the fleshing out of options was deemed its most important function. The committee did not strive to achieve a consensus, but it did take positions and make recommendations in providing advice to the president. L. William Seidman, vice-chairman of the council and economic advisor to the president, described the role of the EPB as that of an "honest broker." He added, "It does not try to set policy, but it sees to it that policy is set. It gets the top level people of the Government involved and it sees that policy options get to the President." [50]

While many of its policy recommendations required legislation or some sort of congressional activity, the EPB and its Executive Committee refrained from an active involvement in congressional relations per se. "We spent less than 10 percent of our time, more on the order of 5 percent, on things that could be loosely related to what might be called legislative strategy," stated Roger Porter, executive secretary of the board.[51] Porter added, "the EPB did not consider itself a legislative strategy board." [52]

Most of the board's studies and option papers were the work of interagency committees and task forces. In contrast to the Domestic Council, the EPB and its Executive Committee operated with only a handful of aides. Created at the time the president was attempting to reduce White House personnel, its staff was kept purposefully small so as not to compete with other departmental and presidential staffs. There was overlap between domestic and economic activities but this was viewed as inevitable.

The president's interest and involvement in economic matters elevated the importance of the Executive Committee within the administration. The committee's option papers provided the framework for presidential decision making and the information on which these decisions were predicated. According to Porter, "President Ford has been willing to make a decision on every major economic issue that has been *presented* to him and every major issue has been *presented* to him." [53]

The presentation of issues and options to the president characterized economic and domestic policy making during the Ford presidency. Rather than having a centralized White House structure which acted on presidential ideas and imposed a presidential perspective, Ford chose to depend on a variety of people, acting individually and collectively, to develop and coordinate the initiatives and put them into a decisional format. This had the effect of maximizing and clarifying his choices but minimizing his direction.

The staffing contrasts are striking when compared with the later Johnson and earlier Nixon years. Whereas Johnson had a small group of policy synthesizers and coordinators and Nixon a large, highly structured and specialized Domestic Council staff system, Ford depended on a more open, flexible mechanism that included the Domestic Council, the OMB, the Executive Committee of the EPB, and various cabinet officials. Whereas the Johnson system was geared to the generation of new policy initiatives from outside the government and the Nixon effort toward presidential control from within, the Ford process was designed to permit a complete airing of views from within and from outside the government.

This had both benefits and liabilities which were magnified by the

1976 presidential election. It distanced the Ford administration from its predecessor and from the more odious associations of the closed presidency. It returned cabinet members to a major role in policy making (to their own and their clientele's satisfaction) and lessened the control which White House staff aides had exercised over priority presidential programing. But it also appeared to make the development and presentation of a comprehensive legislative program more difficult. Collegial advising when combined with a more conservative philosophy, more limited legislative goals, and less success in selling these goals to Congress, produced a less visible and identifiable economic and social program for the Ford administration. The staff's preoccupation with day-to-day decisions from transition through the election made it difficult to design, much less present, a blueprint for the future. Ford's decision-making style also created the impression of a reactive rather than an assertive president.

CONCLUSION

Programing developed from and remained parallel to the legislative clearance operation during the Truman and Eisenhower presidencies. Orchestrated by the White House and staffed by the Bureau of the Budget, the major difference between ongoing clearance and annual programing during this period was the cycling of the latter (in conjunction with the preparation of the budget) to coincide with the beginning of the congressional session and the highlighting of the program itself in the president's State of the Union Address.

While more elaborate White House consideration, packaging, and presentation of the annual legislative program was evident in the Eisenhower administration than in Truman's, both of their programing efforts were oriented towards the departments and agencies. In the Kennedy-Johnson periods this orientation changed. The interest of Presidents Kennedy and Johnson in generating new policy initiatives, combined with their view of the bureaucracy as a pretty conservative place where new ideas were not likely to originate, resulted in a shift of focus from inside the executive branch to outside the government. The high priority placed on legislative proposals in both administrations and the desire of both presidents to be personally involved in program development put an even greater burden of the initiation, coordination, and synthesis on White House aides. Moreover, the size of the programing effort forced an expansion in the number of people regularly dealing with domestic legislative matters. By the mid 1960s, a separate domestic policy staff under Joseph Califano's direction was created to systematize the programing operation. This staff, although small and fairly general by contemporary standards, was the forerunner of the larger, more differentiated structure that functioned as an operating arm of the White House thereafter.

Nixon's Domestic Council staff, organized hierarchically along subject-matter lines, provided an in-house mechanism for generating and analyzing policy proposals. Department and agency interests were clearly distinguished from and subordinate to presidential needs in what became a two-track system. Dissatisfaction resulting from this differentiation, from problems of access, and from shifts in the administration's legislative objectives led to changes in the decision-making structure. These changes basically eroded the Domestic Council's position. Reductions in the size of its staff, combined with the events of Watergate and Ehrlichman's departure, impeded policy planning in general, reduced the council's influence, and allowed the OMB to play a larger and more substantive role.

Under President Ford, the Domestic Council staff never recovered its influence. It had difficulty planning on a large scale and developing a long-range perspective. The inevitable personnel problems of a transition, the size and structure of the operation that Ford inherited, and the president's own style and political objectives kept the council staff focused on immediate problems and rendered its advisory role nonexclusive in the domestic areas. The council's voice was one among several in the new administration and its role and influence actually seemed to shrink as the administration progressed.

Programing during the Ford presidency illustrates and emphasizes both the continuities and discontinuities in the evolution of the process. That the president will propose an annual legislative program and that it will be outlined in the State of the Union Address and amplified in special messages is now an expectation which every contemporary president has met. The operation of a large specialized staff structure in the presidency to coordinate, generate, and package the proposals is also a foregone conclusion. What has changed has been policies, personalities, and the institutional relationships among the White House, OMB, and the executive departments and agencies. These variable elements in the programing process will be examined in the remainder of this section.

Unlike clearance and enrolled bill procedures which have remained relatively stable over time, presidential programing has been much more sensitive to political pressures and personal presidential objectives. Whether a president chooses to emphasize social, economic, or national security issues, how he establishes his legislative priorities, where he looks for his policy ideas, what kind of mechanism he has to coordinate and refine his administration's positions, how receptive he is to outside interests and positions, all make a difference in the form and product of the programing process.

Those presidents who placed greater stress on domestic policy initiatives, who saw their political success closely tied to their legislative record, have naturally tended to produce a more comprehensive program than those who have looked to other policy areas or who have emphasized other executive duties and powers. The legislative presidents have had programing processes that encourage innovation. They have also tended to be more personally involved in the process. Truman's formal establishment of an annual programing cycle and Kennedy and Johnson's extension of it illustrate the legislative orientation of these Democratic presidents in contrast to the Republicans, who met programing expectations without enlarging them.

The quest for legislative suggestions also distinguishes Democratic and Republican presidencies. Kennedy and Johnson's use of outside task forces was more likely to generate new ideas and less likely to be bound to established patterns and interests than was Nixon and Ford's internal group approach. Even Truman's departmental orientation was not nearly as self-serving in its early years as it became toward the end of his and his successor's administrations.

Administrations tend to age, especially when presidents are not seeking reelection. They not only produce fewer innovative programs but they have less capacity to get them enacted. While all presidencies grow old, aging seems to have had a more pronounced effect on those legislative programs that are internally developed. The tendency to conserve gains and not take chances, most obvious in an election year when the president is not seeking reelection, results in programs that tend to be less innovative and administrations that tend to be less willing and able to get them enacted into law. Republican administrations have grown tired of legislating more quickly, in part because they may have begun with more limited objectives. The end of Eisenhower's second term, the beginning of Nixon's second, and much of the Ford period are examples of such presidencies.

The personal involvement of individual presidents also distinguishes the programing efforts of contemporary administrations. Truman, Kennedy, and Johnson were much more active in the formulation of their own programs than were Eisenhower and Nixon. Ford was deeply involved in his budget decisions. Personality rather than legislative philosophy seemed to condition the level of this activity, although for the recent Democratic presidents, personality, legal activism, and a myriad of social goals have been closely related. Nonetheless, active presidents tend to display their activism in the policy-making aspects of their job.

Operating style also impinges on the character of programing since presidential policy making has become basically a White House operation. Whether a systematic, analytic process is created or an ad hoc system developed depends, in large part, on the way presidents like to do business. Programing is more revealing of and dependent on the style of the president than are the clearance and enrolled bill processes which are more executive branch oriented.

Some have suggested that presidential staff flexibility contributes to innovative programing.[54] This seemed to have been the case until the Ford administration where an open senior staff structure combined with specialization at the lower level did not produce the same type of new and innovative programing that was evident in Democratic administrations of the 1960s. Even though Ford did not strive for agreement per se, the consistency of his political views with those of his senior advisors probably contributed to a consensus. Moreover, the design of the Ford policy-making system, the "sending-up" of policy options from concentric circles of advisors, conditioned his choices and the eventual policy. In other words, a president dependent on colleagues of similar political persuasion for making programatic decisions is likely to reflect that persuasion in his decisions regardless of the number and range of options from which he theoretically has to choose.

Ford's difficulties stemmed in part from the transition. Developing an elaborate programing mechanism seems to be a product of experience and time. For the White House especially, transitions are notoriously difficult periods. At the beginning, urgent and immediate presidential tasks take precedence. The first six months are usually a learning period with programing often a hit-or-miss operation. President Kennedy, and to a lesser extent, President Nixon, attempted to minimize the transition effect by using the postelection periods in 1960 and 1968 to collect and refine ideas for their legislative programs from their campaign task forces. Presidents Johnson and Ford did not have the luxury of a two-month respite, much less active outside consulting groups organized along subject-matter lines. The pressures to maintain continuity forced them to use the people and organizations already in place. Developing a distinctive program under these conditions is apt to be a frustrating experience. Alternatives must be thrashed out among old staffers whose loyalty to the new president is still in doubt. The intrusion of new presidential aides onto the ongoing staff structure accentuates the problem.

The OMB has been of critical help during these periods. Its institutional position as a presidential agency, combined with its staff resources and, until the early 1970s, its stability in senior personnel, have provided the White House with an important source of knowledge and experience. The degree of dependence on the OMB has been related to the size of the White House staff. A small White House staff such as that of Eisenhower and Kennedy had no choice but to use the OMB to help coordinate and integrate legislative suggestions. Similarly, the reduced size of the Ford Domestic Council staff during the transition and its high turnover through 1976, combined with the president's budget emphasis, also resulted in a large OMB role. In contrast, the development of a policy staff during the latter years of the Johnson administration and its enlargement, differentiation, and sophistication under Nixon decreased the dependence on the OMB. In addition to the size of the White House, the orientation of the program, the personalities involved, and the extent to which programing is keyed to the budgeting effort impacts on OMB's influence and its access to key points of decisions. The example of the Ford administration suggests how important personalities and policy goals have been to the OMB's ability to wield political influence.

IMPLICATIONS FOR THE FUTURE

While comprehensive presidential programing will undoubtedly continue to be an expectation of the modern presidency, the scope of the program and the orientation of the process is likely to remain reasonably flexible. Scope is conditioned by the political climate and public mood in addition to the president's policy objectives.

The general environment is subject to flux. What a president thinks he can or must achieve within a given Congress will undoubtedly influence what he requests and how hard he tries to get it. Constituency pressures, however, tend to be more constant. The bureaucracy that expanded in response to policy initiatives has a self-generating capacity. Extending existing programs and developing new ones has become a bureaucratic expectation, in and of itself, one with which chief executives have to live. This, in turn, increases the likelihood of public responses and legislative proposals in policy areas, regardless of the president's personal inclinations and, in some cases, regardless of the chances for success.

In deciding on the priorities given to legislative goals, contemporary presidents have had to balance their own costs in time, energy, and political obligations with the political benefits of achieving a legislative record, the psychological benefit of success in the legislative arena, and the societal benefits that the legislation is designed to achieve. In the domestic area, the costs have often been calculated as quite high, especially by presidents who have to contend with oppositional majorities in Congress. In general, the better the opportunities for achieving policy initiatives, the greater the payoffs for taking them. Presidents are encouraged by their potentialities for success. This explains why Republican presidents have and probably will continue to put less emphasis on proposing and packaging comprehensive domestic legislative programs than Democrats. If the differences between the parties' electoral constituencies also persists, they too should contribute to the Democrats placing a higher priority on legislative policy making.

The need to satisfy the president's political constituency and policy objectives affects the kinds of sources that are consulted. The presidential staff system affects how the ideas from these sources are to be integrated into a legislative program. The size, experience, and, to a lesser extent, structure of the White House staff has probably had the most important impact on the way in which policy has been and can be developed.

A large specialized presidential policy staff is necessary if the size of the programing effort, the complexity of modern legislation, and the desire to imprint a presidential perspective continues. There is little alternative so long as priority programing is primarily presidential and not executive in character. While the OMB's participation is necessary to evaluate the large number of department and agency proposals and to coordinate the increasing amount of interagency legislation, its role is not as central to the programing process as it is to clearance and enrolled bill procedures. In fact, OMB's agency orientation and its budget perspective make it less than the ideal presidential agency to stimulate and oversee the development of policy initiatives from outside the government. The OMB is an effective policing agent and an effective unit for integrating budget and policy considerations, but it is not oriented toward generating new policy ideas. To do this, a White House perspective is far more appropriate.

Senior policy advisors officed in the west wing, cycled to presidential duties, and sensitized to the president's political needs are in a more advantageous position to create and articulate a presidential program than are their counterparts in the OMB, who also have to contend with budget and management responsibilities. While some OMB staff support is both necessary and desirable, White House dependence on the OMB in the programing process is not. In the long run, it is the distance from and accessibility to the president that counts.

NOTES

1   Neustadt writes that Truman came to the White House "with his mind set on restoring proper balance between President and Congress." Richard E. Neustadt, *Presidential Power* (New York: Wiley, 1960), p. 173.
2   Harold Smith, Roosevelt's budget director, was alleged to be insanely jealous of his personal relationship with the president. As one White House official saw it, "he and he alone wanted to see the president; anything related to the Bureau of the Budget, he wanted to flow up through him and from him to the president. He stood as a wall; he blocked off contact between staff and the White House staff."

On the other hand, White House aides praised his replacement, James Webb, for his very cooperative attitude:

> Practically the first thing Jim did was to come across West Executive Avenue and see Clifford and Steelman and others on the White House staff and assure them that as far as he was concerned, the Bureau of the Budget staff was White House staff. The talents, knowledge and abilities, data, resources, information—everything in the bureau—was ours for the asking. And he did not insist that we had to go through him or anything of that sort.

George Elsey, interview.

> Jim Webb wanted to do all he could to facilitate cooperation between the White House staff and the Bureau of the Budget. I believe it was his notion that if he

did that this would give BOB the most influence on what happened within the administration. That was a very sound doctrine. I think that is exactly the way it worked out.

Charles Murphy, interview.

3   Richard E. Neustadt, "Presidency and Legislation: Planning the President's Program," *American Political Science Review* XLIX, no. 4 (December 1955): 1006.

4   Ibid., p. 1011. The annual call for legislation thus became a way for departments and agencies to try to elicit presidential support for their pet projects.

5   Clifford mentioned the Point Four Program as one of these gems. (Clark Clifford, interview.)

6   Harry S Truman, *1945, Year of Decisions* (New York: New American Library [Signet], 1955), p. 49.

7   Bernard M. Shanley, interview.

8   Neustadt describes the sessions in the following manner:

> The briefings themselves followed a set form. Typically, as a subject was reached the President would open with some appropriate remarks, then call on the department head (or in some cases the staff member) most concerned; the latter responding with what was, in effect, a redo or refinement of his cabinet presentation (or equivalent), complete with visual aides. Everything was visual and oral; no written summaries, much less bill or message drafts, were passed around. Language, it was explained, remained at a preliminary stage, pending these consultations. During the presentation the President himself would interpose a running commentary; at its close he would invite reactions (not concurrence) from the leaders—equally calling time rather shortly, and passing on to the next subject.

> Neustadt, "Presidency and Legislation," p. 991.

9   Major General Wilton B. Persons, interview.

10   Roger Jones, interview.

11   Lee C. White, interview.

12   Beginning in 1948, Legislative Reference collected material from the campaign to use in its clearance of agency bills. Platform and campaign pledges of the president-elect were assembled in order to determine a presidential position in clearing executive positions and proposals. The year 1960 was the first time this material was used in a systematic way to develop a presidential program.

13   When he saw the list of over 250 items of issues for possible presidential action, Kennedy remarked, "Now I know why Ike had Sherman Adams." Quoted in Theodore C. Sorensen, *Kennedy* (New York: Harper & Row, 1965), p. 238.

14   One strategy which secretaries had employed in the annual call for legislation was to withhold some of their priority items that they feared the BOB would veto in order to make a case before the president and his staff. The sessions with senior White House staff allowed the secretaries to float these ideas directly before the key people although usually in the presence of a BOB representative.

15   There was also a standing rule in the Kennedy administration for White House clearance on all major speeches and congressional testimony. It tended to be enforced, however, only during crisis periods. Sorensen's staff checked out major domestic speeches, while press secretary Salinger and his aides looked over the more routine ones. Legislative Reference approved congressional testimony in the normal course of its clearance work.

16   White, interview.

17   Myer Feldman, interview.

18   Johnson claims that the encouragement of candid and critical analysis was his motivation for keeping the task force reports secret. He wrote, "When a man is preparing a document for public consumption he is far more cautious and concerned about public image, and far more reluctant to be critical, than when he is advising on a confidential basis." (Lyndon Johnson, *The Vantage Point: Perspectives of the Presidency 1963–1969* (New York: Holt Rinehart and Winston, 1971), p. 328.

The president also wanted to avoid another problem that had cropped up during the Kennedy period. The public airing of the task force reports forced the administration to defend them even before they were translated into concrete legislative proposals. Not only did Johnson want the credit for new proposals but he also wanted to avoid being saddled with unpopular and unworkable ones.

Finally, Johnson argued that the development of public reports required considerably more time and effort. Since members of the task forces were busy people, often working under deadlines, he did not want to ask them to take the additional time to produce a public report. Lyndon B. Johnson, "Policy Formulation During the Johnson Administration" (paper obtained from the Lyndon B. Johnson Library), p. 9.

19   Johnson, *Vantage Point*, pp. 326–327.

20   Johnson, "Policy Formulation," pp. 3–4.

21   James Gaither, interview.

Johnson provides an interesting and successful example of a task force's failure to take political consideration into account.

> The model cities program which emerged from the combined efforts of two task forces in 1964 and 1965 was almost rejected by the task forces on the grounds that it could never be passed. Fortunately, however, that group heeded my admonition and made the recommendation as the right thing to do irrespective of their judgment about its political prospects.
>
> Johnson, "Policy Formulation," p. 7.

22   The discussion that follows, based largely on interviews with Joseph Califano and his principal assistants, Lawrence Levinson and James Gaither, substantially corroborates the description of the Johnson task forces made by Norman C. Thomas and Harold L. Wolman in their article, "The Presidency and Policy Formulation: The Task Force Device," *Public Administration Review* XXIX, no. 5 (September/October 1969): 459–471. It does not agree in every detail, however. The Thomas and Wolman article should be consulted for a more in-depth study of the operation of the Johnson task forces.

23   The membership of the internal groups was dictated by the subject matter;

the composition of the outside task forces was determined by the staff with the president's approval. Johnson insisted that there be a geographic balance. "I do not want just a bunch of guys coming out of Harvard and Yale. I want you to draw them from the South and Midwest," he told his aides. Despite the opposition to the Vietnam war which developed during this period, the White House experienced no difficulty in getting people to serve on the task forces.

24   Quoted in Doris Kearns, *Lyndon Johnson and the American Dream* (New York: Harper & Row, 1976), p. 222.

25   Ibid., p. 223.

26   Ibid.

27   Beginning in 1967, an additional step was added. The Office of Legal Counsel in the Department of Justice was asked to examine all legislation after the BOB finished with it. The purpose of this final legal check was to make sure that the legislation did what the president wanted it to do.

The incident that sparked the adoption of this new procedure was the Clean Water Restoration Act of 1966. Interior drafted the legislation and Legislative Reference approved it. In the White House view, however, the bill did not do what the president desired as expressed in his legislative message. "A fairly hefty argument," between Interior and the White House ensued and led to the use of the Justice Department as a final arbiter and legal check.

Justice's role was subsequently abandoned during the Nixon presidency, at least on a systematic basis. There were complaints by professionals within the department of the routine and perfunctory work being done on legislation "much of which was going nowhere anyway." Justice was still occasionally involved in giving advice on drafting statutes, however.

28   Johnson writes:

> Throughout my Presidency I insisted that we brief the Congress fully before our messages were sent to the Hill. We made many mistakes, but failure to inform and brief the Congress was not one of them. My insistence on this practice was rooted in an experience I had in the House in 1941, when I witnessed the negative impact of failure to brief Congressional leaders. I was standing in the back of the House behind the rail as Speaker Sam Rayburn listened to the House clerk read an important new administration message President Roosevelt had just sent to the Hill. Several dozen Democrats were gathered around him. As he finished, a unanimous chorus of complaints rushed forth: "Why, that message is terrible, Mr. Sam—we can't pass that . . . ." "That last suggestion is awful . . . ." "Why in the world did you let the President send one up like that? . . ." "Why didn't you warn us?"
>
> Speaker Rayburn listened to all the criticisms and then responded softly: "We'll just have to look at it more carefully. That's all I can say now, fellows. We'll have to look at it more carefully." The crowd scattered. Mr. Sam and I were left alone in the back. I could see that something was wrong. "If only," he said, "the President would let me know ahead of time when these controversial messages are coming up. I could pave the way for him. I could create a base of support. I could be better prepared for criticism. I could get much better acceptance in the long run. But I never know when the damned messages are coming. This last one surprised me as much as it did all of them." He shook his head sadly and walked slowly away.

I could see that his pride was hurt. So was the President's prestige and the administration's program. I never forgot that lesson.

Johnson, *Vantage Point,* pp. 447–448.

29   Lyndon Johnson as quoted in Kearns, *Lyndon Johnson and the American Dream,* p. 226.

30   Richard M. Nixon as quoted in Dom Bonafede, "White House Report/ Domestic Council Tries to Match Early Promise," *National Journal Reports* VII, no. 50 (December 13, 1975): 1688.

Murray Comarow, the executive director of the council that suggested the reorganization, comments to the same effect: "We saw emphasis on the Domestic Council as a mechanism within which the fragmented Cabinet system could function on problems which cut across departmental lines," as quoted in Louis Maisel, "High Level Domestic Advising: The Domestic Council in the Ford Administration" (Paper presented at the annual meeting of the Southern Political cal Science Association, Atlanta, Ga., November 4–6, 1976) p. 4.

31   Kenneth Cole, interview.

32   I will use the term associate director in referring to the positions that these individuals held.

33   John Ehrlichman, as quoted in Louis Maisel, "High Level Domestic Advising," p. 11.

34   Egil Krogh, Jr., interview.

35   John Ehrlichman as quoted in Maisel, "High Level Domestic Advising," p. 18.

36   Ibid., p. 21.

37   Egil Krogh, Jr., interview.

38   Raymond J. Waldman, a staff assistant on the Domestic Council from November 1970 to February 1973 stated that one of the primary reasons for the Domestic Council's existence was "to gain policy control of the domestic agencies." He observes that it achieved this objective to a large degree. Raymond J. Waldman, "The Domestic Council: Innovation in Presidential Government," *Public Administration Review* XLIV, no. 3 (May/June 1976): 266.

39   Geoffrey Shepard, interview.

40   Cole, interview.

41   They were Edward Morgan and Egil Krogh, both associate directors of the council.

42   Nonetheless, some of the work of the council did result in legislation. The extension of revenue sharing, the transfer of highways funds to mass transportation projects, the new Elementary and Secondary Education Bill, and the 1974 Housing and Community Development Bill were projects on which the Nixon Domestic Council staff had worked.

43   All official correspondence that cabinet secretaries sent to the president was normally routed through the appropriate Domestic Council associate director for comments and any necessary staff work. This procedure was designed to provide the information and expertise the president needed to immediately reply to the secretary.

44   The struggle was between Rumsfeld and Rockefeller and centered on the person who would replace Cole as staff director. Rumsfeld favored Phillip

Areeda, Associate Council to the President, and Rockefeller wanted his long-time associate, James Cannon. Ford's choice of Cannon was a conscious decision to give the vice president oversight over the direction of council policy and activities.

45   The new responsibilities as enunciated by the president were:

> To assess national needs and identify alternative ways of meeting them
> To provide rapid response to presidential needs for policy advice
> To coordinate the establishment of national priorities for the allocation of available resources
> To maintain a continuous policy review of ongoing programs
> To propose reforms as needed

Gerald Ford, "Memorandum for Members of the Domestic Council," February 13, 1975.

46   Within the council itself, the forums received a mixed evaluation. One aide who attended most of the sessions described them as "thought-provoking" and "direction-pointers." "They emphasized the items that we might find it useful to look at," he said. Another Domestic Council staff member, however, viewed the forums as "window-dressing . . . as politically but not substantially useful."

47   The Hatch Act makes it unlawful for most employees of the executive branch to actively participate in political campaigns. Exempted are the president's White House aides and top political appointees in the departments and some agencies. Ambassadors are also not subject to this restriction.

48   The council staff did utilize review goups, a new name for the interagency task forces of the Nixon period. These groups consisted of department and agency representatives in addition to the Domestic Council staff and OMB representation. A major distinction between the Nixon and Ford groups, however, was the level of representation. During the Ford period, the department representatives did not tend to be assistant or undersecretaries but lower-echelon officials.

49   The top officials who were members of the Executive Committee of the EPB were the secretary of the treasury (chairman), the assistant to the president for economic affairs (vice-chairman), the secretaries of state, commerce, and labor, the chairman of the council of Economic Advisers, the director of OMB, and the executive director of the Council on International Economic Policy. Additionally, three other officials of the Executive Office of the President (the assistants to the president for national security and domestic affairs and the executive director of the Energy Resources Council) were given advisory membership.

50   L. William Seidman as quoted in Philip Shabecoff, "What Ford Hopes Carter Will Keep," *The New York Times,* December 12, 1976, p. 17.

51   Roger Porter, interview.

52   Ibid.

53   Ibid. (Italics added.)

54   See, for example, Norman C. Thomas, "Presidential Advice and Information: Policy and Program Formulation," *Law and Contemporary Problems* XXXV, no. 3 (Summer 1970).

CHAPTER 5

Selling the Product: The Congressional Liaison Operation

The president has become a principal legislator.
The Congress does expect and often awaits the
presidential initiatives in major areas. The
congressional activity is usually one of
response. It is significant that you hear a
lot of criticism of the president from time to
time that he hasn't sent up the program so we
can't really do anything. I think this is a
trend that is now irreversible.

Orval Hansen
(Representative, Idaho,
1968–1974)

Merely placing a program before Congress is not
enough. Without constant attention from the
administration, most legislation moves through
the congressional process at the speed of a
glacier.

Lyndon B. Johnson,
The Vantage Point (New York:
Holt, Rinehart and Winston,
1971), p. 448

> **I never expected any member to commit political
> suicide in order to help the President, no matter
> how noble our case. I expected politicians to
> be concerned with their own interests; I only
> hoped to convince them our interests were often
> the same.**

Lawrence F. O'Brien,
No Final Victories (Garden City, N.Y.:
Doubleday,
1974), p. 118

INTRODUCTION

Presidential involvement in the legislative process is a natural consequence of the chief executive's duty to recommend necessary and expedient legislation. This involvement has traditionally taken the form of a presidential address or written message to Congress. It has also, and increasingly, been evident in less direct and formal ways. While the State of the Union Address, special messages, and required reports have served as vehicles for presenting presidential views, they have not, in and of themselves, been the most effective instruments for selling these views to the Congress. Even early presidents realized that they would have to do more than simply pronounce their recommendations in order to get them enacted into law.

A variety of constitutional and political factors combined to limit the legislative role of most presidents in the nineteenth century. The prevailing interpretation of the separation of powers doctrine led to a narrow definition of the president's recommendation role and also discouraged presidential interference in congressional affairs. The difficulty of exerting congressional party leadership and, especially, of influencing it from the White House, had much the same effect. It reduced the president's incentive for creating legislative goals, much less for making them administration priorities. With the exception of the Jefferson, Jackson, and Lincoln presidencies, it was not until the twentieth century that these constraints against presidential activity in Congress were overcome.

The development and institutionalization of the president's policy-making role created needs for more effective channels of communication between Congress and the president and for presidential influence within Congress. The establishment of a White House congressional liaison office in the post-World War II period was both an institutional and political response to these needs. It was designed to provide the president with a mechanism for affecting the legislative process. This chapter will explore the objectives and organization of that office and the ways in which it has operated.

It will begin with a description of the first official presidential liaison office created during the Eisenhower administration. Its legislative goals, structure, and strategy, its integration into the White House policy-making apparatus, and its tactics for influencing Congress will be examined. The chapter will then turn to the enlargement of the operation during the Kennedy and Johnson years, exploring the extension of domestic policy objectives, the expansion of policy-making responsibilities, and the energizing of activities on Capitol Hill. Finally, the legislative priorities and practices of the Nixon and Ford administrations will be explored within the same basic framework. The Nixon attempt to recreate the Eisenhower liaison model, to limit congressional input into presidential policy, and to tailor the administration's legislative tactics to more conservative policy objectives will be reviewed and the modifications that resulted from the Ford presidency noted. The chapter will conclude by contrasting the stylistic differences among liaison offices and by comparing their structural and tactical similarities. In this way, both the unique characteristics of each White House operation and the institutionalized aspects of contemporary presidential-congressional relations will be summarized and their implications for the president's future legislative role suggested.

THE ESTABLISHMENT OF A CONGRESSIONAL OFFICE IN THE WHITE HOUSE: THE EISENHOWER EXPERIENCE

Although Roosevelt and Truman were involved in domestic policy making and began developing structures and processes for formulating legislation, neither extended these very far into the congressional arena. They did not have White House liaison agents per se. Both, however, had key aides maintain contact with members of Congress and help generate support for their legislation. Roosevelt's postmaster general, James A. Farley, dispersed patronage with Congress in mind while Washington lawyers Thomas G. Corcoran, Benjamin V. Cohen, and James Rowe did some "influence peddling" on behalf of the president. Truman appointed two assistants, Joseph G. Feeney and Charles Maylon, in 1949 to help with the more routine political chores such as minor appointments, tickets to the Army-Navy football game, autographed pictures of the president, and the like. Charles Murphy, and to a lesser extent, Clark Clifford and Donald Dawson, conducted informal liaison with Congress on substantive policy matters but their involvement was neither comprehensive nor continuous. While Truman's Senate experience had sensitized him to the needs and desires of Congress, his conception of the president's proper legislative role limited both his personal interaction with Congress and that of his staff. As president, his visits to Congress were on official business only.

Eisenhower too had a traditional view of the president's legislative responsibilities. Like Truman, he believed that the president had a constitutional obligation to maintain the separation of powers and carefully refrain from getting into the legislature's business. Unlike Truman, this particular aspect of Eisenhower's theory of the president's proper role was reinforced by his personal predilection to avoid the wheeling and dealing of the political process whenever possible. Truman enjoyed politics; Eisenhower did not and refrained from active political involvement until his last two years in office.

Fortunately for Eisenhower, both the size and nature of his electoral coalition did not require him to promise a legislative program at the outset of his administration. He did not bring a laundry list of domestic policy goals into the White House. In fact, it was unclear whether he would even continue Truman's annual programing effort. Pressure to do so, combined with his personal desire to stay out of congressional politics, provided much of the incentive for designing the first organized congressional liaison unit in the White House. Eisenhower's military experience helped shape its goals, personnel, and structure.

Formulating Roles, Structure, and a Strategic Approach

The initial objective of the office was to improve congressional relations for the president. "What I really had in the back of my mind," stated Wilton B. (Jerry) Persons, Adams' deputy and first head of Eisenhower's liaison unit, "was to create a mutual understanding between downtown and uptown so that they [president and Congress] would not have all these misunderstandings through the news media." [1] After the Democrats won control of Congress in 1954, there was an additional function: "not just to sell the president's program," as Bryce Harlow, Persons' successor, put it, "but also to keep Congress from doing something different such as the blunting and thwarting of such harmful congressional activities as investigations, speeches, and excessive display of partisan activities." [2]

The approach of Persons and Harlow was low-key and generally bipartisan.[3] Their mutual experience in World War II days in handling the army's relations with Congress, their fear of intruding on the legislature's prerogatives, and their desire not to create a service office inclined them to maintain a low silhouette on Capitol Hill. White House agents tried to remain as inconspicuous as possible. Eisenhower's penchant for the non-partisan, the existence of a congressional Democratic majority for six of his eight years in office, and the unprecedented leadership powers of Johnson and Rayburn also contributed to this soft sell, bipartisan approach. The office operated with a small staff consisting of no more than a half dozen people at any one time.[4]

Integrating Liaison with Policy Making

The senior liaison aides were also policy advisors. Acting in part as a conduit for congressional views, they participated in White House meetings where issues were thrashed out; they were involved in the important signing or veto decisions; and they worked with the departments on the preparation and coordination of legislation. They did most of this on an ad hoc basis, working informally with other White House officials.

In addition to advising the departments, the White House congressional office loosely coordinated some of the departments' liaison work on Capitol Hill. Saturday morning meetings in the Cabinet Room were held to acquaint liaison officers with the administration's priorities and, in turn, to receive information on the departments' congressional activities. This interchange was used to help prepare agenda for the president's Tuesday morning meetings with Republican leaders which the senior liaison officers attended. Eisenhower considered these leadership sessions to be particularly valuable.

The meetings with departmental liaison agents were also used to coalesce them as a group, when necessary, behind key presidential policies. In general, the administration sought to discourage departmental reliance on the White House for what were considered to be matters of limited presidential interest. Harlow mentioned this as one of the great problems in any White House-dominated system: "to keep the departments doing that which they ought to do themselves and stop bothering the White House with their 'bric-a-brac.' So many a time we'd have to tell them to go off and carry their own hods. We were going to work on the big things which didn't happen to be big to them." [6] While the White House felt it essential to disclaim departmental interests and differentiate its own concerns if presidential priorities were to be achieved, this practice also had the effect of "indulging executive anarchy" in matters of lesser concern to the administration.[7]

When performing its liaison activities, the office of congressional affairs also had frequent contact with the Bureau of the Budget, mainly with Legislative Reference, and mostly on presidential clearance of proposed legislation. Budget provided technical assistance: tracking proposals within the executive, clearing congressionally sponsored bills and amendments, and doing the enrolled bill work. The congressional liaison staff also had an input on enrolled bills but usually only on the most controversial issues or in situations where members of Congress specifically requested their views be conveyed to the president. Legislative aides read veto signals for the president even though Eisenhower was not as concerned with the possibility of a veto override as other contemporary presidents seem to have been. "It was a factor but never a controlling one," said General Persons, who added, "He [Eisenhower] judged legislation on its own merits, so the question of whether or not it would pass a veto hardly ever came up." [8] Harlow recollects, however, that Eisenhower privately took careful stock of party associates on the Hill who voted against his disapproval of a bill.

Creating a Friendly Climate

From the perspective of the administration, the most important consideration was to establish priorities and then to seek them in an open, above-board way. Eisenhower did not like "noisy, strong-arm tactics" nor did he consider them productive in dealing with a Democratic majority. His staff followed his lead. "On major presidential initiatives we tried to bring all the influence to bear we could *with propriety,*" Bryce Harlow stated. [9]

The staff engaged in traditional kinds of the liaison activities. They interceded on patronage and impoundment matters. They provided information to Republican members on government projects within their districts. They helped with constituency-related problems, and they did most of this from the White House. The president did not want his top aides roaming the corridors of Congress. Senior staff instead went to specific meetings, usually with congressional leadership groups, then returned promptly to the White House leaving lesser aides to work Capitol Hill. [10]

Eisenhower's concerns were primarily with the substance of the program not its politics. The extent of his involvement in the legislative process was a subject of controversy, even among his own staff. Some felt that the president was too aloof and did not participate enough. One close personal aide stated:

> Eisenhower didn't realize that things weren't just going to happen. We weren't going to get these programs through unless he went in and fought for them. Our problem was a lack of drive and to some extent, leadership on the Hill.

Bernard Shanley commented: "During the eighty-third and eighty-fourth Congresses . . . we did not accomplish nearly as much as we did subsequently due to the president's realization that he had to interfere or we could not obtain passage of the program." [11] But others such as Bryce Harlow felt that Eisenhower was actively involved:

> He was a heavy participant in it, infinitely more than he has been publicly given credit for. A lot of it was off the record. He phoned and had meetings with congressmen at breakfast and dinner and in private sessions in the evenings. A great part of this the press never reported. [12]

Throughout his years as president, Eisenhower was accessible to members of Congress. He was very conscious of maintaining good relations and during the first few months of his administration, he invited the entire Congress for lunch at the White House. "Amazingly," Harlow stated, "at the first of these lunches, one prominent congressman with over 20 years of service, Representative Howard Smith of Virginia, said he had never eaten at the White House while another with over 40 years service, Carl Vinson of Georgia, said his last meal was a breakfast with Calvin Coolidge!" [13]

In the general course of events, most members of Congress were able to talk with the president. Although Eisenhower did not like to use the phone for public business, he gave formal instructions to his staff that any congressmen who wanted to talk to him would be put on the line as soon as it was convenient. Eisenhower rarely made calls himself. In the words of one aide, "he was an eyeball to eyeball kind of fellow." The president personally signed all the letters that were prepared for him in response to letters from senators and representatives, a practice that did not survive his administration.

The congressional leadership could always get to see him. Senator Robert A. Taft was one of three people who did not even need an appointment. Eisenhower got along well with both majority and minority leaderships. He was particularly fond of Rayburn and Johnson. Harlow recalls that the feeling was mutual.

> Their only dislike of Eisenhower related to the fact that he ran as a Republican instead of as a Democrat. But the president was from Texas by birthright and they loved to sit together. I'd get them together about once a month at least. They'd "strike a blow for liberty" a time or two or three and everything would liquidize a little bit. They'd just have a ball, enjoy each other enormously, and be totally candid.[14]

In his memoirs, Eisenhower described the meetings with legislative leaders as the most effective mechanism for developing coordination with Congress.[15] He continued to hold these sessions throughout his administration.

Together, Eisenhower and his liaison staff succeeded in formalizing institutional relationships with Congress and thereby established a presidential presence on Capitol Hill. That the Congress found this palatable may be explained in part by the White House's even-handed attitude and soft-sell approach, in part by the continuing popularity of the president which provided incentive for bipartisan cooperation, and in part by the growing recognition that the mere presentation of the program was not sufficient, in and of itself, to get it enacted into law. Explanation and some persuasion were also needed and would be tolerated, provided that they were kept within bounds.

Eisenhower and his staff tried to avoid alienating Congress. They deferred to the Democratic leadership, pushing hardest on the relatively few issues that were of genuine presidential concern. As a consequence, their legislative record was viewed by some as the product of the lowest common denominator and by others, as low volume, high quality. Presidents Kennedy and Johnson took a different tack and achieved different results.

THE ENLARGEMENT OF THE CONGRESSIONAL OPERATION: THE KENNEDY-JOHNSON YEARS

Liaison activities during the Kennedy-Johnson period extended the boundaries of presidential-congressional relations and added a new dimension to White House efforts on the Hill. The congressional liaison staff became more active and more assertive. There was greater presidential involvement and, throughout, a clear sense of both general and specific goals. Kennedy wanted a well-organized, well-run, aggressive operation, one that would vigorously push his program. "I was up there for fourteen years," he told Lawrence F. O'Brien, his and later Johnson's special assistant for congressional relations, "and I don't recall that Truman or Eisenhower or anyone on their staffs ever said one word to me about legislation." [16] By giving congressional relations a high priority, Kennedy hoped to change that situation. Initial surveys of the Congress indicated that such a change was necessary if the New Frontier program was to stand any chance of passage.[17] Johnson, too, desired a high-powered and well-oiled operation.

Reorienting and Revitalizing the Office

While the original staff of the liaison office had no preconceived notion of how to structure or run their operation, they had drive and purpose.

> We had every intention at the outset to vigorously move in advocating a program which would fulfill the Democratic party platform and pledges over a long period of time . . . so we would have an active White House, hopefully working closely with the Congress. That was the thrust of our activity, and we developed this along the way.[18]

O'Brien believed that he needed a more elaborate and forceful lobbying system than the one Harlow had developed. During the transition he and several of his top aides had met with Harlow for extensive discussions. "He could not have been more cooperative," said one Kennedy official, "but he wasn't particularly useful. He had a completely different situation from us." With a conservative Republican president and a Democratic Congress, the function of the Eisenhower office had become that of stopping legislation rather than passing it—at least that is the way the Kennedy people perceived it. They saw their own role in much more positive terms.

Illustrative of this objective and also reflective of the staff's operation was the early fight in 1961 to enlarge the House Rules Committee from 12 to 15 members. Much of this effort was orchestrated from the White House with the cooperation and support of Speaker Rayburn. Practically the first thing O'Brien did was to get a head count, isolate the undecided, and make an appeal to them. Meeting with Congressmen Richard Bolling (Missouri), Frank Thompson Jr. (New Jersey), and Carl Elliott and Robert Jones (both from Alabama), he worked to compile a list of the representatives and their leanings. A subsequent session expanded this into a file on each member which included "relevant" political information about the representative, his district, his friends, his interests, and his voting record. The file proved useful not only for the Rules battle but for subsequent votes as well.

In addition to canvassing the House of Representatives and focusing on its key people, O'Brien personally met with members at a series of cocktail parties hosted for him by Representative Edward Boland. He then reciprocated with his own cocktail parties at the White House (known as "coffee hours") where representatives had an opportunity to chat with the president. O'Brien saw to it that committee chairmen could get a session alone with Kennedy. A dinner for the Democratic Study Group provided the opportunity for a pep talk to the faithful and an indication of the kinds of rewards they could expect for continued presidential support. "The White House certainly remembers who its friends are and can be counted on to apply significant assistance in the campaign," O'Brien reportedly told the group.[19]

Strong backing by the president supported O'Brien's efforts. The telephone calls that Kennedy received from his friends on Capitol Hill during the first few weeks were tactfully referred to the congressional liaison office with the query, "Have you taken this up with Larry O'Brien?" Soon the calls came directly to O'Brien.[20] From the perspective of the president and his new liaison chief, it was important to establish at the outset that O'Brien spoke for the president.

Thereafter, a system developed that kept the liaison office at the center of communications to and from the president. Calls to the president from members of Congress were monitored by the president's secretary. Whether the call would be put through or not depended on who the member was and the exigencies of the president's schedule. Congressional leaders or important committee chairmen would almost always be put through. The president's secretary would also forward memos of the president's calls from the Hill to the liaison office. Similarly, the mail the president received from members of Congress would be sent to the liaison office. Similar practices were followed in the administrations that followed Kennedy's.

The liaison staff that was established during the 1960–1961 period was younger, had less congressional experience, and was more overtly partisan than were their Republican predecessors. O'Brien felt that years in Congress could create liabilities, especially in the form of ties to groups and policy positions, so he opted for people with "sound political judgment" regardless of their previous experience.[21] Rejecting Harlow's advice that he eschew partisanship, O'Brien chose a staff with solid Democratic credentials. His two principal aides were Mike N. Manatos who had worked in the Senate for 23 years and Henry Hall Wilson, a member of the Democratic National Committee from North Carolina and a participant in John Kennedy's presidential campaign in 1960.

Interaction among these three liaison agents and Presidents Kennedy and Johnson was frequent and easy. O'Brien and Henry Hall Wilson stated that they could always speak to the president. In fact, O'Brien's phone was directly connected to the telephone on the president's desk. Johnson had even issued a standing order with the switchboard that any time O'Brien called, he was to be put through regardless of the hour. The calls went in both directions.

Liaison aides reported that memos submitted during the day would be part of the president's night reading and replies could be expected the next day. Memos were used frequently to describe the evolving political situation on the Hill. Johnson also developed a red tag system whereby any memo that was so tagged would be brought to the president's attention immediately, whether he be in conference, out of town, or whatever. Red tag memos were used sparingly. They alerted the president to things he needed to know right away: which members were waivering prior to a crucial vote, what phone calls he could expect in the immediate future, what developments might affect his program, and other similar problems.

In addition to their access, the chief liaison officers could speak and even make commitments for the president. Kennedy delegated more authority than Johnson. O'Brien recalled an incident early in his tenure that indicated the scope of his discretion:

> I can remember vividly meeting with Speaker Rayburn and others involving a minimum wage bill and being confronted with the decision whether we compromise the $1.15 and the extent of coverage. Everyone in the room turned to me and said, "well what's the president's view?" Well, I wasn't going to pick up the phone and ask the president, when I was in a better position at that moment to make a judgment perhaps than he was. It was up to me to do it and I made the judgment.[22]

The ability of O'Brien and his senior aides to speak for the president greatly enhanced their influence in Congress. They could and did make substantive and strategic decisions without checking with the White House. And they had the assurance that the president would back them, although under Johnson, their authority was conditioned to some extent by his personal involvement in many of the details of bargaining.

Introducing a Congressional Perspective into Policy Making

Throughout the Kennedy and Johnson presidencies, the liaison staff had a substantial involvement in the formulation of policy. O'Brien described his staff's role as, "an involvement in determining what the program should contain, an involvement significantly in the thrust of the messages and launching the program and, of course, an involvement in the follow-through." [23] Wilson usually attended the White House sessions in the fall of the year when the president's program was created. He provided a congressional viewpoint. "I had to make judgments that no one else in the room had to make and that is, how do you get this through the Congress," he said.[24]

The closer the proposal came to its actual submission to Congress, the greater was the liaison aides' role. It was their job to assess the potential Hill response in view of lobbying pressure, committee sensitivities, the chairman's inclination and preferences, and general congressional moods. Decisions such as what should or should not go into a particular bill depended in part on this evaluation.

White House liaison aides made frequent use of the Bureau of the Budget for tracking legislation. The Legislative Reference Division prepared and sent to the liaison staff one-page summaries of bills that were moving through or coming out of Congress. These short synopses highlighted the status of the bill and substantive changes that had been made in it in the congressional process.

The office of congressional affairs was not, as a general rule, involved in departmental clearance decisions although sometimes liaison agents requested a clearance decision for a proposal or amendment submitted by a member of Congress. It was the White House staff, not the Budget Bureau, that was consulted for the policy judgments. Similarly, while senior liaison officials participated in the decisions on controversial enrolled bills, it was usually at the request of the special counsel or the president himself. Their recommendations normally took political factors into account in assessing the effect a veto or signing might have on Congress. Unlike Eisenhower, both Kennedy and Johnson were very conscious of having their vetoes sustained. Indeed to have a Democratic Congress override a Democratic president's veto would have been a source of great embarrassment.

While contact with the BOB was intermittent, White House liaison officials interacted frequently with their counterparts in the departments and agencies. They worked closely not only in the preparation of legislation but in the coordination of legislative activities. O'Brien believed that if the administration's program were to be achieved, and if the White House liaison office were to remain small, then there was no alternative but to utilize the department's liaison agents. This meant convincing every departmental agent that he had a stake in the president's program, that his proposals were only a part of the total package. Similarly, it involved a willingness on the part of the White House to work on behalf of some departmental legislative objectives even if they did not conform to the administration's priorities.[25]

Rejecting Bryce Harlow's contention that reaching out to the departments and agencies might dilute the administration's legislative focus, O'Brien and his staff became involved in the selection and removal of department agents, the assignment of some of their lobbying activities, and the receipt of their legislative reports. These reports provided valuable information for assessing the political climate and constructing a legislative strategy. They were summarized and presented to the president weekly, prior to his meeting with congressional party leaders. O'Brien and his staff also held monthly meetings with the department agents and had frequent contact with them on a one-to-one basis. This continued throughout the eight-year period, with the meetings becoming more frequent from 1966–1968.

During the Johnson presidency, the agenda of every cabinet meeting included an item on legislative activities. The congressional liaison office reported on the status of the White House's legislative program and, additionally, secretaries might be asked to report on their department's legislative activities. Johnson regarded this congressional work as an important departmental responsibility and was constantly urging his secretaries to go up and tell their story and to stay informed on legislative matters.

The departments were charged with lobbying for their own legislation and were primarily responsible for it when it was in committee. The longevity of departmental-committee relationships, the overlap of clientele pressures, plus the ability to concentrate efforts in a few committees in both houses enabled the departments and agencies to exert more effective pressure than the White House could at this particular point in the process. The White House liaison staff became increasingly involved as the bill moved from committee to floor action to final vote. They worked primarily with the leadership and floor managers of the bill. Areas of jurisdiction were not exclusive, however. Department liaison agents were occasionally asked to approach members they knew on nondepartmental bills. In some instances, the While House took responsibility at each stage for an administration proposal.[26]

Bargaining, Lobbying, and Servicing

In mobilizing congressional support, the liaison staff utilized a variety of lobbying tactics. This included direct contact by the staff and president and indirect influence through state, city, or interest group leaders. A direct personal appeal by or on behalf of the president was naturally one of the most persuasive techniques. "It was just amazing to me," Larry O'Brien asserted, "how often that a decision would be favorable to us not on the substance of the bill but really on the Congress' desire to be helpful to the administration." [27]

Involving Kennedy and Johnson in congressional affairs was not difficult when the liaison staff found it necessary. Neither president shared Eisenhower's philosophical or psychological reluctance to participate in congressional politics. Kennedy devoted considerable time and energy to legislative relations although his aides were careful not to overinvolve him in details.[28] Johnson, however, displayed almost a fetish about being informed and involved about everything. He was interested in all aspects of the legislative process. He read a specially prepared summary of the *Congressional Record* daily. He continually wanted status reports, sometimes even four or five times a day. He would go over weekly charts of administration legislation with the Democratic congressional leadership always urging them to do more. Larry O'Brien writes:

> No detail of the legislative process was too minute to involve him [LBJ]. Kennedy would give congressional affairs whatever time I requested. Kennedy had other interests as well. For Johnson, Congress was a twenty-four hour a day obsession. One morning I called him to inform him about a vote we'd lost late the night before.
>
> "Why didn't you call and wake me up and tell me, Larry?" he demanded. "When you bleed, I want to bleed with you." [29]

Wilson stated that he called Johnson after every major vote in the House.[30]

Involving the president in liaison activities might include him meeting with a recalcitrant committee chairman, or more likely, phoning a member. Johnson had a very effective telephone manner. He tended to be disarmingly informal and ultimately persuasive. In describing his own telephone tactics, Johnson wrote:

> When I made these phone calls, I had no set script. Sometimes I would start with: "What's this I read about your opposing my bill?" Other times I would ask: "What do you think of this bill?" Or: "Say, Congressman, I haven't seen you around in a while, just wondering how you've been." [31]

Presidential phone calls were not a regular occurrence. Because they had such a large impact, the staff did not want them to become commonplace. Henry Hall Wilson suggested that it was an extremely rare thing that President Kennedy or Johnson ever called congressmen about votes.[32] However, when Johnson did, he usually called right before critical votes, concentrated on key senators and representatives, especially those who were wavering or uncommitted, and armed himself with a good deal of information not only about the bill but also about the person he was calling.[33]

In addition to direct personal appeals to individual members, there were other ways in which the president could bring his influence to bear. Social events at the White House, popular with members of Congress, were occasions for informal conversations with the president. Each year an annual congressional reception was given at the White House. Kennedy held a number of cocktail parties during his first year to which most congressmen were invited. Johnson had buffet dinners which he hosted for approximately 50 members and their spouses. White House liaison aides drew up the invitation lists. After cocktails, Johnson would invite members of Congress into the East Room where they would be briefed by the secretaries of state and defense, the national security advisor, the director of the budget, and the chairman of the Council of Economic Advisors. The briefing would then be followed by a question-and-answer period. Spouses were taken on a White House tour by Mrs. Johnson or otherwise entertained.

The amount of interaction between president and Congress was actually quite extensive. In his book, Lawrence O'Brien summarizes Kennedy's contacts in 1961:

> He held thirty-two of the Tuesday morning leadership breakfasts and about ninety private conversations with congressional leaders, the type that lasted an hour or two. Coffee hours brought five hundred members of the House and Senate to the White House, and bill-signing ceremonies brought in the same number. All in all, Kennedy had about 2,500 separate contacts with members of Congress during his first year in office, exclusive of correspondence. Then, he used to thank the Democrats who'd helped on a bill with a personal note—that they could use in their campaigns. But he thanked the occasional Republicans who needed thanking by a phone call, which could not be reproduced for campaign purposes.[34]

As in the Eisenhower period, the meetings with the party leaders of each house continued. They were usually held weekly when Congress was in session. Senior liaison officials prepared the agenda and always attended the meetings. Strategy, tactics, and the substance of legislation would be discussed. For example, the president might stress a particular legislative priority that he felt was not getting adequate emphasis or he might want to enlist the support of the leadership in scheduling what he considered priority legislation for floor action. He or his aides might even suggest the kind of amendments the administration would be willing to accept. The meetings were viewed as extremely valuable by all participants. They gave the leadership an opportunity to contribute to administration policy, both substantively and strategically, and thus become part of the administration's team. In the end this paid large dividends. Similarly, the president was able to persuade and cajole, thereby enlisting support of the most powerful members of Congress.

White House liaison agents also attended strategy sessions in the majority leaders' offices. They worked together with the whips on head counts and used their friends on Capitol Hill to gain support for the administration. Having a partisan majority helped. One Kennedy aide commented: "I doubt if Sam Rayburn permitted Bryce Harlow to sit up there in his office when he was trying to get votes for a bill." The Democrats played on partisanship, especially in the House, using their numerical advantage as much as possible. They viewed Charles Halleck, the Republican leader from 1959–1964, as a staunch partisan and saw most Republican representatives as opposed to the New Frontier and Great Society programs. In the Senate, there tended to be a greater possibility of compromise and bipartisan support. In both houses, there seemed to be little discernible Vietnam spillover into domestic issues.

The White House office also performed a variety of services for the benefit of Congress, all of which worked directly or indirectly to improve the atmosphere for the president on Capitol Hill. Announcements of government contracts, traditionally a source of congressional and executive concern, were given exclusively to Democrats. This required that members be informed of the project grants almost immediately before the word leaked out. Project announcements were one area where departmental and presidential interests often conflicted. Patronage was another. "Very early we had to instill the understanding that all good news comes from the White House and bad news from the departments," stated Henry Hall Wilson.[35]

White House tours became a major attraction and headache for the liaison office. Tickets for the small guided tour in the early morning were particularly sought after. The liaison office set up a quota system for their distribution, keeping enough in reserve for "effective and good use." "Sometimes the pressures were just unbelievable," remarked Henry Hall Wilson. H. Barefoot Sanders who headed the White House liaison office during the last years of the Johnson presidency echoed a similar sentiment:

> If you are dealing with Congress, if you're asking them to support administration programs, if you're getting acquainted with them and forming friendships, if you're their contact in the White House, then they are going to call you. And I would have found it impossible to say, "I'm sorry, I can't talk to you about this tour. I'll send you down to the tour office." [36]

Rewarding supporters with patronage, projects, public credit, and valuable services were inducements for others to be cooperative. These "goodies" could not and were not easily bartered for votes per se. O'Brien writes:

> A folklore arose that pictured me and my staff trading dams and post offices for votes. In truth, we didn't have much patronage to dangle before anyone's nose. For example, the allocation of most public works projects was in the hands of powerful members of Congress.[37]

Johnson sang a similar refrain. "I could not trade patronage for votes in any direct exchange. If word spread that I was trading, everyone would want to trade and all other efforts at persuasion would automatically fail." [38] Nonetheless, there were persistent rumors of subtle and not so subtle pressures being exerted. Representative Gerald R. Ford (Michigan) piously complained on the floor of the House of Representatives in 1962 that the Kennedy administration threatened to cancel military contracts in his district if he did not support the administration's position on legislation to raise the debt ceiling. In investigating this charge, the *Congressional Quarterly* reported that a high-ranking Defense Department official during the Kennedy period recalled that such tactics were discussed. "This was done rather blatantly," said the official. "It happened two or three times on a massive scale." [39]

The allocation of funds for military bases and, especially, the projected closing of those bases has always been a highly charged political issue for members of Congress, one on which "deals" seem to have been made. Representative Edward F. Hebert (Dem., Louisiana), a member of the House Armed Services Committee, admitted that he personally prevented the closing of a large naval base in New Orleans after the Defense Department publicly stated that it would be closed for reasons of economy. At a party at the White House on the day the closing was announced, Hebert said to the president, "Jack, they're hauling down the flag in New Orleans." Kennedy replied that he would talk with Secretary of Defense McNamara. Hebert reported the next day that he got a call from McNamara who said, "We'll work something out." The base was not closed. [40]

According to Doris Kearns, Lyndon Johnson thought congressmen were guided by two emotions, their desire for recognition and their fear of losing hold:

> Desire opened the door to the exercise of presidential power; fear closed it. The desire for recognition could persuade a legislator to risk allying himself with the effort to bring about change so that he might receive acknowledgment of his good works. Fear of losing the struggle immobilized him, influencing him to stand pat, to leave things as they were. Johnson's success in winning congressional support for change depended upon his ability to reduce the fear and increase the desire . . . . [41]

A president's promise not to forget and to provide help when needed has frequently been employed as an implicit or explicit inducement for support. Representative Porter Hardy, Jr. (Dem., Virginia) mentioned an instance when Johnson telephoned him and requested his vote on a particular bill. According to the *Congressional Quarterly,* Hardy had made up his mind to vote for the bill but told Johnson that he would support it as a favor to the president. Later, while requesting the president's help for one of his projects, Hardy reminded Johnson of the favor he had done him. [42]

The potential for being helpful has always been a key to effective liaison. Barefoot Sanders stated it simply:

> We generally tried to be helpful to everybody but obviously if someone was voting with us 100 percent of the time as contrasted to 60 percent, we'd be liable to be a little more helpful to him. I think that's a rule that everybody understands. Johnson was not the type of fellow who was going to wreak vengeance on anybody.[43]

Sanctions were not viewed as a particularly useful bargaining tool. The general rule, never to force a voting decision that would jeopardize a congressperson's political future, was strictly followed. Larry O'Brien put it this way:

> I never expected any member to commit political suicide in order to help the President, no matter how noble our case. I expected politicians to be concerned with their own interests; I only hoped to convince them our interests were often the same.[44]

By the end of the Johnson presidency not only had presidential programing become an expectation of Congress but so had some congressional participation in that effort. Advocacy was also recognized as a presidential right and responsibility. In fulfilling this responsibility, the congressional liaison office effectively institutionalized a presidential presence in Congress. This institutionalization had an insulating effect. Despite the growing unpopularity of Johnson's policy in Southeast Asia, the servicing and lobbying of Congress continued unabated. While there was less personal involvement by the president, there seemed to be no lessening of efforts by his staff.

In contrasting the development of congressional liaison during the Eisenhower, Kennedy, and Johnson periods, differences in style not function distinguished the operations. While all had small staffs, Kennedy-Johnson liaison was conducted in a more partisan and forceful manner. The Democratic presidents were more personally involved in liaison activity and there was a greater attempt to generate congressional support for presidentially initiated legislation during their administrations. Furthermore, lobbying techniques had become more sophisticated with the White House offering a variety of goods and services which were eagerly consumed by Congress. Even though the expansion of services could be attributed in part to, the presence of Democratic majorities in both houses and to the more activist presidency of the 1960s, when Bryce Harlow was reappointed as head of the Nixon congressional relations staff, he soon found that there was no turning back.

THE INSTITUTIONALIZATION OF PRESIDENTIAL-CONGRESSIONAL RELATIONS: THE NIXON-FORD PERIOD

Harlow's original intent was to rebuild an Eisenhower-type office but the growth of the operation in intervening years and, most particularly, the expansion of its services effectively prevented this. Harlow viewed the greatly enlarged service as "fawning" to Congress. He cited the special White House tour for distinguished persons as an example of a "goodie" that had been so enlarged as to compete with the public tour in size. "I thought this was terrible," he said, "and I tried to cut it back as well as undo others but couldn't." [45]

In the end, the congressional office assumed most of the functions that had come to be regarded by the end of the Johnson period as traditional liaison responsibilities. In addition to the services, these included gathering intelligence, tracking legislation, coordinating department and agency activities, and working with the leadership on priority programs.

Modifying the O'Brien Model

Nixon and Ford's legislative objectives fell somewhere between the limited goals of the Eisenhower liaison office and the more extensive ones of Kennedy and Johnson. Trying to steer a middle course between the softer sell, bipartisan approach and the harder sell, partisan one, the Nixon and Ford liaison offices attempted to maximize Republican strength while at the same time appealing to certain Democrats,[46] largely by taking an issue-oriented, "ideological" line. "We couldn't just play a party game," stated William Timmons, Harlow's chief assistant and eventual successor, "we had to play a philosophical one as well. We talked about what was right and wrong." [47]

The situation which the Republican liaison team encountered was very different from that of its Democratic predecessors. To have dealt only with the minority leadership would have given the liaison staff less influence over the legislative machinery such as the scheduling of committee hearings, the calling of witnesses, the timing of legislation, and positioning of amendments. As a consequence, they had to be less overtly partisan in their approach.

In structure and organization, the office continued to be small, but during Nixon's first administration, it appeared to become distanced from the president. Assisting Harlow was William Timmons, who had 12 years of experience in the House and Senate in addition to his political activities in several Republican electoral campaigns. Timmons subsequently became operational head of the office on February 4, 1970, when Harlow was elevated to the position of counselor to the president and relieved of day-to-day liaison responsibilities.[48]

Difficulties, brought on in part by Harlow's early departure, Timmons' lesser stature with members of Congress, and Nixon's growing inaccessibility, complicated the task of conducting relations with Congress.[49] Harlow had enjoyed a special relationship with the president; Timmons did not, at least not during Nixon's first term. While Timmons could and did get to speak with the president and saw him as many as two or three times a week, he had to go through Haldeman and later Haig to do so. Haldeman was not viewed as a friend of Congress.

Timmons had no problem with this arrangement, viewing it as both necessary and satisfactory. He explained:

> There is a distinction between controlling the president's time and controlling congressional relations. It is proper for the chief of staff to maintain order in the president's schedule, improper to use it to direct legislative (or any other) affairs. I felt the former was the case with Haldeman and Haig.[50]

Timmons added that he was never denied access when he wanted it. Nixon, he noted, called him on many issues.[51]

Members of Congress of both parties, however, had a different perspective. They viewed the president's senior aides with hostility and saw Timmons as a subordinate. House Republicans questioned his effectiveness in conveying their views and implementing their suggestions. One Republican representative commented sadly:

> I suspect that Timmons had access when the matters for which he had responsibility were under discussion but otherwise in terms of policy I would guess not. I think if I were to contact Timmons and say, "I've got a red hot candidate for one of the commission's openings and I'd like you to communicate this to the president," I would not expect this to happen.

Democrats, however, were suspicious of Timmons' almost exclusive ties with Republican organizations and representatives prior to his joining the Nixon White House; they saw his office as more overtly partisan than Harlow's.

The ability of White House liaison aides to have face-to-face contact with the president improved substantially during the Ford administration. Timmons and his successor, Max L. Friedersdorf, had no difficulty seeing Ford. Even their aides had considerable contact with the president. Vernon C. Loen, White House liaison for the House of Representatives, commented:

> I served under President Nixon for almost exactly a year. I was with him in the Oval Office exactly three times, always when I escorted a member of Congress to see him. I saw him only at public ceremonies like bill signings. When President Ford came in, I would see him four or five times a day.[52]

Improved access could only help but increase the effectiveness of the liaison staff.

Under President Ford, White House liaison responsibilities were divided in a similar but not identical fashion to the way they had been during much of the Nixon period. Friedersdorf, who took over for

Timmons in 1975, had operational responsibility while John O. Marsh, Jr., a former member of Congress, oversaw both public and congressional liaison activities. As counselor to the president, Marsh did some trouble-shooting on critical and controversial issues, but his principal role was that of advisor. He was also the main link between the congressional liaison office and President Ford.[53]

Restricting and Regulating Policy Input

The degree to which the congressional relations staff participated in policy making varied considerably in the Nixon and Ford administrations. Bryce Harlow, in his capacity as assistant to the president for legislative and con-gressional affairs and later as counselor, had some policy input; Timmons had less during the 1969–1972 period, at least as it pertained to the sub-stance of the legislative package. He described his staff's contribution as "relatively minor":

> We're not really qualified to determine or to recommend to the president different kinds of programs. We don't have the staff nor the knowledge to get involved with the policy development. Our job was to determine and advise the president and his other policy people what might get through Congress, what is "do-able." In that sense, we have a policy role.[54]

While Timmons' position as congressional chief, and especially his role as a presidential advisor, was upgraded approximately six months before the beginning of Nixon's second term, the emergence of Watergate and the president's growing estrangement from Congress made presidential advising and lobbying difficult. During the Ford period, however, the top legislative aides, first Timmons and later Friedersdorf and Marsh, participated in the consideration of major domestic policy decisions.

The larger role of President Ford's congressional aides in policy making was both a product of Ford's work style and a consequence of his congressional sensitivity. His more open manner of decision making encouraged the interchange of views from a variety of quarters. One high liaison official stated that in developing policy, the president's first instinct was to determine whether or not it was practical and what the Congress' reaction was likely to be. Nixon, on the other hand, worked within a closed hierarchical system in which neither he nor his top aides encouraged the consideration of congressional views.

Although the Nixon congressional relations staff had a small role in policy formulation, it did have a larger and more systematic input into the enrolled enactment process than had liaison aides in previous adminis-trations. Timmons saw all enrolled bill files and was expected as a matter of course to add a recommendation. The recommendation was couched in terms of Congress' potential reaction to the signing or vetoing of the bill. Timmons commented:

> It is not my own personal view on whether the bill has merit. Since I am not basically a policy maker, I cannot agree on the substance of so many of the bills. . . . I am influenced by the support or lack of support a particular measure gets.[55]

Timmons estimated he concurred with the OMB the great majority of the time. When he disagreed, it generally was with respect to an OMB recommendation to veto what he regarded as a relatively unimportant bill.

> There are some very minor bills that come down here, either private relief bills or small amendments that have little impact on the budget, but OMB is concerned about the precedent it sets down the line in the future and therefore they come down and recommend a veto. On the other hand, I don't want to waste the political capital on the Hill, particularly when the sponsor of the bill is one of our best friends up there.[56]

The practice of involving the liaison staff in enrolled bill decisions continued in the Ford administration. Friedersdorf also routinely checked each file before it went to the president. "I initialed it 'O.K.' if I agreed with it," he stated. "If I didn't feel that the congressional attitude or viewpoint was adequately presented, then I'd do a cover memo for the president, especially if there was a possibility of a veto." [57]

Implementing a Veto Strategy

A potential veto constituted an important part of both administrations' legislative strategy. Liaison aides used the threat of a presidential veto to influence the Democratic majority to tailor its legislative proposals so that they would be acceptable to the president. Timmons estimated that there were 20 to 30 measures that were "cleaned up sufficiently" due to the threat of a veto. Since it made little sense to push for legislation that the president might veto, the congressional staff tried to get veto signals as early as possible. In the domestic area, OMB, in conjunction with the Domestic Council, gave the signs.

In order to make the veto threat credible, the liaison staff had to be able to sustain presidential vetoes. This became the major strategic objective of the Ford liaison operation. The tactics used in this effort did not differ markedly from those employed in other legislative situations and by other administrations although the stakes from the president's point of view were higher.

Appeals were made directly to individual congressmen by liaison agents or were exerted by and through outside groups. In a few instances, state party leaders and large financial contributors were requested to intercede, usually causing considerable consternation on Capitol Hill in the process. Even the threat of adverse political consequences generated hostility. In one highly publicized incident, a Ford liaison aide predicted trouble for a Republican member of Congress if he voted against a particular bill which the president favored. The congressman cast a vote against the president and returned to his office to find a telephone message that he need not turn to the White House for any future favors.[58]

Ostensibly, liaison aides could only offer information, couched in terms that were philosophically or politically compatible. "We couldn't take members to lunch or dinner;" one aide noted, "we had no expense account." Extending extra presidential help to congresspersons in campaigns or responding to particular requests for a presidential phone call or nonelection visit to their districts was done, however, sometimes even on an implicit quid pro quo basis. While some representatives complained of strong-arming by the administration,[59] White House liaison aides noted similar congressional pressures. One high official commented:

> Quite often they [members of Congress] will make their vote contingent on whether you come through with this request. I had a congressman tell me that he would vote to sustain an important veto if, and only if, we would get a CAB route into his town. I told him, "Congressman, that is impossible. We can't touch regulatory agencies." He went in and voted right against us.

Nixon's relations with Congress were much more limited than were President Ford's. While Nixon initially evidenced some appreciation for "stroking" and other congressional niceties, his interchange with Congress tended to become more formal and less frequent as his administration progressed. Nixon had telephoned committee chairmen and spoken with Republican and Democratic leaders when he was president-elect. His choice of Bryce Harlow as liaison chief was applauded on both sides of the aisle. However, as time wore on, he became less accessible to those who were neither close friends nor party leaders. While Nixon made telephone calls to members of Congress throughout his administration, he usually would call people he knew and mainly for small talk. Unlike Johnson, he could not bring himself to ask for votes. Timmons recalled that the president would frequently end meetings with members by saying, "I know you're going to do what you have to do anyway and that's fine. Whatever you do is O.K. with me." [60] The liaison people found it difficult to twist arms after this kind of presidential statement.

Calls to the president were carefully screened. Timmons estimated that over 90 percent were handled by the congressional relations staff and did not require involvement of the president. In those instances where the staff felt the call merited Nixon's attention, they would apologize for the president's unavailability and advise the caller that the president would return the call. Prior to phoning back, Nixon would be briefed on the subject to be discussed.

There was widespread feeling on the part of representatives of both parties that the president would not be informed of their calls or written correspondence. In fact, there was considerable doubt as to whether it was possible to reach Nixon at all. In the words of one House Republican:

> I pretty well concluded that there was almost no way to contact him except if you had a personal relationship. You'd write letters and send telegrams and be as emphatic as you could. You'd normally get back the polite reply that your letter would be brought to the president's attention and you knew very well that it would never be. There were some that enjoyed a personal relationship but they were relatively few.

The inability to get to Nixon created considerable frustration in Congress and naturally resulted in great difficulties for the president's liaison staff.

The Ford presidency offers a marked contrast. Ford was not at all hesitant to use the phone. He displayed no hesitancy in calling members, especially before critical votes, when his prestige was on the line. In fact, at the beginning of his administration, he occasionally used the phone more than his aides desired. This presented some difficulties for congressional relations officials who were not always sure when and with whom the president had spoken. Timmons noted that each day he would ask Ford, "Did you speak to any members of Congress? Is there anything that I should know about?" Ford was very good about this, Timmons added, and often kept notes of his conversations.[61]

In addition, the new president greatly increased the amount of personal contact with the Congress. He instituted a congressional hour. Held every two to three weeks, it gave members of Congress an opportunity to introduce important constituents to the president. There were also more White House events to which members of both parties were invited during the Ford period. One Republican member noted that he had never been asked to a single signing or veto ceremony during the entire Nixon period, even though some of the bills he had sponsored were signed into law by the president; but, during the first week of the Ford presidency he had been invited to one. "The main difference between the Nixon and Ford periods," stated another representative, "was that it was the friends of Richard Nixon who got to the White House; in Ford's case everyone got invited." There was also a perceptible difference in the behavior of the two presidents. Ford mixed easily and informally and seemed to enjoy himself; Nixon did not. He even had formal receiving lines at his White House prayer breakfasts.

While the degree of personal interaction between Nixon, Ford, and the Democratic Congresses was markedly different, the operation of their congressional liaison offices was strikingly similar. For example, the practice of coordinating departmental liaison activity, which required weekly reports and forecasts from agents in the field, continued. During the early years of the Nixon presidency, Timmons met with departmental liaison officials, as a group, on a more or less regular basis. These large meetings were later discontinued in favor of individual sessions between White House and departmental liaison staffs. Most of the contact between the legislative agents continued to occur on the telephone.

In keeping with previous practices, administrative proposals were pushed hardest at the committee stage, usually by department agents who were coordinated by the White House. The Nixon administration, especially, desired to have the departments assume the major lobbying effort. Floor action saw a more direct lobbying role for the president's agents.

When operating on the Hill, the congressional liaison aides of both administrations would either work out of their own briefcases or from the whip's office in the House and the vice-president's nonceremonial office in the Senate. The congressional offices would be used for meetings or telephone calls. A page-type buzzer system alerted the president's aides to contact the White House. For floor votes, the liaison aides would try to position themselves strategically. One high liaison official described his favorite location as "between the Speaker's lobby and the rest room," commenting, "inevitably during the debate most of those guys have to go to the rest room."

While the departments administered some of the usual legislative services that had been centralized under Kennedy and Johnson such as contract announcements and minor patronage appointments, the White House still interceded on important questions, some political appointments, and major public works projects. Liaison aides of both administrations routinely checked the political qualifications of potential appointees. Allegations that some appointments were tied to congressional favors continued to be made.[62]

Because of the Democratic majority in Congress, both White House liaison offices had to perform many of their constituency services on a bipartisan basis. Information on pending government contracts was not handled in a strictly partisan manner as it had been during the Kennedy-Johnson period. The White House alerted Republicans and Democrats in order of their seniority.

The president's congressional aides also continued to be involved in the tour and entertainment business. The *Sequoia* remained a popular form of congressional entertaining, as did seats in the president's box at the Kennedy Center. In general, the liaison staff saw social occasions as opportunities for a relaxed discussion of legislative issues. "We didn't try to pitch any particular legislation," stated one aide, "but we were able to talk with them in an informal setting about their problems and how they saw Congress moving and so forth."

The summer of 1973 put a temporary stop to these activities. As

Watergate began to unravel and impeachment loomed as a distinct possibility, members of Congress were reluctant to partake of social invitations from the White House congressional relations office, largely for the sake of appearances. In fact, members of the House Judiciary Committee "didn't want to talk about much of anything," according to a senior liaison official. The hearings, especially those in the House, impeded the liaison staff's ability to contact congresspersons even though they made a conscious effort to avoid discussing Watergate-related matters.[63] Social activities were resumed under Ford.

The contrast between the Nixon and Ford liaison efforts illustrates the extent to which style can affect the general character of presidential-congressional relations. Nixon's standoffish manner and his desire not to get involved in the intricate details of legislative activities created great burdens for his staff and ultimately limited their effectiveness in dealing with Congress. Ford's ability and willingness to interact easily and frequently with members of both parties and branches, despite strong policy differences, earned much praise for his administration's liaison with Congress. His staff was generally well respected and if judged by the president's personal popularity on the Hill, or by the large number of vetoes sustained, it was highly effective. That the same key staffers served in both administrations reemphasizes the impact that the president alone can have on executive relations with Congress.

Watergate provides another illustration, albeit a negative one. Despite the awesome political and personal consequences of the congressional investigation and the legal controversies, Timmons believed the effect of Watergate on pending legislation was minimal. He said, "I don't think that the hearings by the Ervin Committee first, and later, by the House Judiciary Committee, in any way affected the president's legislative program. I can't cite one bill that should have been passed or could have been passed or defeated because of the Watergate issue." [64] Others supported his view.[65]

That much lobbying during the Nixon period was not tied directly to the president undoubtedly mitigated the effect of Watergate on presidential-congressional relations. A myriad of other factors such as party, constituency, and ideology, that normally influence the legislative process served also to minimize its ramifications. Nonetheless, the fact that Watergate failed to spill over into the congressional arena testified to the weakness of President Nixon in Congress. Simply put, a chief legislator whose waning popularity did not appreciably affect his influence could not have had very much influence.

The similarity between the two administrations' liaison efforts suggests the degree to which congressional relations had become institutionalized. That the structure of the office remained essentially the same and that the bulk of its activities continued, despite the different legislative strategies, indicates the degree of consensus surrounding the functions of the office and the way they were performed. From the perspective of both the White House and Capitol Hill, congressional relations had come to be recognized as an expectation of the modern presidency.

CONCLUSION

Like other aspects of the legislative presidency, the congressional liaison operation has become a standard and accepted component of the policy-making process. Developed out of the need to improve the chances for the president's proposals on the Hill, the White House liaison office has provided a channel for the interchange of executive and legislative views as well as a vehicle for exerting presidential influence in Congress.

Unlike other presidential policy-making staffs, this office has neither grown appreciably in size nor changed in structure. Run by a small group of aides, most of whom have had prior experience on the Hill, it has maintained a simple hierarchical structure with areas of functional responsibility divided between House and Senate. Figure V-I diagrams the formal organization.

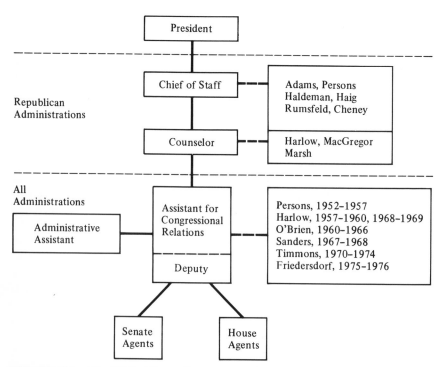

FIGURE V-I.   The White House Congressional Liaison Office

The head of the office has always had a dual policy and operational role, although in the Nixon and Ford administrations some of these responsibilities were divided among senior White House officials. In general, the operational heads of the congressional relations office have enjoyed a closer and more direct relationship to the president under Democratic than Republican administrations. This can be attributed in part to the personality of the presidents and their aides, to the relative importance of achieving legislative goals, and to the structure of White House decision making. Presidents Kennedy and Johnson were always accessible, rated legislative objectives highly, and ran a fairly loose bilateral staff system in the White House. Eisenhower and Nixon were more aloof, not nearly as oriented toward domestic legislative objectives, and had a more formal, hierarchical arrangement. While Ford's White House was more open and he personally was more accessible and involved than his Republican predecessors, his policy-making organization still retained many of the structural features of the Nixon presidency. As a consequence, his relationship with his liaison chiefs fell somewhere between the Kennedy-Johnson and Eisenhower-Nixon patterns.

The similarities in the structures of the liaison offices themselves extend only partially to the legislative objectives they sought and the basic strategic approach they utilized. Usually, the objectives were a product of each president's political philosophy, the demands emanating from the policy process in his administration, and the partisan composition of Congress. From a practical standpoint, Republican presidents, saddled with large Democratic majorities, could hardly have expected the same kind of support for their proposals that Democratic presidents received. Not only did Presidents Eisenhower, Nixon, and Ford make fewer demands for innovative social legislation—the kind that generally requires the greatest effort to get enacted—but they went about soliciting support in less partisan ways.

In general, the approach that liaison staffs have adopted have resulted from the fit between their specific legislative goals, congressional environment, the president's operating style, and, increasingly, the expectations of the liaison function itself. While Eisenhower's traditional view of the executive's legislative role and his regal leadership style did not produce a great quantity of new and different legislative proposals, the institutionalization of programing did elicit, on an annual basis, White House initiated legislation beginning in 1954. The need to generate support for these proposals within a Congress that was controlled by Democrats for six of eight years led the Eisenhower White House to adopt a moderate, bipartisan liaison approach that neither resulted in a large and visible presidential presence on the Hill nor required very active participation by the president himself.

This soft-sell, low-key appeal contrasted markedly to the harder-sell, more partisan strategy of the Kennedy-Johnson presidencies. With a more innovative and comprehensive program, more partisan congressional support, more direct presidential interest and involvement, and more congressional demands for White House services, the liaison staff greatly increased the temper of its Capitol Hill activity. Its expanded operation in turn produced demands for programs and services in the next administration, eventually thwarting the desire of President Nixon and his liaison aides to revert to an Eisenhower-type operation, one that was more consistent with his conservative philosophy and isolationist psychology. The middle ground that was eventually adopted sought to maximize the administration's issue-oriented, ideological appeal in the face of the partisan Democratic Congress. It was more effective in discouraging legislation that the White House opposed and in preventing veto overrides than in generating backing for presidential proposals.

Presidential-congressional relations seemed to improve during the Ford presidency, despite the political differences between president and Congress. Since the structure, personnel, and approach of the liaison office did not differ markedly from the Nixon effort, much of the improvement can be attributed to President Ford himself—to his personality, to his sensitivity, and to his method of interacting with Congress.

Throughout the years, presidential style has always been a crucial independent variable, directly contributing to the president's popularity on the Hill and indirectly to his ability and that of his staff to achieve their legislative objectives. The amount of accessibility, level of involvement, and degree of personal interaction are three criteria by which presidential style may be evaluated. When judged by these criteria, Johnson and Ford's styles were the most responsive to the exigencies of Congress; Nixon's was the least. Johnson and Ford were the most reachable; Kennedy and Eisenhower less so; Nixon the most remote.

Johnson and Ford had the greatest personal contact with members of Congress and the most detailed involvement in the legislative process. In this respect, their congressional careers stood them in good stead. Both were gregarious. They displayed considerable sensitivity to congressional needs and desires. Johnson worked hard at building and maintaining his influence, and Ford labored to keep good personal relationships despite his strong policy differences with both the Democratic leadership and the rank and file.

In contrast, Eisenhower lacked both the background and the inclination to appreciate and cater to the political needs of senators and representatives. However, he displayed a healthy respect for Congress' constitutional prerogatives, acknowledged the limits of his own powers, and made fewer demands on Congress. His reluctance to have a great deal of personal contact with Congress was mollified to a large extent by his willingness to work with and through the elected congressional leadership. Besides, his was an era in which less personal involvement was expected and required.

Kennedy's more innovative and extensive policy proposals demanded a greater presidential effort, one that he accepted but did not necessarily relish. His legislative experience had given him an appreciation for the intricacies of the congressional process but, unlike Johnson and Ford, he had never been an insider who thrived on internal politics and procedures. Nixon was the most distant. Coming after Johnson's presidency with its high level of presidential interest and involvement, his disinterest in details and his disinclination to personally lobby for his proposals complicated the tasks of his legislative staff. Liaison seemed to be relegated to a secondary status within his administration at the very time that presidential-congressional relations were undergoing serious strain.

Despite these stylistic differences, most of the Capitol Hill activities of the individual liaison offices have remained basically the same from the Kennedy period on. Certain tasks and tactics came to be recognized and accepted while a variety of services were now regularly demanded.

The institutionalization of lobbying functions occurred mainly in the Kennedy-Johnson period. While the limited goals, low-keyed approach, and lack of precedent during the Eisenhower presidency enabled its liaison officials to downplay the care and feeding of members, the Kennedy-Johnson office had less choice given the political objectives and operating style of the Democratic administrations. Projects, patronage, and a variety of other goods and services became a part of the regular liaison effort. This enlargement of services created expectations from which succeeding administrations found it hard to retreat.

Moreover, as the president's legislative role expanded and became institutionalized, Congress increasingly demanded to have a regular and systematic voice in executive policy making. This too became the job of the liaison staff whose senior officials were increasingly consulted on the administration's proposals before they were presented to Congress, almost always involved in the president's negotiations on Capitol Hill, and regularly given an opportunity to recommend action on enrolled bill decisions.

Finally, and most importantly from the president's perspective, presidential advocacy for priority programs has also become a congressional expectation. So long as the sanctity of legislative independence is not publicly violated and executive lobbying remains discreet, aboveboard, and out of the public eye, presidential influence in Congress is regarded as a legitimate responsibility of the chief legislator and a recognized function of his liaison staff. Just how effective particular liaison staffs have been in exerting this influence and affecting votes is difficult to say, however. Before examining the implications which this liaison function may have on the structure and operation of presidential policy making, a brief discussion of the problems of measuring presidential influence in Congress will be presented.

THE DIFFICULTY OF MEASURING PRESIDENTIAL INFLUENCE IN CONGRESS

Does the White House liaison operation really make a difference? Does it help the president get his program enacted into law? Which liaison staffs and which approaches have been most effective and which tactics seem to reap the greatest payoff? These, of course, are critical questions, but ones which are very hard to answer.

Presidents obviously feel that their congressional office makes a difference. So do their liaison aides. Each can easily point to instances where they believe they have influenced votes and affected the outcome of a congressional decision. While interviews with White House liaison agents will naturally exaggerate this influence and its impact on Congress, interviews with members of Congress will do the opposite. Representatives and Senators who are expected to render a considered and independent judgment that is responsive to the interests and wishes of their constituents are unlikely to admit that their vote on a particular bill was influenced by a phone call from a liaison official, a promise of future help from the president, or even the simple White House request, "we need you on this one."

Trying to determine presidential influence through more objective measures is also very difficult and fraught with danger. The authors of two such studies, John W. Kingdon and Aage R. Clausen, both found very little presidential influence on congressional voting decisions, but neither was willing to conclude that presidents and their staffs could not change votes or affect outcomes. Both, in fact, suggested they could.[66]

Three fairly simple measures have frequently been employed as indicators of presidential effectiveness in Congress. They are (1) presidential support scores, the percentage of agreement between Congress and the president on recorded votes where there is a discernible presidential position; (2) presidential box scores, the number and percentage of presidentially initiated programs enacted into law; (3) presidential vetoes and congressional overrides.

Table V-I indicates presidential support scores from 1953 through 1976 as calculated by the *Congressional Quarterly.** Table V-II lists box

* Presidential messages to Congress, press conferences, and other public statements are used to determine the president's position. The roll calls are substantive votes. The *Congressional Quarterly* includes procedural votes only if they reflect a substantive issue. Votes on appropriations are generally not included. Only members

TABLE V-I. **Presidential Support Scores, 1953–1976**

Eisenhower		Nixon	
Year	*Percent*	*Year*	*Percent*
1953	89.0	1969	74.0
1954	82.8	1970	77.0
1955	75.8	1971	75.0
1956	70.0	1972	66.0
1957	68.0	1973	50.6
1958	76.0	1974	59.6
1959	52.0		
1960	65.0	*Ford*	
		1974	58.2
Kennedy		1975	61.0
1961	81.0	1976	53.8
1962	85.4		
1963	87.1		
Johnson			
1964	88.0		
1965	93.0		
1966	79.0		
1967	79.0		
1968	75.0		

Source: *The Congressional Quarterly* XXXIV, no. 44 (October 30, 1976): 3092.

scores on congressional enactment of presidential programs from 1954 through 1975, the last year in which the *Congressional Quarterly* compiled and published such scores.† Table V-III simply presents the total number of presidential vetoes and congressional overrides.

While each of these tables may provide a crude indication of the president's effectiveness in Congress, each has also serious shortcomings as a quantitative measurement of that influence. The presidential support scores do not indicate the criteria for presidential position taking, much less the positions about which presidents felt most strongly.

who cast a yea or nay are counted in calculating the scores. The final percentage combines House and Senate support for the president.

† The proposals which the *Congressional Quarterly* includes in its box score are only the specific legislative requests contained in the president's messages to Congress and other public statements. Policy emanating from the executive branch that is endorsed by the president but not specifically requested by him is not included. When policy proposals are substantially amended by the Congress, The *Congressional Quarterly* makes the judgment whether the legislation amounts to an acceptance or rejection of the president's initial request.

TABLE V-II.   Presidential Programs Enacted into Law, 1954–1975

Year	Proposals Submitted	Approved by Congress	Percent Approved
1954	232	150	65
1955	207	96	46
1956	225	103	46
1957	206	76	37
1958	234	110	47
1959	228	93	41
1960	183	56	31
1961	355	172	48
1962	298	133	45
1963	401	109	27
1964	217	125	58
1965	469	323	69
1966	371	207	56
1967	431	205	48
1968	414	231	56
1969	171	55	32
1970	210	97	46
1971	202	40	20
1972	116	51	44
1973	183	57	31
1974 (Nixon)	97	33	34
1974 (Ford)	64	23	36
1975	110	30	27

Source: Congress and the Nation, Vol. II (Washington, D.C.: The Congressional Quarterly, 1969), p. 625, and as updated in the *Congressional Almanacs.*

TABLE V-III.   Presidential Vetoes and Congressional Overrides, 1945–1976

President	Number of Vetoes	Number of Vetoes Overriden by Congress
Truman	250	12
Eisenhower	181	2
Kennedy	21	0
Johnson	30	0
Nixon	43	5
Ford	66	12

Lyndon Johnson is a good example. While his influence undoubtedly declined from its peak in the 1964–1965 period, he still wielded considerable authority in the Congress throughout his presidency. Yet, Kennedy's scores from 1961–1963 were higher than Johnson's from 1966–1968 and Nixon's were almost as high during his first two years. Were the three presidents approximately equal in influence? What high support scores may reveal is presidential positioning on bills Congress really wants and has initiated. Pork barrel legislation would be an example. In other words, a high score may indicate that Congress is persuading the president to support, or at least not to oppose, its most popular bills. The decline in the scores as some administrations have progressed may suggest that the so-called honeymoon has ended.

In order to pin-point the president's success with the policies he really wants, Table V-II calculates the percent of those presidentially initiated programs that have been enacted into law. What these figures do not indicate, however, is anything about the programs themselves. Were they innovative? Did they require greater efforts at consensus building? Were they priority programs in which presidential prestige was on the line or relatively minor legislation introduced for the record? Did Congress make any changes in the president's proposals, and if so, how did these changes affect its character? Did it accord with the president's original suggestion or had it been substantially modified?

Presidents who took less chances by introducing fewer and less controversial bills and were more willing to accept congressionally proposed changes, might have a high percentage. Look at Eisenhower, for instance, who submitted 232 proposals in 1954 and got 65 percent enacted while Johnson proposed more than double the number in 1965 and had success with 69 percent. Who was doing better? Kennedy received only 27 percent of his proposals in 1963 and Ford the same percentage in 1975, yet Kennedy proposed almost four times as many measures. Ford, a Republican, was saddled with a Democratic Congress; Kennedy, a liberal Democrat, faced a conservative Democratic-Republican coalition. Which liaison office was most effective? The figures in the table do not reveal the answer.

Finally, the number of vetoes and/or congressional overrides can also be misleading. The common adage, the more vetoes the less effective the president, is not always or even necessarily true. Presidents and their aides frequently do not have the time to follow relatively minor public bills and private bills of which they may subsequently disapprove for a variety of reasons. That some presidents have evidenced greater concern than others about having their vetoes overriden may also affect the number of bills they actually veto or how hard their liaison aides work to sustain them. Obviously, the partisan composition of the legislature also has a lot to do with the number of bills that are disapproved and the number of these that are overridden. Readers can draw their own conclusions from these tables. It would be difficult, however, to hypothesize about the influence of the liaison operations from these figures. Unless and until a closer tie can be established between specific liaison activity and congressional voting behavior, the effectiveness of the liaison function in general, and any administration's operation in particular, will remain the subject of considerable speculation and controversy.

IMPLICATIONS FOR THE FUTURE

It is reasonable to assume that the president's legislative responsibilities will remain at least as large as they have been in the past 15 years. Even if a comprehensive legislative program is not presented to Congress every year, the need for appropriations, reauthorizations, and some new legislation will require a presidential presence in Congress. The domestic policy-making structure is simply too interrelated for the executive to disregard the legislature, a lesson that Nixon learned only too well during his first administration.

Not only have evolving governmental roles made it important for the president to try to influence Congress to get his policies adopted, but they have also made it important from a congressional perspective to affect the formulation of those policies. Influencing the executive is now fair game for Congress. While the procedures for factoring in Congressional views may vary from administration to administration, the conduit role has come to be regarded as a functional requisite of the legislative presidency.

The White House has also become tied into the time-consuming job of helping to service congressional constituency needs. Naturally, departments and agencies provide a major source of aid. But increasingly, the White House has functioned as a court of last resort in much the same manner as it is the final arbiter on policy questions. From the perspective of the presidency, this role, which has only minimal impact on the generation of policy support, is not likely to decrease.

Saddled with these obligations and in all likelihood encountering or generating more, the White House liaison effort and office is unlikely to shrink. In fact, the small number of aides will probably be forced to increase unless some operational responsibilities are assumed by other staffers. There are several options. It would be possible, for example, to have lower-level political appointees or even civil servants handle more of the routine constituency service functions. The creation of White House tour and personnel offices were steps in this direction. Another possibility is to have the departments assume greater lobbying and/or servicing responsibilities so long as the tension between their interests and those of the president's could be satisfactorily resolved on a continuing basis. While White House officials would still coordinate department agents on major policy initiatives, especially those that crossed agency lines, they would no longer hear all final appeals for executive branch issues. The dictum adopted in the Kennedy administration "that all good news comes from the White House and bad news from the departments" would have to be abandoned.

A third alternative and one not necessarily at variance with the other two would be to have the White House policy staff, whatever its form, get involved in more of the congressional activity within their respective policy spheres. This would place those officials who had a major role in formulating policy in a better position to respond to congressional critics. It would better sensitize them to the interests of Congress and would probably open up additional lines of communication between the White House and the Hill. It might improve the chances for the president's program in Congress, but it might also dilute that program. It might make it difficult to maintain a presidential perspective in the formative stages of program development. It could also adversely affect presidential-congressional relations if domestic policy staff rejected members' policy suggestions.

No matter how the legislative operation is handled, the president is likely to continue to have an important role to play. The interaction between executive and legislative branches occurs within a framework that encourages the president to set the tone of that relationship. Presidential initiative conditions the legislative response within the context of the political and institutional environment.

At least three factors have a bearing on this initiative: the president's philosophy on how presidential-congressional relations should be conducted, the time he has or takes to conduct them, and the way he interacts with members of Congress. To some extent, a president exercises control over these factors and to some extent, he does not. Personality may be the critical variable. While a president's appreciation for the legislative process may be gained through the congressional experience that most have had prior to taking office (Eisenhower and Carter being the exceptions), his personality is developed before that experience and undoubtedly conditions it. Personality, in short, distinguishes between presidencies and between presidential-congressional relationships. Despite the institutionalized aspects of congressional-presidential interaction, there is no escaping the fact that the character of the relationship is very much affected by the president himself.

NOTES

1   Wilton B. Persons, interview.
2   Bryce N. Harlow, interview.
3   The senior liaison staff's background was not strongly Republican. In fact, Persons alleged, when he first took over in 1953, he knew more Democratic

members of Congress than Republicans. During World War II, he served the army in a legislative capacity where he had to develop relationships on both sides of the aisle. Harlow worked with him in the same office and later received his first job in the House of Representatives from a Democratic congressman.

4 Initially, Persons was assisted by Gerald Morgan and Bryce Harlow, both of whom he had worked with previously, and by Homer Gruenther. Later, I. Jack Martin, formerly administrative assistant to Senator Robert A. Taft, joined the staff when Harlow became the president's full-time speech writer in 1953. Martin covered the Senate and Morgan the House. When Morgan became a special counsel, Harlow took over the House job again. After Persons succeeded Adams in 1958, Harlow became director of the office.

5 The senior members of the liaison office attended these meetings. Dwight D. Eisenhower, *Mandate for Change* (Garden City, N.Y.: Doubleday, 1963), p. 194.

6 Harlow, interview.

7 Ibid. Abraham Holtzman maintains in his book, *Legislative Liaison,* that the Eisenhower congressional office was not able to shape the departmental agents into a unified and powerful force on Capitol Hill. Harlow contends that "the process was deliberately selective and did produce supporting departmental activity where presidential 'must legislation' was at stake." (Harlow, interview.) See Abraham Holtzman, *Legislative Liaison: Executive Leadership in Congress* (Skokie, Ill.: Rand McNally, 1970), p. 259.

8 Persons, interview.

9 Harlow, interview. (Italics added.)

10 Ibid.

11 Bernard Shanley, interview.

12 Harlow, interview. Neil MacNeil quotes Harlow: "In this game, it's what you've done lately that counts." MacNeil continues, "Harlow worked closely with 'every friendly influence' that he could find, principally the conservative lobbies, to help enact President Eisenhower's program." Neil MacNeil, *Forge of Democracy* (New York: McKay, 1963), p. 235.

13 Harlow, interview.

14 Ibid.

15 Eisenhower, *Mandate for Change,* p. 194.

16 John F. Kennedy as quoted in Lawrence F. O'Brien, *No Final Victories* (Garden City, N.Y.: Doubleday, 1974), p. 109.

17 Henry Hall Wilson, an original member of the Kennedy liaison staff, prepared a detailed study of prospects in the House for the Kennedy program. He concluded that the prospects were very bleak. For another analysis of the initial problems that Kennedy faced see Holtzman, *Legislative Liaison,* p. 241.

18 Lawrence F. O'Brien, interview.

19 Lawrence F. O'Brien as quoted in MacNeil, *Forge of Democracy,* p. 260.

20 O'Brien, *No Final Victories,* p. 112.

21 Ibid., p. 101.

22 O'Brien, interview.

23 Ibid.

24 Henry Hall Wilson, interview.

25 Johnson told his cabinet members that the most important appointment they would make in their departments was head of the congressional liaison post. He expected a real "hot shot" in this job.

26 In their dual responsibilities to their departments and the White House, liaison agents sometimes got caught in the middle between conflicting loyalties. In cases of patronage, for example, the departments naturally wished to make their own appointments and take credit for them while the White House liaison office also wished to intercede.

27 O'Brien, interview.

28 Not only did they want to save the president's time and maximize his influence for the most critical issues, but they also wanted to protect their own influence. Involving the president in a lot of detail would certainly not have maximized their own discretion.

29 O'Brien, *No Final Victories,* p. 170.

30 Wilson, Interview.

31 Lyndon B. Johnson, *The Vantage Point: Perspectives of the Presidency 1963–1969* (New York: Holt, Rinehart and Winston, 1971), p. 459.

32 Wilson, interview.

33 O'Brien wrote of one instance where Johnson telephoned 22 members of the House and asked them to sign a Discharge Petition on a Home Rule Bill for the District of Columbia. "He persuaded and cajoled and pleaded. He spoke movingly of the inequality of denying democratic government. He got the signatures, personally and single-handedly. It was a remarkable performance," O'Brien stated, although he should have also noted that the petition failed. O'Brien, *No Final Victories,* pp. 112, 173.

34 Ibid., p. 111.

35 Wilson, interview.

36 H. Barefoot Sanders, interview.

37 O'Brien, *No Final Victories,* p. 119.

38 Johnson, *Vantage Point,* p. 457.

39 Donald Smith, "Turning Screws: Winning Votes in Congress," *Congressional Quarterly* XXXIV, no. 17 (April 24, 1976): 950.

40 Ibid., p. 952.

41 Doris Kearns, *Lyndon Johnson and the American Dream* (New York: Harper & Row, 1976), pp. 221–222.

42 Smith, "Turning Screws," p. 954.

43 Sanders, interview.

44 O'Brien, *No Final Victories,* p. 118.

45 Harlow, interview.

46 One small indication of the change in goals between the Eisenhower and Nixon administrations was Timmons' strong preference for the title congressional relations rather than congressional liaison. He viewed liaison as merely a messenger service. "The office has become much more than that," he said. William E. Timmons, interview.

47 Ibid.

48 Kenneth Belieu, formerly an assistant and undersecretary of the navy during the Kennedy and part of the Johnson period, became Timmons' prin-

cipal aide. There were five others on the original Nixon liaison staff which grew to eight professionals by the end of the president's first term and which also experienced considerable turnover during this period.

49   Harlow resigned in December 1970. Some of his responsibilities were subsequently assumed by Clark MacGregor, who was named counsel to the president for congressional relations and served from January 1971 to July 1972 when he took John Mitchell's place as head of the Committee to Reelect the President. Harlow returned briefly in June 1973 and stayed until the end of the Nixon presidency, becoming increasingly involved in Watergate-related matters. He had no congressional responsibilities during his second tour in the Nixon White House. Timmons remained in charge of the congressional operations and directed most of its Hill activities.

50   Timmons, interview.

51   Ibid.

52   Vernon C. Loen, interview.

53   Friedersdorf and Marsh were considered to be senior White House staff. The early morning meeting schedule in the White House illustrates the hierarchy in the congressional liaison office and the linkage between various levels of the Ford presidency. The 7:30 A.M. meetings with the associate directors of OMB and the Domestic Council were attended by William T. Kendall and Vernon C. Loen, liaison aides, who were in charge of the Senate and House respectively. Friedersdorf and Marsh would go to the senior staff meeting at 8:00 and then Friedersdorf would hold a meeting with his own staff at 8:30.

54   Timmons, interview.

55   Ibid.

56   Ibid.

57   Max L. Friedersdorf, interview.

58   Smith, "Turning Screws," p. 947.

59   Ibid.

60   Timmons, interview.

61   Ibid.

62   In an incident that aroused considerable public attention, Douglas Bennett, head of the White House personnel office during the later part of the Ford administration, was accused by two Republican congressmen of pressuring them to support a presidential veto in exchange for favorable consideration of the reappointment of an ex-governor of their state as chairman of the National Transportation Safety Board. Bennett denied that he linked reappointment to the vote. The reappointment was not made.

63   The president's counsels, Fred M. Buzhardt and James St. Clair, acted as the main conduits to the House Judiciary Committee. While the congressional relations office was available to provide information and arrange meetings, it did so on a request only basis. "We were suspect," stated one official "so we didn't take the initiative although we did some canvassing of Senate opinion as the hearings progressed in the House."

64   Timmons, interview.

65   A member of the House put it this way: "The world just went on. These matters were handled as they had been before. Except perhaps for those last

few days, the Watergate hearings were more of a distraction than anything else." Since a representative sample of congressional opinion was not surveyed, it is not possible to ascertain whether this was the prevailing view.

66   John W. Kingdon, *Congressmen's Voting Decisions* (New York: Harper & Row, 1973), pp. 169–191; Aage R. Clausen, *How Congressmen Decide: A Policy Focus* (New York: St. Martin's Press, 1973), pp. 192–212.

CHAPTER 6

Overseeing the Administration: The Business of Implementation

The executive power shall be vested in
a President of the United States of
America . . . he may require the opinion,
in writing, of the principal officer
in each of the executive departments,
upon any subject relating to the duties
of their respective offices, . . . he
shall nominate, and, by and with the
advice and consent of the Senate, shall
appoint ambassadors, other public
ministers and counsuls, judges of the
Supreme Court and all other officers
of the United States, whose appointments are not herein otherwise provided
for, and which shall be established by
law, . . . he shall take care that the laws
be faithfully executed, ...

Article II,
United States Constitution

We have no discipline in this bureaucracy.
We never fire anybody. We never reprimand
anybody. We never demote anybody. We
always promote the sons-of-bitches that
kick us in the ass.

Richard M. Nixon, April 19, 1973

We have nothing to do with policy. Much as we love the President, if Congress, in its omnipotence over appropriations and in accordance with its authority over policy, passed a law that garbage should be put on White House steps, it would be our regrettable duty, as a bureau, in an impartial nonpolitical and nonpartisan way to advise the Executive and Congress as to how the largest amount of garbage could be spread in the most expeditious and economical manner.

Charles G. Dawes, *The First Year of the Budget of the United States* (New York: Harper & Row, 1923), p. 178

INTRODUCTION

The implementation of legislation enacted into law has always been conceived as an executive function but one which has been left largely to the departments and agencies to handle. Presidents have tended not to get deeply involved in operational details. Discouraged by the size of the bureaucracy, the time and energy it takes to influence it, and their limited potentialities for affecting decision making on a continuing basis, they have eschewed an active administrative role in favor of a more general supervisory function. Only recently, with the development of policy-making initiatives by and in the White House, have chief executives and their closest aides become more directly concerned with how those initiatives are being implemented. This concern has been sporadic and that leadership has remained uncertain.

Presidential power is not easily exerted within the bureaucracy. While presidents have the authority to intervene directly, their influence is difficult to exert for extended periods and over a wide range of issues. The experience and tenure of bureaucratic personnel, combined with their tendencies to adhere to established routines and abide by formal procedures, has made a presidential impact hard to achieve. Moreover, the pressures exerted by outside groups on the existing structure often work against the implementation of innovative presidential policies. As a consequence, presidents have often had to resort to the creation of new agencies within the Executive Office to administer their pet programs [1] and crisis interventions by their White House staff to settle controversial administrative issues on their behalf.

The need to construct a bureaucracy within the presidency poignantly testifies to the weakness of a president in his role as chief executive. It also reflects White House suspicion and, to some extent, hostility toward the established administrative structures, especially evident during the 1960s and 1970s. The simple fact is that presidents do not have the tools at their disposal to permit a comprehensive and systematic oversight of departmental and agency activity.

In many respects, Congress is better able to exercise more continuous and direct supervision. Through its committee structure, which parallels much of the executive branch organization, members of Congress and their staffs are often placed in a better position to observe and check bureaucratic activity than are the president and his staff. The longevity of service on committees, encouraged by the seniority system, has facilitated close personal ties between congressmen and career civil servants in the departments and agencies.[2]

Congress has provided for direct operational oversight in a variety of ways. It has written into statutes requirements for advanced reports, and consultations. In some cases, it has required actual committee clearances of anticipated agency actions prior to the time such actions are to be taken. This has been particularly effective in preventing the elimination or alteration of public works and defense projects that have been proposed by the president in the interests of economy and efficiency. Moreover, Congress has used the annual appeal for appropriations to scrutinize past and prospective bureaucratic decisions. Not only have appropriation hearings been employed as part of Congress' oversight mechanism but so have authorization requests for new programs or the renewal of existing ones.

Whether a program is initiated or continued, for how long, and with what administrative restrictions, is of obvious interest and concern to the departments and agencies. While Congress does not exact tribute, it can and does use committee hearings to praise and scold, reward and sanction. The Senate has used confirmation hearings to the same end. Investigations, or even their threat, have also been employed to compel what congressional committees consider to be necessary "corrective" behavior. The bureaucracy's responsiveness to these political pressures explains some of its resistance to presidentially initiated change. It also indicates the magnitude of the task that presidents face.

The development of legislative policy making in the presidency has made the job of management more critical from the president's perspective, but the way in which it has developed has also made it more difficult. The centralization of the policy-making machinery in the White House and the OMB, the relegation of the departments and agencies to more of a supportive role, and the emphasis that some contemporary presidents have placed on new ideas, have all engendered management expectations and have created complex administrative problems for chief executives.

How presidents have attempted to cope with these expectations and problems will be examined in the remainder of this chapter. The next section chronicles White House management initiatives. It describes the interest and involvement of presidents and their staffs in matters of policy implementation. The development and enlargement of the OMB's management role is discussed in the following section.

Particular emphasis is placed on recent attempts to institute management-oriented systems to promote efficiency in the departments and agencies. The conclusion assesses the problems and prospects of presidential management and the implications that they have for the legislative presidency.

PRESIDENTIAL MANAGEMENT INITIATIVES

Although most presidents have ritualistically voiced concern about the need for efficiently implementing policy objectives, in practice few have devised effective methods for doing so. Except for crisis intervention, the White House has generally taken a hands-off attitude and presidential involvement has been essentially limited to reorganization, recruitment, and reaction to specific "hot" issues.

The emphasis on developing new policy initiatives, translating them into a legislative package, and marketing that package for Congress and the public has consumed an increasing amount of time and effort. It has also kept White House attention riveted on the legislative rather than administrative stages of the process. Not until the late 1960s, did presidents and their aides evidence much concern over the manner in which their programs were implemented or evaluated by the departments and agencies.

Presidents Truman and Eisenhower were interested in the organization of the executive branch and proposed a relatively large number of re-organization plans to Congress,[3] but they did not extend this interest much beyond general structural concerns. President Eisenhower even decentralized personnel selection, allowing his cabinet heads maximum flexibility in choosing their own aides. His White House staff rarely got involved in appointments at the department and agency level, except for refereeing jurisdictional disputes over which agency should exercise primary responsibility over what position.[4] The president himself was neither interested in nor played an active role in lower-level appointments, in keeping with his tendency to avoid involvement in these kinds of issues.[5] Truman was more directly involved although not in any systematic way.[6]

Both presidents had little choice even if their inclinations had pushed them toward a more active role. The size of their White House staffs and the orientation of their Budget Bureaus would not have permitted much direct presidential oversight to be exercised. They had to be more or less content to have the departments and agencies that developed the legislation be primarily responsible for its execution.

While the Kennedy White House started the trend toward reducing the departments' roles in the initiation and development of legislative policy, it did not effectively reduce their role in administering that policy. There were times when Kennedy became impatient with the bureaucracy's stately processes and would try to expedite matters with telephone calls placed to lower-echelon officials. Kennedy felt that presidential intervention and persuasion were useful, but he was under no illusion that he or the White House could substitute for the departments and agencies on a regular basis. "The President can't administer a department, but at least, he can be a stimulant," Kennedy is quoted as saying.[7]

Johnson operated on much the same level with the departments and agencies, although his personal interest in operational detail was more pervasive than Kennedy's. During the last two years of his administration, Johnson's White House staff also began to get more involved in following legislative policy once it had been enacted into law. James Gaither, a deputy special assistant to the president on Califano's staff, commented on the need for this White House involvement:

> We got increasingly involved in day-to-day policy direction of the various programs that had been developed so that they didn't just sit there, so that something was done about them.[8]

Using the BOB as its principal resource, the White House was able to monitor domestic programs. In some instances, the Budget Bureau submitted reports on how departments and agencies were administering these programs. Inside and outside task forces also checked on what had been done to the recommendations of previous task forces. Evaluation began to be built into some of the newly developed social programs.

During this period, however, White House oversight of domestic policy was haphazard and uneven. Aides of both the Kennedy and Johnson administrations did not evaluate their own management efforts very highly. Thomas Cronin writes that of the 50 former White House aides he interviewed, most of whom served during this period, "not one of them praised the quality of White House domestic policy monitoring and evaluation." [9] He goes on to report, "more than one-quarter of the aides . . . thought White House policy evaluation and monitoring capabilities were mediocre, and nearly two-thirds responded that in their experience, such capabilities were 'poor,' terrible or virtually non-existent." [10]

Systematizing the Selection Process: Kennedy and Johnson

Both Presidents Kennedy and Johnson showed more concern with personnel selection than did their immediate predecessors. While neither believed that his appointments would ensure a responsive bureaucracy, both concluded that having capable administrators operating on the same political wavelengths helped, especially for implementing new social legislation.

Kennedy was active in choosing his own cabinet and frequently made the final decision in selecting lower-level appointments; Johnson took an avid interest in all aspects of recruitment. He would choose the applicant from a list provided by his staff and then personally invite his choice to join his administration after it was determined that the individual would accept.

Kennedy and Johnson both established personnel offices in the White House and moved toward a more systematized method for choosing executive officials. The Kennedy administration developed contacts in various professional communities and used these contacts to generate lists of candidates. G. Calvin Mackenzie in his study of the appointment process describes the Kennedy system:

> Efforts were made to identify executive vacancies before they occurred. The personnel office began to talk to people in the administration to get a clearer sense of what capabilities they ought to look for in a candidate for a particular office. The importance of establishing effective working relations with agency heads was recognized as an essential foundation for a centralized personnel operation. A roster of names of potential nominees was drawn up from a great variety of sources. Regular political and security clearance procedures were instituted, and efforts were undertaken to clarify the basic criteria for service in the administration and the specific criteria for nomination to particular offices.[11]

This process was further developed and sophisticated under Johnson. Search procedures were improved. A computerized list of names that reached 16,000 by the end of 1968 was compiled and was cross-referenced by candidate skills and position profiles.[12]

Both presidents also showed some concern for structure, Johnson more so than Kennedy. During the 1961–1963 period, Kennedy proposed one new department—Urban Affairs and Housing, which was defeated— and created several new units within the Executive Office of the President. Johnson got two new departments approved, Housing and Urban Development and Transportation; recommended without success the merger of two others, Labor and Commerce; and further expanded the Executive Office of the President.

While interest in administration grew during the Kennedy-Johnson period, it never became a major presidential priority. Both chief executives seemed to be more concerned with individuals and programs than with structure and policy implementation. The presidential emphasis on management did not really begin until after the Nixon presidency got underway.

In the postelection planning and during the first few months of the new administration, policy implementation was not a major White House concern. The president's view was that administration was the proper role of the departments and agencies. Nixon initially saw a cabinet government as adequate for handling domestic matters. Fairly soon after becoming president, he modified this view.

Centralizing the Instruments of Presidential Control: Nixon

As chief executive, Nixon voiced the traditional concern for the efficient and economic administration of government. However, during most of the first year of his presidency, the emphasis seemed to be more on generating new initiatives than worrying about how they were to be implemented. By the winter of 1969–1970, this emphasis had begun to change.

A variety of factors contributed to increased presidential interest in management questions. Nixon's domestic legislative initiatives had been given a hard time on Capitol Hill. Naturally, he and his aides looked to the president's executive powers to help promote his policy objectives. More importantly, the concentration of power within his own staff and the limited access to the president sparked the tension that was developing between a White House and cabinet approach to government. Nixon had seriously overestimated his ability to sustain a unified team in a cabinet system. He had underestimated his desire to run a tight ship. So when the Ash Council submitted its reports on executive reorganization, the president greeted them with enthusiastic support.

In order to improve the president's management capabilities, the Ash Council proposed the creation of the Domestic Council, the reorganization and orientation of the Bureau of the Budget, and the restructuring of ten domestic departments into four. President Nixon was able to implement the first two recommendations under his reorganization authority subject to congressional veto. The cabinet proposal, however, required new legislation which Congress failed to enact.

The major structural changes, announced in the President's Reorganization Plan No. 2, took effect on July 1, 1970. Policy-making and policy management responsibilities were divided between the White House and the OMB staffs. It was Nixon's contention that increasing White House involvement in presidential management during the Johnson administration had blurred staff responsibilities and resulted in intermittent interest and, in some cases, avoidance of key management decisions. By placing responsibilities squarely in the hands of the newly enlarged Office of Management and Budget, the president hoped to prevent a repetition of this problem. While the plan's well-publicized division between formulation and execution did not work out in the policy-making area, it was more evident in policy implementation.

For the most part, the Domestic Council stayed out of the day-to-day work of the departments and agencies. Its intervention was essentially limited to crisis or catalyst situations in which specific political problems arose. John Kessel quotes a council staffer to this effect:

> We define areas where action should be taken, and get policy decisions made. Then, to the extent that we have to, we monitor agencies to make sure that action is being taken and then we get out. Our job is to catalyze action.[13]

Egil Krogh, Jr., an associate director of the Domestic Council during the 1970–1972 period, stated simply, "In general, it was more crisis management than ongoing management. . . . The Domestic Council was too small to do ongoing and long-term management." [14]

Under Ehrlichman's direction, the council staff was still more directly involved in management than previous White Houses had been. There was an attempt in the 1970–1972 period to follow through on programs until the regulations governing their implementation were issued. The regulations themselves had to be cleared with the appropriate council staffer. In some cases, they were actually rewritten. Richard Nathan, a former OMB official and undersecretary of the Department of Health, Education and Welfare (HEW) in the Nixon administration, described two such incidents during this period: one where the new regulations increased federal controls, and the other where they reduced them.

> The new rules . . . required that funds [to aid the poor] only be used for people with defined and specific conditions of need, and then only under a system of detailed accounting for the services provided. Here the aim was to reduce the options available to social-work professionals, long subject to Administration criticism and strongly entrenched in the welfare bureaucracy of HEW. On the other hand, in the manpower field . . . the aim . . . was to decentralize by implementing the Administration's plan for manpower special revenue sharing through administrative action in the form of changed regulations under existing statutory authority.[15]

The practice of involving the Domestic Council staff in administrative regulations was practically terminated by the reorganization that severely cut the size of the council staff and sent a number of its principal members to positions in the departments and agencies at the beginning of 1973. After that, one staffer who remained, noted, "The management role has been nothing except to nag and bitch."

One of the purposes of the 1973 reorganization was to respond to the criticism that the White House had grown too powerful. Another was to further extend presidential influence in the departments and agencies. These objectives were hardly complementary. In the light of the Watergate hearings, the latter seemed to be the primary motive.

Before the 1972 election, the administration had been sufficiently concerned with executive branch responsiveness to contemplate and initiate a program to get the departments and agencies in line behind the president's reelection efforts. The White House was interested in policy, publicity, and operations. The operations included a wide range of administrative activities, especially those that had direct political impact. Specified were "positive decisions (e.g., project grants, contracts, loans, subsidies, procurement and construction projects), and negative actions (e.g., taking legal or regulatory action against a group as government body, major cutbacks in programs, and relocation of Department operations)." [16]

The department responsiveness program and the 1973 Domestic Council staff reshuffle clearly indicated that the Nixon administration had come to the conclusion that management operations involved policy making and therefore required a presidential perspective. Nixon hoped to accomplish this by instituting high-level personnel changes that would achieve in fact what the president's proposed domestic department reorganization plan hoped to encourage in form:

> The President would put his own trusted appointees in positions to manage directly key elements of the bureaucracy with elaborate White House or Executive Office staff machinery to encumber their efforts. The new appointees would be the President's men. They would be arranged so that there would be clear lines of authority. The bureaucracy would report to them. They would be held accountable. [17]

Personnel became even more important than structure as the administration progressed.

More than other presidents before him, Nixon tied personnel and organization to his management needs. His White House developed an elaborate personnel operation and he instituted major structural changes in the executive office.

The development of a White House recruitment system was not without its difficulties. In his initial enthusiasm for a cabinet approach to government, Nixon delegated primary responsibility for filling political-level vacancies to the departments and agencies. He further asserted that ability not loyalty should be the major consideration for appointment. [18] At the same time, he set up a personnel office in the White House office. It began compiling its own list of applicants and creating its own procedures. This engendered considerable friction between cabinet and White House that did not easily dissipate. In fact, the continuing tension undoubtedly fueled White House attempts to centralize the appointment authority in order to gain influence over the bureaucracy.

Despite the president's increasing desire to have the White House flex its muscles, he personally displayed little interest and involvement in the selection process except for the top positions. Mackenzie writes, "The President often took no part in personnel selection decisions." [19] And when he did, it was to approve or reject usually the one candidate which his personnel office felt was most qualified for the position. "The President can turn it [the appointment] down if he wants to," stated Harry S. Flemming who initially headed the White House personnel operation, "but he doesn't." [20]

The administration's most concerted attempt to relate the needs for effective management to the recruitment of executive officials came in the 1970–1972 period when Frederic V. Malek headed the White House personnel office.[21] A student of management by training and experience, Malek sought to achieve the president's policy objectives through the appointment of loyal, competent administrators.

In a *Federal Personnel Manual* written in the White House during Nixon's first term, this connection between policy management and partisanship was forcefully stated. The *Manual* read in part:

> You cannot achieve management, policy or program control unless you have established political control. The record is quite replete with instances of the failures of program, policy and management goals because of sabotage by employees of the Executive Branch who engage in the frustration of those efforts because of their political persuasion and their loyalty to the majority party of Congress rather than the Executive that supervises them.[22]

The question of loyalty was continually raised throughout the Nixon period. The president became preoccupied with it. His preoccupation, to the point of paranoia, is illustrated by a remark he made to Ehrlichman in the spring of 1973:

> We have no discipline in this bureaucracy. We never fire anybody. We never reprimand anybody. We never demote anybody. We always promote the sons-of-bitches that kick us in the ass.[23]

Ehrlichman's resignation, Nixon's increasing beleaguerment, and the growing disenchantment of Congress and cabinet with White House dominance made these policy objectives impossible to achieve. The small and less potent council staff was not able to exert centralized leadership on policy making or on administrative matters. The aides who had moved to major positions in the departments and agencies now found their White House experience a liability. As a consequence, not only were departments and agencies not brought within a White House perspective but they acquired increasing autonomy in dealing with administrative issues on their own. This continued through the transition and into the Ford administration as the new president moved to improve the access and initiative of his department heads and to further enlarge their sphere of responsibilities.

Maintaining the Management Focus: Ford

While Ford did not come to the presidency with an articulated management strategy nor with much executive experience, he displayed a strong management orientation and considerable interest in management activities. One associate director of OMB, Donald G. Ogilvie, found him "more interested in management and ensuring implementation of his initiatives than President Nixon. President Ford is very concerned that when he asks that something get done, that it in fact gets done." [24] Ford tended to delegate less authority than Nixon. He did not share his predecessor's disinclination for becoming personally involved. On balance, he also displayed a greater emotional commitment to the implementation of domestic policy.

Nonetheless, the White House's management role did not appreciably alter. While the Domestic Council staff continued to take management factors into account in developing policy, most particularly in designing procedures for evaluation, it did not as a general rule attempt to participate in administrative decisions. Nor did the council staff tend to follow legislative policy through to the regulations as had been done during part of the Nixon period. Crisis management remained the rule, not the exception.

President Ford also did not emphasize structural reform as President Nixon had done. He could not. The president's reorganization authority lapsed in 1973 and Congress showed no enthusiasm for renewing it during his presidency. Moreover, the pressures to resist organizational changes, as reflected by the Congress' failure to seriously consider Nixon's proposals to reorganize the executive departments, made administrative restructuring a high-risk, low-priority venture. There was little incentive to push ahead with major reorganization. Instead, President Ford chose simply to change personnel within the existing organization, replacing Nixon cabinet officials, in some cases belatedly and brutally, with his own appointees.[25]

Ford also continued to use the existing machinery in the OMB. The Budget Bureau had always enjoyed a more active oversight role than the White House staff. Even before the introduction of the word "management" into its title in 1970, the bureau had viewed administrative management as part of its officials' tasks, albeit not a large part.

OMB AS MANAGEMENT OVERSEER

The Budget and Accounting Act that created an executive budget bureau in the Department of the Treasury in 1921 also authorized it to conduct organizational studies of departments and agencies at the behest of the president. During the 1920s and 1930s, however, little attention was devoted to management concerns. After the report of the President's Committee on Administrative Management (the Brownlow Committee) and the establishment of a separate Bureau of the Budget in 1939, greater emphasis was placed on improving bureaucratic organization and management.

In the new organization of the BOB, a Division of Administration Management was set up to conduct research, advise departments and agencies, and aid the president in the administration of government. Training executives in the skills of management also became an important task during the war years, but, by the end of the 1940s, this program had been substantially reduced in size.

As a consequence of the first Hoover Commission Report [26] and a management improvement program instituted in 1949, the BOB also began to provide guidance for departments and agencies in reviewing their management improvement programs and operations. These functions were quickly made a part of its ongoing responsibilities under the provisions of a 1950 law which required the president through the Budget Bureau to devise and evaluate proposals to promote efficiencies in government.

The bureau's work, however, was short lived. Its attempts at interesting departments and agencies in developing improvement plans and conducting management reviews met with difficulties and some resistance, and were eventually abandoned. Despite the urgings of the second Hoover Commission (1955) and the Rockefeller Committee to place greater emphasis on management,[27] the BOB did not exercise strong centralized controls. It continued to view management as essentially an internal department and agency affair. While the 1950s saw some new organizational studies and the early 1960s the enlargement of staff, improvement of management training, and the further development of technical skills and data-processing methods, the bureau's role in management remained subordinate to its budget and legislative functions. At no time did it exercise the same kind of influence over how policy was to be administered as it did over how it was made and funded.

Concern with escalating costs during the Kennedy-Johnson years, however, kept the Budget Bureau involved in various management programs. By 1965, its emphasis had shifted from cost reduction to cost effectiveness. Stressing the importance of program evaluation, President Johnson issued an executive order in 1965 requiring 20 domestic departments to use the Planning, Programing Budgeting System (PPBS) that had been first introduced by Robert S. McNamara in the Department of Defense.[28] The BOB was primarily responsible for its implementation.

PPBS' promise of improved analytic capabilities and informational services were thought to represent a significant management advance. However, the system soon became mangled in bureaucratic confusion (and resistance) and bogged down in paperwork. It was quietly abandoned by the Nixon administration although one of its objectives, improved management, was to be given an even greater emphasis.

Making the Budget Bureau into a Management Office

The management function was clearly conceived as the principal task of the new Office of Management and Budget.[29] The intent of the Ash

Council's recommendations had been to upgrade its management functions and downgrade its budget responsibilities.[30] Reflecting these priorities, President Nixon stated in his message describing the plan:

> While the budget function remains a vital tool of management, it will be strengthened by the greater emphasis the new Office will place on fiscal analysis. The budget function is only one of several important management tools that the President must now have. He must also have a substantially enhanced institutional staff capability in other areas of executive management—particularly in program evaluation and coordination, improvement of Executive Branch organization, information and management systems, and development of executive talent. Under this plan, strengthened capability in these areas will be provided partly through internal reorganization, and it will also require additional staff resources.[31]

The wide range of activities thought to be management responsibilities extended from the establishment of organizational goals and the creation of functionally oriented structures to the designation of specific procedures and processes for monitoring these objectives. The recruitment and training of personnel, the development and operation of informational retrieval and processing systems, and the sophistication of statistical techniques and measures were all part of OMB's management responsibilities. Evaluating programs that crossed agency lines also became a major objective.

In carrying out this expanded role, the office's initial structure sharply delineated between budget and management operations. An associate director with operational responsibilities over the five management-oriented divisions was appointed. In a subsequent restructuring two years later, this rigid demarcation was eliminated and four new program associate directors with ongoing budgetary, legislative, and management responsibilities were established.

These directors were given a broad mandate within their respective areas. This included the job of program evaluation. To assist the associate directors with this function, a new position, that of management associate, was established and organized into a separate unit in each of the four operating divisions. The management associates were to have general oversight responsibilities in contrast to the specific departmental assignments of the budget examiners. Initially, considerable tension was created between the two groups, but within two years this tension had largely dissipated.

The role of the management associate evolved along the lines set by each associate director. In some divisions, the management associates operated as a kind of ad hoc, project-oriented group, addressing special projects almost like consultants. In others, they functioned closely and in conjunction with the budget examiners in different issue areas. In one division, a separate management unit was eliminated entirely and the associates were effectively integrated into the existing structure.

Instituting Management Systems: MBO and PMI

While the mechanism for providing oversight continued to evolve, OMB attempted to introduce a more systematic method for integrating the administration of agency programs with presidential objectives. Replacing PPBS was a new system called Management by Objective (MBO). Its aim was to build a consensus behind the president's policy goals and then try to measure progress toward achieving them. Departments and agencies were asked to submit lists of their objectives for the next year. They were to be stated in a way that permitted evaluation of progress. OMB's job was to review these lists, order priorities, eliminate duplication, and specify concrete legislative needs.

Unlike its implementation of PPBS, however, the OMB maintained a light hand and low profile in coordinating the MBO program. It deliberately deferred to the departments. It viewed its role as a consensus builder not a presidential enforcer. As a consequence, departments and agencies had a relatively free hand in establishing their own goals within the context of very broad presidential guidelines. Some produced large and diverse lists and reproduced the same goals each year; others had a great deal of difficulty in defining goals, much less in establishing concrete and measurable performance indicators.

Top OMB officials did not spend much time reviewing the department and agency lists. Their lack of involvement caused the system to lose much of its direction and thunder. It soon became a captive of the departments. Presidential goals were not easily distinguishable from those of the issuing agency with the result that the exercise became much less useful for the president and OMB.

Periodic attempts to revive the MBO system in one form or another were proposed during the Ford presidency. The last, in July 1976, directed the 20 largest departments and agencies to develop with the help of OMB a comprehensive plan to promote management efficiencies in five target areas: (1) decision making and departmental organization; (2) evaluation of current programs; (3) reduction of federal reporting and regulation; (4) outside contracting and overhead costs; and (5) personnel management. The program known as Presidential Management Initiatives (PMI), had as a major goal the integration of these management efforts into the budgetary process. Four months after the program was instituted, President Ford claimed it produced a savings of nearly $500 million.[32]

Improving program evaluation also continued to be a principal objective of the OMB during both Republican administrations. Studies of how to improve evaluation in the executive branch, how to build it into particular administration policies, and how to solve a particular evaluation problem were the job of its Evaluation and Program Implementation Division. Providing a service for both budget examiners and those departments and agencies that wished to utilize its expertise, the division's work was largely advisory.

The OMB's decision not to mandate most aspects of its management activity was consistent with the general conglomerate view of government expressed during the Nixon and Ford administrations. It also represented both the strengths and weaknesses of the office's management role. While departments and agencies were provided with information and advice, they retained the freedom to experiment and adopt organization, styles, and processes to fit their own particular needs. From the department's viewpoint, this was a welcome relief from what had traditionally been regarded as OMB's "negative" role. From a presidential perspective, however, maintaining continuous oversight, much less achieving a political consensus, was made difficult by this "service" approach to management.

Management without budget lacks clout. The impact of the functional divisions, especially, has been dependent on the support they received from those involved in the budgetary process. One official of the Information Systems Division stated simply: "Our credibility with the agencies is limited to the extent to which they believe what we're saying is at least nominally subscribed to by the budget examiners." Clifford Graves, deputy associate director for evaluation and program implementation during the Ford administration, spoke to the same point when he commented:

> The ability of OMB on its own or for the president to execute its overall management responsibilities is limited. . . . Its authority in general management is much vaguer [than its budgetary authority] and has relatively few handles. . . . The only way we can seriously affect them [the departments and agencies] is through the budgetary process. We can write circulars but enforcement power is through the budgetary process.[33]

Without budget, OMB provided a management service and the departments and agencies generally chose when and how to use it. Most of them did not use it very much.

CONCLUSION

As the bureaucracy has grown in size and as legislation has become more complex, the job of managing those presidential initiatives that have been enacted into law has become a more prodigious and time-consuming undertaking. Lacking the instruments, expertise, and, until recently, the incentive to get directly involved in policy implementation, presidents and their staffs have tended to leave the day-to-day business of management to the discretion of the departments and agencies. The White House has become involved when it has had to, mainly when crises impel a presidential response. A variety of factors, both institutional and political, have contributed to the reluctance of the White House to exercise a stronger influence in all but the most critical management decisions.

By its very nature, the implementation of policy demands time, which has traditionally been in short supply in the White House. Moreover, the creation of workable rules that conform to established administrative procedures requires considerable know-how, the kind that senior bureaucrats are likely to have but that White House staffers, especially new ones, are not. The president's closest aides are normally recruited from his political associates. While they have usually undergone the rigors of the campaign, they do not necessarily possess the skills required for administrative management. Where concrete procedural and substantive management issues are involved, bureaucrats have an advantage.

In addition to their qualifications for dealing with specific and often detailed implementation problems, careerists are, and departmental political appointees often become, sensitized and responsive to the interests of the publics most directly concerned with the legislative policy. Servicing departmental clientele is necessary and usually yields political benefit for departments and agencies but may be less critical to presidential needs. In some cases, in fact, it may even present political problems. Few presidents wish to alienate organized interest groups by making unpopular administrative decisions.

There have been other incentives for the White House to remain aloof. In addition to the time, energy, and political constraints, the payoffs for presidential involvement are not great. Mismanagement makes news but good management does not. Public attention is normally focused on what goes wrong or what is new. This is why contemporary presidents have directed their energies toward the development of new programs rather than the administration of old ones. Only recently has management itself been acknowledged as an important presidential priority.

The emphasis on management as a presidential goal has produced only a marginally more active and energetic White House approach to policy implementation, however. There are primarily two reasons for this. First, the traditional authority at the chief executive's disposal (such as his appointment and removal power, executive orders, proclamations, and the like) does not permit a continuous and comprehensive oversight of the executive branch. Second, the budget and legislative policy-making processes have not been used as effective management tools. Whether they can be is another question.

As a consequence, presidents have had to utilize recruitment and reorganization in the hopes of creating a more responsive bureaucracy. Personnel operations under White House supervision have become more centralized and systematized while reorganization proposals have been designed to streamline administrative structures and, more recently, extend presidential influence. While the power to appoint and the ability to reorganize, both subject to congressional controls, are only indirect ways in which presidents can promote better management, there is little alternative. Jimmy Carter realized this when as president-elect he met with members of Congress to plead for a restoration of the president's reorganization authority. The reliance that contemporary presidents have placed on personnel and structural change to effect management goals suggests how little direct impact chief executives usually exercise over the implementation of legislative policy.

The increasing importance of management as one of the Budget Bureau's most important functions also testifies to the priority which recent presidents have placed on overseeing legislative policy and to the impossibility of their doing it from the White House.

The Budget Bureau had a long history of promoting the efficiency and economy of government. The Budget and Accounting Act of 1921, which created the bureau, prescribed these goals as official functions. They have remained the agency's *raison d'etre*. In recent times, the OMB has sought to expand its management role and provide for more services. It has presented information on management systems, program evaluation, statistical techniques, and information retrieval and data analysis systems. It has helped condition and implement special studies on executive organization and procedures. It has even gotten involved in the training of federal executives.

In addition to providing these services, the office has tried to tie management objectives to presidential policy initiatives but it has done so in a loose and nonbinding way. Rather than impose a presidential perspective on the bureaucracy, its approach to management has reflected a bureaucratic perspective. This has made it difficult to distinguish presidential interests in the management area from those of the departments and agencies.

IMPLICATIONS FOR THE FUTURE

Presidents will have to profess a greater concern for management and devote more attention to it than they have in the past. In a larger and increasingly complex government where the number of programs crossing traditional department and agency lines has also grown, management problems are unavoidable, and they are unavoidably presidential. They can and do have significant political impact for the chief executive.

Diverting the public's attention to new policy is less likely to enable present and future presidents to evade responsibility for programs they have developed or inherited. Nor is the restitution of a more decentralized approach to policy making likely to relieve the president of this responsibility. As a consequence, the business of management will undoubtedly continue to be an even more pressing presidential obligation for Democrats as well as Republicans.

If presidents try to institute greater oversight over administrative decision making and become more actively involved in certain administrative decisions, they will need a presidential agency to do this. A White House policy staff is probably not the most suitable unit for this purpose. It would have to be larger than it has been in the past and at least as highly differentiated. The political and administrative liabilities of having such a size staff make it unlikely and perhaps unwise for presidents to look to their policy aides for anything more than emergency intervention on controversial implementation issues.

What are the alternatives? Thomas Cronin has suggested the creation of an Office of Planning and Program Evaluation in the White House, separate from, but adjunct to, the policy staff. The reason that the office must be separate, he argues, is that policy makers often have or develop a stake in the policy they help formulate.

> Aides who might have been fairly objective on questions of policy formulation often become unrelenting advocates and lieutenants for fixed presidential policy views in the implementation stages, especially after substantial amounts of their time have been committed to bureaucratic combat work or when the president desperately wants to accomplish at least a few of his promised objectives before the next election.[34]

Cronin sees the differentiation between policy-making and policy-evaluation roles as absolutely critical if the proposed office is to carry out its tasks in an objective and neutral fashion.

A second possibility would be to upgrade the OMB's efforts. It already has the staff resources, institutional structure, political loyalty, and most importantly, a presidential perspective. It is also not as subject to the kind of clientele pressures that departments and agencies experience, although the more visible it becomes, the more likely it will experience such pressures.

For the OMB to exert a presidential view on the administration of policy, however, would require a far more assertive stance by the office than it has heretofore taken. The OMB's clout clearly lies in its role in the legislative and budgetary processes. Getting departments and agencies to adopt certain evaluation procedures, streamline their management techniques, tailor their own goals toward presidential initiatives, and generally implement policy with the president's interests in mind, requires persuasion but cannot be accomplished by persuasion alone. The possible use of sanctions is necessary if change is to be effected or control exerted. This is not without its dangers, however. Having one executive agency affect the way in which others go about their business is always potentially hazardous for a responsive government. It could produce adverse political fall-out.

There is another, even more basic problem. Imposing a single perspective on the implementation of public policy may itself be dysfunctional. It is not always the case that presidential interests differ from those of the departments and agencies, but, even when they do, achieving uniformity does not always improve the administration of government.

This suggests another alternative. Simply continue past attempts to promote better management from within the departments and agencies by using the traditional tools of appointing competent, loyal administrators, eliminating duplication and consolidating responsibilities by reorganization, and achieving procedural shortcuts through red tape and complex administrative regulations. Whether this approach would be sufficient to improve management is open to some question based on recent history; whether it would enable the president to exercise sufficient oversight on the implementation of policy proposals is even more debatable issue.

The president has a management dilemma. The government is simply too large and too complex for the chief executive and a few personal aides to run it alone. That is why there are departments and agencies. But how can these departments and agencies be kept responsive to the president's interests and needs? In the policy-making sphere, the answer seems to lie in the influence of sizable presidential staffs and agencies and centralized coordinating and clearing processes. In the policy-implementation sphere, the staffs are not nearly as involved or as influential and the processes not nearly as centralized nor controlling. How to oversee the executive branch without overinvolving the White House and OMB and without overwhelming the departments and agencies is a critical problem that every contemporary president has and will continue to face.

NOTES

1   Roosevelt was the first president to do this, using authority granted him under the Executive Reorganization Act of 1939. Under the terms of this act and its subsequent revisions, presidents were permitted to initiate changes in the executive subject to congressional veto. The Reorganization Acts lapsed in 1973, largely as a product of congressional restiveness over the growing centralization of power in the presidency and its alleged abuse by the president. During the period in which they were in effect, however, major additions to the Executive Office included the Office of Science and Technology in 1962, the Office of Economic Opportunity in 1964, the Special Action Office for Drug Abuse Prevention in 1971, and the Federal Energy Office in 1973.

2   In a well-known study published in 1955, J. Leiper Freeman described a subsystem of executive bureau-legislative committee relations which minimized presidential influence. Freeman generalized that the structure, personnel, and interest group pressure work to reinforce this relationship, contributing to its stability. Students of the American political system generally subscribe to this

view. J. Leiper Freeman, *The Political Process: Executive Bureau-Legislative Committee Relationships* (New York: Random House, 1955).

3 **Reorganization Plans, 1939–1973**

President	Plans Proposed	Plans Enacted	Plans Rejected
Roosevelt	5	5	0
Truman	48	32	16
Eisenhower	17	14	3
Kennedy	10	6	4
Johnson	17	17	0
Nixon	8	8	0
Total	105	82	23

SOURCE: Jennifer Brandt, The Office of Management and Budget Library.

4 G. Calvin Mackenzie, "The Appointment Process: The Selection and Confirmation of Federal Political Executives" (Ph.D. diss., Harvard University, 1975), p. 79.

5 Sherman Adams described patronage matters as "a constant annoyance to Eisenhower . . . Ike wanted no part of it." Adams insists that Eisenhower made the final decision on appointments although Adams also notes that cabinet members and his own staff made the recommendations on capabilities and qualifications. Sherman Adams, *First-Hand Report: The Story of the Eisenhower Administration* (New York: Harper & Row, 1961), pp. 57–58.

6 The need for personal trust remained Truman's foremost criterion when selecting people for major positions in his administration. Mackenzie notes, "As the president slowly undertook the process of replacing these people, he sought to ascertain that their successors would be personally loyal to him and would vigorously support his programmatic goals." Mackenzie, "The Appointment Process," p. 69.

7 John F. Kennedy as quoted in Arthur M. Schlesinger, Jr., *A Thousand Days: John F. Kennedy in the White House* (Boston: Houghton Mifflin, 1965), p. 685. Theodore C. Sorensen, *Kennedy* (New York: Harper & Row, 1965), p. 282.

8 James Gaither, interview.

9 Thomas E. Cronin, "Presidents as Chief Executives," in *The Presidency Reappraised*, eds. Rexford E. Tugwell and Thomas E. Cronin (New York: Praeger, 1974), pp. 237–238.

10 Ibid.

11 Mackenzie, "The Appointment Process." p. 91.

12 Ibid., pp. 93–101.

13 John H. Kessel, *The Domestic Presidency* (North Scituate, Mass.: Duxbury Press, 1975), p. 102.

14 Egil Krogh, Jr., interview.

15 Richard Nathan, *The Plot that Failed: Nixon and the Administrative Presidency* (New York: Wiley, 1975), p. 75.

16   Frederick V. Malek, "Departmental Responsiveness Memorandum for H. R. Haldeman," March 17, 1972 as it appears in Executive Session Hearings, *Select Committee on Presidential Campaign Activities*, U.S. Senate, Ninety-third Congress, Second Session, Book 18, p. 8315.

17   Nathan, *The Plot that Failed*, pp. 61–62.

18   Mackenzie describes a Nixon cabinet meeting in 1969 in which the president allegedly gave department heads the responsibility to fill positions within their agency:

> The President had engaged in a discussion of administration appointment procedures. Unprepared to discuss this matter and still imbued by his campaign pledge to revitalize the Cabinet, he impulsively delegated the primary responsibility for filling appointive positions in each department to the cabinet officers themselves. He further specified that these jobs should be filled on the basis of ability first and loyalty second. He recognized almost immediately that in granting this discretion, he had made an error in judgment. As he left the Cabinet room after the meeting, he said to an aide, "I just made a big mistake."
>
> "The Appointment Process," p. 107.

19   Ibid.

20   Harry Flemming, Ibid., p. 110.

21   Malek further systematized the recruitment procedures. He generated a larger list of candidates, had security and political clearances conducted, and circulated the names of the best qualified to Haldeman for final decision or for submission to the president. Ibid., p. 115.

22   "Federal Personnel Manual," Ibid., p. 340.

23   Richard M. Nixon, transcript as published in *Washington Star-News*, July 20, 1974.

24   Donald G. Ogilvie, interview.

25   During the so-called Sunday night massacre on November 9, 1975, President Ford fired his secretary of defense and CIA director, announced the resignation of his secretary of commerce, and indicated that his secretary of state, Dr. Kissinger, would no longer be his assistant for national security affairs.

26   The Hoover Commission was established by act of Congress in 1947. Chaired by former President Hoover, it was charged with examining the administrative structure and process of the executive branch of government. Among its 277 recommendations was a suggestion that Congress permanently give the president the authority to reorganize the executive branch. Congress did review and even extend the jurisdiction of the reorganization authority but kept it subject to the veto of either house.

27   The second Hoover Commission was created in 1958. Also headed by the former president, it too was charged with examining the organization of the executive branch. One of its recommendations was that the BOB expand its management functions.

A more extensive recommendation along these lines was proposed by a committee headed by Nelson Rockefeller. It actually urged the abolition of the BOB and its replacement by an office of Executive Management. The Rockefeller Committee argued that the BOB as presently constituted could not effectively provide direction and leadership in the management area.

28 PPBS was designed to measure the costs and benefits of alternative programs. It was a system intended to define specific objectives, quantify them whenever possible, and then calculate the costs of resources needed to achieve them. Alternate ways of reaching these goals were also evaluated on the basis of costs and benefits. The system was designed to replace the more incremental, item-line budget approach whereby individual items were grouped by subject category rather than by programing functions.

29 There had even been a suggestion that the title of the new agency be simply Office of Executive Management. Members of the House Appropriations Committee and most particularly its chairman, George Mahon, objected. At his insistence, the word "Budget" was retained and "Management" added.

30 Larry Berman, "The Office of Management and Budget That Almost Wasn't," *Political Science Quarterly*, XCII, no. 2 (1977), p. 298.

31 Richard M. Nixon, "Message from the President of the United States transmitting Reorganization Plan No. 2 of 1970," Ninety-first Congress, Second Session, Document No. 91-275 (March 12, 1970), pp. 4–5.

32 President Gerald R. Ford, statement released by Office of the Press Secretary, November 18, 1976.

33 Clifford Graves, interview.

34 Thomas E. Cronin, *The State of the Presidency* (Boston: Little, Brown, 1975), p. 276.

CHAPTER 7

Epilogue: The Carter Transition

I believe in Cabinet administration of our government.
There will never be an instance while I am
President where the members of the White House staff
dominate or act in a superior position to the members
of our Cabinet.

Jimmy Carter
National Journal
February 12, 1977
p. 234

Carter is quite accessible. Johnson was also; the
only problem was he did all the talking. It took
an act of God to reach Nixon.

Sen. Frank Church
July 20, 1977

[Patronage] is like a beauty contest. You choose
one person and you make 434 mad because their candidate
wasn't selected. Patronage should be given
to the losers.

James Free
Congressional Associate
(House of Representatives)

INTRODUCTION *

The Carter transition began before the 1976 election. It is difficult to say exactly when it ended. After winning the Pennsylvania primary, Carter designated campaign aide Jack H. Watson, Jr. to head a transition office. Watson's charge was to examine the problems the new administration would face if Jimmy Carter were elected as the 39th president of the United States. During the remainder of the primaries and the presidential campaign, Watson and his staff studied the structure and operation of the executive branch of government. Task forces concerned with recruitment, government organization, and substantive policy questions were created. Experts from universities, research institutions, and past administrations were consulted. After Carter's victory, extensive briefings with Ford officials were conducted.

In the period from the election to the inauguration, the transition staff was enlarged to over 100 people and moved from Atlanta, Georgia to Washington, D.C. Policy analysis, government organization, agency liaison, and personnel appointments were its principal areas of concern. The president-elect studied large briefing books prepared by the transition team and consulted with Watson and other senior aides on the shape of the new government. A separate personnel operation headed by Hamilton Jordan made recommendations on appointments. By January 20th, the new president had fairly definite ideas in mind about the kind of staff system he wanted to create and the orientation of the policy processes he had to develop.

CREATING A CABINET APPROACH
TO POLICY MAKING

Carter wished to reverse the flow of people and power to the White House. He wanted a more open and less imperial presidency, one that was more symbolic of his grass roots campaign. He desired to redesign policy making by providing his department and agency heads with greater presidential access and more individual discretion.

To achieve these objectives, the president proposed to cut the White House in size, eliminate many of its perquisites, and resurrect the concept of cabinet government. In his first fireside chat on February 2, 1977, Carter announced, "I am reducing the size of the White House staff by nearly one-third, and have asked the members of the Cabinet to do the

---

* This epilogue covers the period from Carter's inauguration on January 20, 1977 through September 30, 1977.

same at their top staff level. Soon I will put a ceiling on the number of people employed by the Federal Government agencies, so we can bring the growth of government under control." [1]

Eliminating some of the pomp of the office and the mystery surrounding the White House was also a major presidential aim. Symbolizing this desire, Carter walked rather than drove down Pennsylvania Avenue from the Capitol to the White House following his inauguration. Limousine service for senior White House aides was terminated. "Government officials can't be sensitive to your problems if we are living like royalty here in Washington," he said. [2] The president was seen carrying his own luggage when he traveled and holding his own umbrella in the rain.

Dress was also more casual. During his first fireside chat which was nationally televised, Carter wore a cardigan sweater. He was frequently seen in a sport shirt and slacks on weekends away from the White House. These informalities carried over to his staff and influenced the style of the White House.

By making the White House a smaller and less formal institution, Carter sought to recreate a better balance between presidential assistants and department and agency heads. "I believe in Cabinet administration of our government," he declared. "There will never be an instance while I am President where the members of the White House staff dominate or act in a superior position to the members of our Cabinet." [3]

By giving his new department heads access [4] and encouraging their policy initiatives, Carter hoped to revitalize the cabinet system. Department and agency heads could establish their own priorities. Cabinet members had authority to make most of their own political appointments subject to White House veto, except for deputies and undersecretaries. [5] As in previous administrations, they exercised a free hand in implementing policy decisions.

While the role of individual cabinet members was enhanced, the institution of the cabinet did not become a policy-making or consensus-reaching body. Weekly cabinet meetings, also attended by some agency heads and senior White House staff, were held with the president presiding. These sessions were mainly informational. They provided a forum for the discussion of issues that crossed departmental lines.

A cabinet secretary provided staff support. In addition to taking and circulating the minutes of the meetings, the secretary also helped to coordinate cabinet matters. Jack Watson, who held this position in the new administration, arranged meetings between cabinet members and the president. He also supervised the paper flow. All cabinet correspondence to the president was routed through White House staff for comment. It was Watson's job to make sure that information was accurate and complete and that department heads were kept informed of pending issues.

STAFFING AND STYLIZING THE WHITE HOUSE

The revitalization of the cabinet system did not markedly decrease the responsibilities of the White House staff. On the contrary, the Carter White House retained many of the traditional functional divisions that had come to be associated with a large staff system. In form, the White House bore a striking resemblance to the one it replaced. It was highly differentiated in organization. There were relatively clear lines of authority. Even the placement of offices was similar to that of the previous administration. Presidential assistants sat at their predecessors' desks. Many even retained their predecessors' secretaries.

In size, the Carter White House initially exceeded Ford's. Despite the new president's promise to reduce its size, start-up demands required more rather than less staff. By May 30, 1977 there were 561 people on the White House staff or detailed to it from other departments and agencies compared to 485 at the end of the Ford presidency.[6]

While structural similarities exceeded the differences, there were some new staff positions and one major deletion. In addition to the cabinet secretary who also handled intergovernmental matters, an energy office, responsible for the development of administration policy and organization in this area and the forerunner of the new energy department, was created. Eliminated was the position of chief of staff, although the title, assistant to the president, was retained.

From Carter's perspective, a chief of staff was both unnecessary and undesirable. So long as White House administration, personnel, and appointments were in the hands of capable people, there was no need for an "executive president," it was argued.[7] In the Carter White House separate offices of administration and budget, and organization took care of the more routine management and personnel functions which the chief of staff had handled in the Nixon and Ford administrations. The president's desire to be accessible and close to his staff also seemed to profit from a flexible, bilateral staff structure in which no one came between Carter and his senior aides.

The internal coordination which the chief of staff and his deputy had achieved in the previous administrations became the joint responsibility of the senior staff. Meeting three times a week, Carter's senior advisors helped plan the president's schedule, discussed emerging policy issues, and generally oversaw staff activities. Robert Lipshutz, counsel to the president, presided over these meetings. The president usually attended once a week.[8]

Nine members of the White House were considered senior staff. (See Figure VII-I). They were presumably equal in rank and salary ($56,000). Some White House aides, however, regarded Hamilton Jordan, assistant to the president, as a *de facto* chief of staff.[9] His office in the West Wing, the

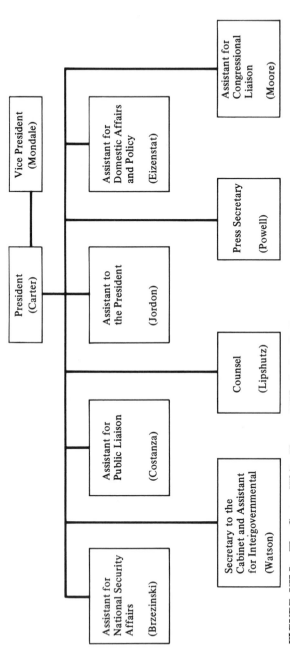

FIGURE VII-I. **The Carter White House, 1977: Senior Staff**

same one that was occupied by Richard Cheney, Ford's chief of staff, became a hub of activity. However, Jordan's responsibilities were primarily political and not administrative.

Each senior aide had direct access to the president. Several, such as Zbigniew Brzezinski and Frank B. Moore, had regularly scheduled morning meetings to brief the president on developments within their areas. Jody Powell and Jordan, probably Carter's closest personal advisors, could see him whenever he was free. They did so frequently. Others on the senior staff also had little difficulty talking with the president.

Influence, however, was not solely related to personal access. In the Carter White House, being on the paper loop in a position to affect presidential options was deemed even more important. The president made many of his decisions alone and off paper although meetings of key officials often preceded important policy decisions. Decision documents took the form of option papers in which arguments and recommendations were presented. Carter would simply check the options he desired, often writing succinct notes in the margin.[10]

Exhibiting a thirst for information and a memory for detail, Carter read and absorbed quickly.[11] While he periodically complained about being overwhelmed by the amount of paper, he did little to discourage its flow.[12] Not only did the president seek involvement in a wide range of issues, but he also seemed to have difficulty letting go of them. He was decisive, energetic and knowledgeable. According to his aides, he had a keen, analytical mind.[13]

Since Carter was a formal decision-maker, the White House operation was geared to a paper flow system. The staff secretary handled the circulation of written memoranda and option papers except for some classified national security documents that went directly from Brzezinski to the president. The secretary's job was to make sure that all bases were touched, that the papers were on time, and that they were complete. Circulation loops were quickly developed which alerted principal members of the White House staff to pending policy issues. "Most of the flow accords with the natural division of functions," stated staff secretary Rick Hutcheson who added, "If I have a question whether someone should see something or not, I show it to them." [14] There was no circumvention of senior aides as there had been in the last six months of the Ford White House.

The president's day was scheduled so as to maximize his time to work alone. Care was taken to keep ceremonial functions to a minimum. Carter would usually arrive at the Oval Office between 6:30 and 7:00 A.M. and work uninterrupted until 8:00 A.M. After his national security council and congressional briefings, he would frequently also find time for his paper work. "His schedule is not all that full," stated one White House aide, who added, "we try to limit his appointments to a maximum of 15 minutes."

The Carter White House seemed to operate smoothly. Senior aides were able to anticipate the president's needs, understand his reactions, and sense his broad policy goals. Amongst themselves, they interacted with a minimum of friction. Only the initial division of responsibilities between Stuart Eizenstat, assistant for domestic affairs, and Watson, cabinet secretary and assistant for intergovernmental affairs, posed some problems, but the backbiting and internal conflict that occurred in the last year of the Ford White House did not develop. The newness of the administration, the idealism that naturally permeated its first few months, and the close working relationships that had developed among Carter aides during the campaign all contributed to the spirit of cooperation. The president's own demeanor, his informality, and his intolerance of internal staff conflict also helped set the tone. Stated one White House aide:

> This is not a president who believes in a competitive staff structure. People have extolled the competitive staff system of Roosevelt and Kennedy. They have said it brought forth this greater brilliance. But the fact of the matter is, when you have a situation where people are trying to protect themselves against other people, you have to devote a certain amount of energy each day to try to beat somebody else, to try to cover your ass. That just doesn't produce very harmonious working relationships. . . There is a sense in this administration that it would be a great sin to undermine some senior staffers.

The president did not chew out his aides. In fact, he rarely expressed emotion. His style was to understate: "He flashes his intent in a number of ways," stated one aide. "If you are absolutely so dense as not to pick up what he is signaling, he will tell you or have someone else tell you." Senior White House officials who had been with Carter throughout the campaign had little difficulty interpreting the signals. There was no Haldeman-type tickler system in the Carter White House as there had been in Nixon's although the president kept abreast of what his aides were doing.

COORDINATING LEGISLATIVE POLICY MAKING

The flexibility of the White House structure and the informality of staff interaction extended to legislative policy making in the domestic and economic spheres. In addition to cabinet participation, the OMB and the president's Domestic Policy Staff were regularly involved in the formulation, clearance, and presentation of new proposals to Congress.

Other White House and executive branch offices had some legislative input as well. The counsel's office participated in all matters that related to the Department of Justice, including intelligence questions. The assistant for intergovernmental affairs dealt with legislation that pertained to disaster relief and various state and urban policy problems. An Economic Policy Group evolved to handle cross-cutting economic matters. This group, a successor to the Economic Policy Board of the Ford administration, consisted of the principal economic advisors and domestic department secretaries. Its executive committee, chaired by secretary of the treasury W. Michael Blumenthal, met once a week to discuss major economic issues and make recommendations to the president.

The OMB and the Domestic Policy Staff, however, remained the principal presidential units for coordinating the development of administration policy. Structurally, the OMB was reorganized. The political layers not only were retained, they were augmented by two new positions of executive associate director. Harrison Wellford, one of these new executive associate directors, was charged with reorganization and management matters. He was one of the major architects of the president's first reorganization plan. W. Bowman Cutter, the other executive associate director, exercised supervision in the budget and legislative areas and functioned as a head of the four operating divisions. Deputy director James T. McIntyre had responsibility for instituting zero based budgeting, a technique he had used in Georgia as Carter's budget director.[15] Bert Lance, Carter's first director of the OMB, was not as directly involved in day to day operations, but he maintained a close personal relationship with the president and had wide contacts with the business community. He was forced to resign in September, 1977.

The Domestic Policy Staff resembled the Ford Domestic Council in size, form, and functional responsibilities. It was even stuck with the title "Domestic Council" until Carter's first reorganization plan took effect. Congress had authorized a staff of 40 which the Carter unit could not exceed. The internal division and hierarchy were also similar to the Ford Council as indicated in Figure VII-II.

Within the staff, the associate directors continued to operate with considerable autonomy. They performed most of the same jobs that their predecessors had. A formal meeting was held for exchange of information and views, but there was a good deal of informal interaction.

One of the major differences between the Ford and Carter domestic staffs seemed to be the relationship between the director and the president. Stuart Eizenstat, touted as one of the "heavies" of the new administration, was closer to and more influential with Carter than Cannon had been with Ford or Cole with Nixon.[16] This helped to bolster the staff's position in domestic policy-making spheres. Moreover, the Economic Policy Group did not impinge on its jurisdiction the way the Economic Policy Board had on the Ford Domestic Council's. Said one associate director:

> I've literally never had what you'd regard as a turf dispute. By and large because more people have more to do than they can, whoever wants to take an area where there is overlap usually ends up taking it.

Once routines and procedures became established, the formal operating processes functioned in their customary fashion. There was some ini-

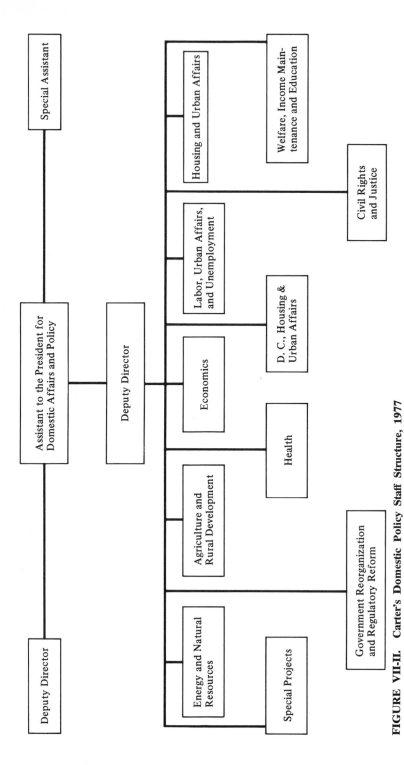

FIGURE VII-II. Carter's Domestic Policy Staff Structure, 1977

SOURCE: Federal Organization and Personnel Directory, June 1977.

tial confusion over the need for presidential clearance of legislation. Some departments and agencies, taking the president's proposal for a cabinet government literally, began developing positions and testimony on their own. At an early cabinet meeting Carter indicated that it was necessary to get clearance and suggested that testimony be sent to Stuart Eizenstat. According to one OMB official, "Bert Lance then told the president that the OMB ran a clearance process. The president responded that he did not want to reinvent the wheel". As a result, Carter and Lance each sent memos to all cabinet and agency heads explaining the need for clearance and clarifying the procedure. After these memos were circulated, adherence to the process became routine.

Within the OMB, the Legislative Reference Division, which was made part of a new legislative affairs office, handled clearance matters, consulting with domestic policy aides on all policy questions. The Division's analysts were instructed to "find out your counterparts on Eizenstat's staff and get in touch with them on anything of policy significance or unsettled policy." [17] This caused some initial problems for a domestic policy group that found itself overwhelmed with a large number of clearance decisions, some of which they regarded as trivial. Complained one domestic staff official, "People in OMB who make these clearance decisions don't have a very good sense of what is an important decision and what isn't."

The enrolled bill process also followed what had become standard practice. Legislative Reference summarized department and agency comments and wrote the OMB memo. The associate directors continued as the key decision-makers for the OMB on controversial bills within their subject matter areas. In the White House, the enrolled bill file, complete with executive branch recommendations, was sent to an associate director on the Domestic Policy Staff for review and analysis.

Bertram Carp, deputy director of the Domestic Policy Staff, assumed over-all responsibility for the staff's recommendation. Other White House opinion was also solicited from the congressional liaison and counsel's offices. Naturally, in the first six months of the Carter administration, the number of enrolled bills was small and the threat of a veto remote.[18]

The cabinet orientation of domestic policy making, combined with Carter's style of decision making, created the need for a presidential staff that coordinated the development of administration priorities. Domestic policy aides functioned more as brokers than advocates. Carp described their responsibilities as follows:

> What we try to do is see that the paper that goes into the president is in decent shape; that people develop the options that should be developed; and, as best we can, that arguments that the president ought not to have to resolve are resolved among the parties.[19]

The Domestic Policy Staff did not impose solutions. Its influence was gained from its proximity to the president. "We will exercise the influence we do have and take something to the president if others don't decide among themselves," stated a senior staff official.

In helping to coordinate presidential policy making, the domestic staff avoided direct involvement in policy formulated by a single department. "The agencies have greater resources," noted an associate director. "We're not going to write their legislation but we have to stay on top of it so we can understand it." Carp indicated that the policy staff might make suggestions to an agency, or in exceptional circumstances, have the president do it. "We would not propose policy directly," he added.[20]

On interagency matters, the president's policy staff was more actively involved. Its associate directors participated in internal work groups, although there was no formal mechanism for creating and staffing these groups. They tended to develop on an ad hoc basis.

Vice President Mondale played a major role in establishing administration priorities and scheduling them. During his early months in office, he created, in effect, a rough blueprint for the president and his senior advisors to follow. A more comprehensive planning effort began in the spring of 1977. A Domestic Policy Staff memo to all assistant secretaries in charge of planning called for proposals for new legislation to be submitted at the same time as the spring budget review was being conducted. The spring review, which begins the budget cycle, is the time when expenditure ceilings are established for the larger executive branch units. Each department and agency was asked to propose its "wish list" of programs. These lists provided domestic policy and OMB officials with a basis for evaluating the proposals in conjunction with the budget for the next fiscal year.

The bulk of the policy staff's work in program development was devoted to coordinating and generating options for the president. No separate, long-term planning operation was contemplated or established. Said one domestic policy official:

> Long-term planning tends to be undirected work unless it is of immediate relevance to a policy maker. This is not to say that long term, futuristic kinds of looks are not valuable. They are, but there is no reason for them to be performed by a staff of this proximity to political executives.

As in the past, little of the staff's time was spent on tracking decisions the president made. "At some point you have to let go and start focusing on the next issue," explained one associate director. Evaluation of existing programs also did not consume much time. That the departments and agencies remained principally responsible for implementing presidential policy presented Carter with some of the same problems his predecessors had encountered in making sure that their objectives were achieved and their interests protected.

ESTABLISHING RELATIONS WITH CONGRESS

Of all the components of the president's legislative policy mechanism, the congressional liaison office seemed to get off to the shakiest start. Severe criticism on Capitol Hill greeted the initial effort by Frank Moore and his small staff to act as conduit between the Democratic presidential candidate and Democratic members of Congress. The problem was two-fold: Moore's inexperience in dealing with Congress and Congress' overanxiousness to deal with Carter.

Designated as Carter's personal representative, Moore came to Washington in July, 1976. He was quickly inundated with phone calls, messages, and requests for appointments. Some of the phone calls were not returned, messages were lost, and appointments were missed. Criticism of Moore, although muffled by the campaign, began to emerge after Carter's victory. The beginning of the congressional session three weeks before the inauguration further complicated the new liaison chief's tasks. "When we came into this office on the 21st, we got 1,100 letters from members of Congress in our first week on the Hill," he stated.[21]

The expectations of Democrats in Congress clearly exceeded the administration's capacity to fulfill. "Sixty percent of the Congress had never dealt with a Democratic White House so they didn't have realities in mind," suggested a top liaison official. "They looked for a rubber stamp White House. It was a learning process on both sides of the street."

Patronage and projects constituted the bulk of the congressional requests. The liaison office passed on personnel suggestions to the White House and checked with appropriate members on many appointments which the White House was considering. However, the large number of requests and potential candidates, and the relative independence of the personnel operation from the liaison effort, made patronage a high-risk, low-return operation for the president's agents on the Hill. There was persistent congressional criticism throughout the first five months of the administration. In June, Speaker O'Neill even held a "bitch" session in his office for 50 Democrats and 3 Carter aides (Jordan, Moore, and James King, head of the personnel office). "We won the election but you'd never know it," O'Neill said to the group.[22] Walter Flowers, a Democrat from Alabama, commented much to the same effect. "I busted my butt for Carter and there's nobody I know who got an appointment. I call up [the agencies] and I'm talking to the same people I talked to under Nixon and Ford."[23]

From the perspective of the president's liaison aides, patronage created more enemies than friends. "It's like a beauty contest," stated James C. Free, one of three White House assistants for the House of Representatives. "You choose one person and you made 434 mad because their candidate wasn't selected. Patronage should be given to the losers."[24] Other members of the administration supported Free's view.

Relations with Congress also suffered from an early presidential decision to eliminate, without congressional consultation, 19 major public works projects that had been authorized and funded. The liaison staff had the unenviable task of notifying members in whose districts the projects were located. Predictably, there were loud protests.

In size and structure, the liaison operation resembled those of previous White Houses. The size remained fairly small. In addition to Moore who headed the office, there were five other assistants who worked in the Congress (three in the House and two in the Senate).[25] A supporting staff of approximately equal number was housed in the White House's East Wing handling congressional correspondence, constituency problems, and requests for information.

The lobbying strategy was similar to the Kennedy and Johnson years when the Democrats controlled both ends of Pennsylvania Avenue. The Carter office adopted a high visibility, partisan approach. Contact was almost exclusively with Democratic members.

Both president and vice president took an active role in liaison activities. Before his inauguration, Carter had invited the congressional leadership to Plains, Georgia, and after becoming president, he continued the practice of hosting leadership breakfasts every other Tuesday. He also held a series of meetings for the party rank and file. Within a few months every Democratic member of Congress had been invited to the White House.

Liaison agents facilitated other contacts on an individual basis. They helped arrange appointments with the president, and they monitored phone calls to him from members of Congress. Valerie Pinson, a presidential liaison agent for the House, indicated that Carter was fairly accessible by phone. "There's no problem with a member just picking up the phone and calling the president. If he's there and free, he'll talk to them. If it is something that can wait, we'll go through the usual process." [26] Normally, if the matter required presidential attention, calls would be routed through the appointments secretary for a specific time on the president's schedule.

Congressional aides prepared talking papers for the president. Also briefed by his policy staff, Carter was well armed with information when conversing with members of Congress. "It constantly amazes me how he can speak across issues," Pinson commented. "He never answers in one or two words, always a paragraph." [27]

The president's contacts with Congress tended to be strictly business.[28] By minimizing the ceremonial aspects of the office, the opportunity for inviting members of Congress to the White House on social occasions decreased. In the first six months there were only a few state dinners and other affairs. Even the presidential yacht, the Sequoia, was sold.

Vice President Mondale was also active as an administration lobbyist. He dealt primarily with Democratic members of the Senate and occasionally, with the House leadership. "He's served a good purpose," stated one liaison aide. "He's a big shot that a Congressman can blow off steam to and know that he's getting his word to the top."

In general, White House liaison performed the traditional functions of information gathering, legislative servicing, and lobbying for major administration proposals. Extensive use was made of department liaison agents, especially at the committee stage of the legislative process. Meetings between the White House and department's liaison staffs were held every Friday morning. The distinction between executive branch and presidential interests was not perceived to be a major problem.

In lobbying for administration policy, White House liaison agents felt that they had few tangible chips with which to deal. "It really presents a problem for use," stated Pinson. "We can ask for a vote, but there is nothing to trade off." [29] As Governor of Georgia, Carter had refused to trade in patronage and special favors. His administration continued this practice in Washington.[30]

Increasingly, members of Congress sought an input into policy formulation. Most of this was channeled to the Domestic Policy Staff. Occasionally, the policy staff would contact members directly. The administration viewed congressional incursions into its legislative sphere as a mixed blessing. The negatives were: it required more time to consider congressional views; it could dilute the president's proposals; and it could actually alienate Congress if some suggestions were not incorporated into policy. On the other hand, the members' views might improve the legislation and enhance its chances for passage.

The liaison office had some input of its own. It provided political soundings. There were also joint meetings between the policy and liaison staffs. Nonetheless, congressional liaison aides did not exercise a regular and continuing influence on the substance of most presidential policy initiatives.

Similarities in the functions and methods of the White House liaison office over the years indicate the extent of its institutionalization. For much of the other legislative machinery in the presidency, this also seems to be the case. Despite new presidential leadership, the institution of the presidency has evidenced considerable stability in its policy processes. New personnel obviously have affected objectives, orientation, and style, but structures, functions and procedures have remained remarkably constant.

REORGANIZING THE STRUCTURES AND PROCESS

In evaluating the transition phase of Carter's legislative presidency, one basic need stood out: to better coordinate the cabinet system of policy formulation by making it more consistent with the president's decision-making style and more protective of his political interests. Three separate but related process-oriented problems emerged by July 1977. They concerned the range of available options, the weighting of political consequences, and the monitoring of presidential decisions.

While departmental proposals were usually well staffed, alternatives sometimes were not. It was natural for departments and agencies to emphasize positions they favored. To some extent, this was true for some of the White House staffs as well. The way options were worded or even the way they were scheduled could ultimately affect the president's decision. Lack of time, for example, could narrow his range of possible choices, giving advantage to the initiators. The system seemed to be skewed in the direction of the advocates. There were not always countervailing forces. For the president's sake, better coordination and more neutral brokering was needed. Carter wanted a fuller range of choices.

With policy initiative resting in the departments and agencies, there was no systematic mechanism for evaluating political consequences for the president. Simply because there was overlap between the president's electoral constituency and some bureaucratic clienteles (such as Labor; Health, Education and Welfare; and Housing and Urban Development) did not guarantee that policy developed by these departments would be to the president's political advantage. The congressional liaison office in the White House did not have a regular input into policy-making. Hamilton Jordan and his small staff saw many of the papers going to the president, but their being on the loop did not insure, in and of itself, that they would have sufficient time to study an issue, understand it and make a judgment, and have an impact on the options. Jordan's staff had to pick and choose. A more systematic process for considering the political ramifications of policy choices was required.

As in previous administrations, implementation remained in the hands of the departments and agencies. There were no procedures for insuring that the president's decisions would be implemented in a manner that was consistent with his objectives and that protected his interests. From Carter's perspective, some follow-up mechanism was desirable.

The first reorganization plan of the new administration spoke to each of these problems as well as to other organizational objectives which Carter had voiced before taking office. Congress had reinstituted the president's reorganization authority in 1977.[31] In a conscious attempt to put his own house in order as a prelude to other reorganization plans, the president recommended structural and procedural changes that would reduce the size of the Executive Office of the President, including the White House staff, shift functions within the presidency, and enlarge the policy-making responsibilities of the Domestic Policy Staff and the policy implementation responsibilities of the cabinet secretary. (See Appendix C for chart of the new Executive Office of the President). The reorganization reduced the number of permanent positions in the White House from 485 to 351. This was a 28% cut, close to Carter's preinaugural promise of reducing the size of the White House by 30%. "I'm very much opposed to having a concentration of people and authority in the White House staff," he stated in announcing the change.[32]

The decrease involved some administrative personnel, people who handled such tasks as mail, accounting, payroll, and personnel matters. They were moved to a newly created Central Administrative Unit in the Executive Office of the President. The offices of most senior staff also suffered some loss of positions but their functional responsibilities remained pretty much in tact. The cabinet secretary's role of preparing the distribution of the minutes of cabinet meetings was consolidated under the staff secretary and a conscious decision was made not to institutionalize the Economic Policy Group.

In order to create a more structured approach to policy making, a new domestic policy system was instituted. Premised on the concept of the cabinet system, the new policy mechanism was designed to improve the development, coordination and implementation of department and agency policy *for the president* without establishing a competing bureaucratic organization. While the functions of the departments and agencies in the early stages of policy formulation were not to be diminished, the vice president and senior White House advisers were charged with a more active role in establishing and scheduling priorities, the assistant for domestic affairs and policy with managing the process, and the cabinet secretary and assistant for intergovernmental affairs with monitoring the president's decisions.

The procedural changes were designed to protect the president's interests as well as better systematize the entire process. While the vice president and senior staff together shared responsibilities for setting the basic policy guidelines, the Domestic Policy Staff became in effect the process manager. Since most major policy was developed in interagency groups, under the new system the president was to approve the composition, the charge, and even the target deadlines of these groups (see Appendix D). A similar procedure had been utilized for groups operating in the national security area.

Once established, the Domestic Policy Staff was to provide these groups with administrative support. An official of the Domestic Policy Staff had the job of insuring that a variety of alternatives were discussed and presented to the president in an option memo. After Carter made his decision, the same official would be in charge of immediate follow-up with longer-term responsibilities in some cases given to the cabinet secretary and assistant for intergovernmental affairs.

Unlike the Domestic Council operation of the Nixon, and to a lesser extent, the Ford periods when the staff ran the work group, a cabinet officer, usually at the level of assistant secretary, would be the chairperson of the Carter interagency teams. Implementation of policy remained with the appropriate department or agency. The new monitoring procedure, however, was designed to keep tabs on this implementation, alerting the White House to potential problems and providing a basis for interceding, if necessary.

The OMB was also asked to assume a greater management role. In his reorganization message to Congress, Carter stated that he had ". . . asked the OMB to reorganize its management arm to emphasize major presidential initiatives such as reorganization, program evaluation, paper work reduction, and regulatory reform." [33]

Whether the structural and procedural changes produced by Carter's first reorganization plan will effectively tighten and streamline legislative policy making in the presidency remains to be seen. While the plan addressed some pressing organizational and procedural problems of the new administration, it was not intended as a panacea for all the tensions that inevitably develop between presidency and bureaucracy. In the past, these tensions have raised serious governing problems, especially for presidents who have oriented legislative decision-making toward cabinet initiative.

How can department and agency heads, for example, be encouraged to take a presidential perspective and maintain credibility with their departments at the same time? The plan does not directly deal with this question nor with others that have afflicted previous administrations. How can jurisdictional disputes between different executive branch units be minimized and a team approach to policy making generated? How can creative policy options continue to be encouraged as an administration ages? How can programs be evaluated to determine whether or not they have been successful and who will do the evaluating? Can the president's information be broad and his interests be protected without the growth of a sizable presidential bureaucracy? Carter seems to think so, but only time will tell if he is right, and if his reorganized policy-making machinery works to this end.

If the past is any indication, centrifugal forces will increase and the president and his aides will try to combat them. The tendency of department and agency heads to see presidential policy in terms of their own interests will become more pronounced. This will make the job of the president's assistants more difficult. Accumulated frustrations of consensus building will wear down some initial White House idealism. The policy-making process is likely to become more routinized which should improve the analysis but not necessarily the oversight of domestic policy. As the next election nears, however, the president will probably have to spend more time prioritizing his goals and directing his influence in Congress rather than presenting a laundry-list of legislative measures. Score cards of his achievements will be computed and promulgated by the White House, while Republicans will point to unwise and mis-managed policy—blaming both Congress and the president. The need for better management and more effective government will be voiced by everyone but what is better management and how can more efficient government be accomplished will continue to be very difficult questions to answer.

NOTES

1   Jimmy Carter, "Report to the American People, February 2, 1977," *Presidential Documents* XIII, no. 6 (February 7, 1977): 141.

2   Ibid, p. 142.

3   Jimmy Carter as quoted in "Carter White House Staff is Heavy on Functions, Light on Frills," by Dom Bonafede, *National Journal* IX, no. 7 (February 12, 1977): 234.

  Presidential assistant Hamilton Jordan commented to the same effect: "The problem is too many presidents have tried to deal with all of the problems of the country from the White House. The first line of offense or defense is the Cabinet. That's where the problems should be dealt with, in the departments and agencies. You can't do it all from the White House. . ." "No One Tries to Roll Over Jordan in the White House," by Dom Bonafede, *National Journal* IX, no. 16 (April 16, 1977): 584.

4   Cabinet members could regularly get to see or speak with the president. According to Jack Watson, designated as cabinet secretary for the new administration, department heads could meet or talk with the president within 24 hours if necessary, although appointments scheduled a week in advance were preferred. Joel Havemann, "The Cabinet Band—Trying to Follow Carter's Baton," *National Journal* IX, no. 29 (July 16, 1977): 1106.

5   Joel Havemann, "The TIP Talent Hunt—Carter's Original Amateur Hour?," *National Journal* IX, no. 8 (February 19, 1977): 268.

6   John Osborn, "White House Watch: Ringing the Changes," *New Republic* (June 25, 1977): 11.

7   Landon Butler, interview.

8   Senior staff meetings occurred Monday, Wednesday, and Friday mornings. The junior staff, the deputy directors of the major White House offices, met on Tuesday and Thursday. The meetings at both levels served two purposes: They enabled staff to know where everything was and what was coming up and to coordinate congressional activities.

9   Bonafede, "No One Tries to Roll Over Jordan," p. 580.

10   Sometimes these comments were so succinct that they provided problems for the staff, especially lower level officials who had been charged with preparing the basic document. Commented one such Carter aide:

  When you get a memo back that says simply "redo" or "explore other options," that's a very ambiguous basis from which to proceed. Personally, I find that unnerving. It's tough to call him up and say "What do you mean?" I would never do that.

Senior aides who had known Carter for years had less difficulty interpreting the comments and less hesitation in calling him when necessary.

11   In order to fulfill a campaign promise to read every bill that came before the legislature, Carter took a speed reading course when he was elected a state senator in Georgia. James David Barber, *The Presidential Character* (Englewood Cliffs: Prentice Hall, 1977), pp. 522–523.

12   One administration official commented: "He has an insatiable appetite for information. In my judgment that leads him into spending time on things he shouldn't be spending time on. Yet he continues to demand the stuff."

13   In contrast to Ford who tended to have an intuitive sense of what to do, Carter seemed to be more analytical. He was also more prone to seeking out decisions than Ford was. Carter preferred to be in the "thick and thin" of policy making rather than waiting to stop the buck at his desk.

14   Rick Hutcheson, interview.

15   Zero based budgeting is a process that requires the justification of existing programs for continued funding. In the past a common assumption has been that on-going programs, having a policy objective and usually having built up a clientele, would continue. Attention focused on the budget increment, with departments and agencies competing for incremental gains. Under the new system, this assumption would no longer be valid. Rather, existing programs would compete with new programs for funds. All programs would have to be periodically justified or else be terminated.

16   In an article on Eizenstat, *Newsweek* magazine states, "no man in the Carter White House exerts more influence on more matters of state than Eizenstat." The article goes on to quote Hamilton Jordan to the same effect: "If Jimmy had to throw everybody else away and keep one guy, he'd keep Stu." "Clear It with Stu," *Newsweek* (June 13, 1977): 18–19.

17   James Frye, interview.

18   The Domestic Policy Staff expected the OMB recommendation to be primarily substantive not political, "They are not supposed to be political. Even their political people are not political, at least not in the same way we are," stated one White House aide.

The Domestic Policy Staff saw its recommendation as independent of and a check on the OMB. "The whole purpose of the process," said Carp "is not just to piggy back the OMB. We don't just rely on their memo." Carp, interview.

19   Ibid.

20   Ibid.

21   Frank Moore as quoted in Spencer Rich, "Shakedown Cruise," *Washington Post* (February 25, 1977): A2.

22   Thomas (Tip) O'Neill as quoted in Martin Tolchin, "An Old Pol Takes on The New President," *New York Times Magazine* (July 24, 1977): 9.

23   Walter Flowers, Ibid.

24   James C. Free, interview.

25   House agents divided their responsibilities along subject matter lines rather than geographically as had been done in previous administrations.

26   Valerie Pinson, interview.

27   Ibid. In contrasting his own experience in reaching presidents, Senator

Frank Church commented: "Carter is quite accessible, Johnson was also; the only problem was he did all the talking. It took an act of God to reach Nixon." Frank Church, statement made to Robert A. Taft Institute of Government Seminar, July 20, 1977.

28   In discussing Carter's relations with the Georgia legislature when he was Governor, James David Barber quotes Hamilton Jordan as follows: "Jimmy is not easy to get close to. He doesn't have enough time in his life to let people get close. He doesn't understand the personal element in politics, though nobody is better at campaigning." Barber, *The Presidential Character,* p. 533.

29   Pinson, interview.

30   Barber, *The Presidential Character,* p. 533.

31   Congress passed a new reorganization act on March 31st. The president signed it into law seven days later. The statute authorized the president to initiate executive reorganizations for a three-year period subject to congressional veto.

32   Jimmy Carter, "Remarks to Reporters on Transmitting a Reorganization Plan to Congress, July 15, 1977" *Presidential Documents* XIII, no. 29 (July 18, 1977): 1007.

33   Jimmy Carter, "Message to Congress Transmitting Reorganization Plan No. 1 of 1977, July 15, 1977," *Presidential Documents* XIII, no. 29 (July 18, 1977): 1012.

APPENDIX A

The Size of The White House 1934–1976

FULL-TIME WHITE HOUSE EMPLOYEES

Fiscal Year	Salaries and Expenses	Special Projects	Total	Detailed Employees	Grand Total
1934	45	—	45	120	165
1935	45	—	45	127	172
1936	45	—	45	115	160
1937	45	—	45	112	157
1938	45	—	45	119	164
1939	45	—	45	112	157
1940	63	—	63	114	177
1941	62	—	62	117	179
1942	47	—	47	137	184
1943	46	—	46	148	194
1944	47	—	47	145	192
1945	48	—	48	167	215
1946	51	—	51	162	213
1947	190	—	190	27	217
1948	245	—	245	23	268
1949	220	—	220	26	246
1950	223	—	223	25	248
1951	257	—	257	40	297
1952	252	—	252	31	283
1953	262	—	262	28	290
1954	250	—	250	23	273
1955	272	—	272	28	300

Fiscal Year	Salaries and Expenses	Special Projects	Total	Detailed Employees	Grand Total
1956	273	78	351	41	392
1957	271	93	364	59	423
1958	272	80	352	51	403
1959	275	79	354	31	385
1960	275	80	355	33	388
1961	270	72	342	134	476
1962	253	56	309	123	432
1963	249	69	318	111	429
1964	236	70	306	125	431
1965	235	59	294	154	448
1966	219	37	256	219	475
1967	209	42	251	246	497
1968	203	47	250	206	456
1969	217	97	314	232	546
1970	250	95	345	287	632
1971	547	8	555	17	572
1972	522	28	550	34	584
1973	483	13	496	24	520
1974	505	—	505	47	552
1975	500	—	500	23	523
1976	471	—	471	26	497

SOURCE: Dr. James Connor, staff secretary, Ford White House.

APPENDIX B

Clearance and Enrolled Bill Procedures

EXAMPLES OF ADVICE USED IN CLEARING PROPOSED LEGISLATION

Standard

You are advised that your proposed legislation would be (would not be) in accord with the President's program.
You are advised that your proposed legislation would be (would not be) consistent with the Administration's objectives.
You are advised that there is no objection to the presentation of your proposed legislation to the Congress from the standpoint of the Administration's program.

Qualified, conditional, or affirmative

Subject to the above (amended along the lines outlined above) (unless amended along the lines set forth above) (subject to your consideration of the views and recommended amendments of the Department of _____),
you are advised that, etc.
Confirming advice given informally to a member of your staff, you are advised that there would be no objection to the presentation of your proposed legislation and that its enactment would be in accord with the program of the President.

Source: "Legislative Coordination and Clearance Functions," Office of Management and Budget, September 1975.

EXAMPLE OF AN ENROLLED BILL MEMORANDUM

EXECUTIVE OFFICE OF THE PRESIDENT
OFFICE OF MANAGEMENT AND BUDGET
Washington, D.C. 20503

MEMORANDUM FOR THE PRESIDENT

Subject: Enrolled Bill H.R. 8000—Tort claims suits
Sponsor—Rep. Celler (D) New York

Last Day for Action

June 5, 1961—Monday

Purpose

A very concise statement in 1-2-3-4- style of the principal features of the enrolled bill. Usually not more than one or two sentences. Comments, views, issues, agency differences, urgency, etc., should go into the two following sections.

Agency Recommendations

Office of Management and Budget	Approval
Department of Justice	Approval (Signing statement attached)
Postal Service	Approval
Department of State	No objection
Department of the Treasury	No objection
Department of Commerce	Disapproval (Veto message attached)
Department of the Interior	Defers to Justice

Discussion

The discussion should be as brief as possible and yet contain the essential background information and basic data which the President should have in deciding action on the bill. If pertinent and significant, such matters as the following should be covered here: (1) origin of the bill, (2) differences, if any, from the Administration's proposal, (3) changes in policy or deviations from established policy, (4) important agency comments or differences, (5) significant provisions of the bill, (6) estimates of costs or savings, and relationship to the budget, (7) references to any attached draft veto message, memorandum of disapproval, or signing statement.

Assistant Director for
Legislative Reference

Enclosures

EXAMPLE OF A SIGNING STATEMENT

Statement by the President

I have signed S.J. Res. 98, which provides that the flag of the United States of America may be flown for twenty-four hours of each day in Valley Forge State Park, Valley Forge, Pennsylvania.

Enactment of this measure is a fitting tribute to the determination and valor of the men who served in the Continental Army at Valley Forge. These men endured the rigors of cold, disease, and starvation during the winter of 1777–1778, to later fight and win the Battle of Monmouth, an important victory in the struggle for independence. As we approach the year of our Nation's Bicentennial anniversary, this Joint Resolution by Congress reminds us again of the unselfish sacrifices made by many American men and women who have served in our Country's Armed Forces. They have fought to establish and preserve, for Americans and free people everywhere, the right to liberty justice, and the pursuit of happiness.

EXAMPLE OF A VETO MESSAGE

To the House of Representatives:

I am returning without my approval H.R. 4035, the Petroleum Price Review Act, because it would increase petroleum consumption, cut domestic production, increase reliance on insecure petroleum imports and avoid the issue of phasing out unwieldy price controls.

H.R. 4035 would go counter to the Nation's need to conserve energy and reduce dependence on imported oil. It would increase petroleum imports by about 350,000 barrels per day in 1977, compared to import levels under my phased decontrol plan. It would even increase imports by about 70,000 barrels per day over continuation of the current system of mandatory controls through 1977.

The provisions in this bill to roll back the price of domestic oil not now controlled, to repeal the "stripper well" exemption from price controls and to establish a three-tier price system which would require even more complex regulations would be counterproductive to the achievement of energy independence.

The bill does contain an Administration requested provision which would continue the coal conversion program through December 31st. Since coal conversion authorities authorized last year in the Energy Supply and Environmental Coordination Act expired June 30th, I urge rapid enactment of a simple one year extension of these authorities.

Last Wednesday, July 16, I submitted to Congress a compromise plan to phase out price controls on crude oil over a thirty-month period. Coupled with administratively imposed import fees, this plan will reduce the Nation's imports by 900,000 barrels per day by 1977. It will reduce our vulnerability to another embargo by adding slightly over one cent per gallon to the price of all petroleum products by the end of 1975 and seven cents by 1978.

If Congress acts on this compromise and on other Administration proposed energy taxes, including the "windfall profits" tax and energy tax rebates to consumers, the burden of decontrol will be shared fairly, and our economic recovery will continue.

I veto H.R. 4035, because it increases our vulnerability to unreliable sources of crude oil and does not deal with the need to phase-out rigid price and allocation controls enacted during the embargo. I urge Congress not to disapprove my administrative plan of gradual decontrol. If it is accepted, I will accept a simple extension of price and allocation authorities. If decontrol is not accepted, I will have no choice but to veto the simple six-month extension of these authorities now being considered by Congress.

For too long, the Nation has been without an energy policy, and I cannot approve a drift into greater energy dependence.

THE WHITE HOUSE
July 1975

APPENDIX C

Executive Office of
The President
1977

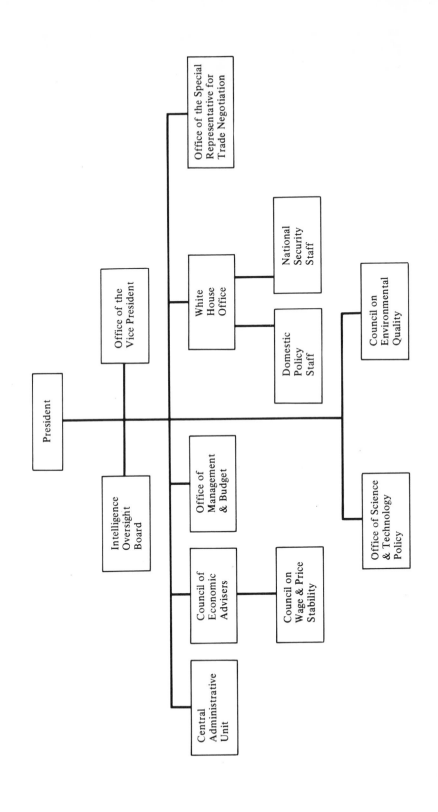

APPENDIX D

Presidential Domestic Policy Review System

Presidential Domestic Policy Review System

Memorandum for the Heads of Executive Departments and Agencies.
September 14, 1977

Memorandum for the Heads of Executive Departments and Agencies

Subject: Establishment of the Presidential Domestic Policy Review System

The Presidential Domestic Policy Review System is hereby established to coordinate the work of the Departments and Agencies in developing the Administration's position on selected key domestic policy issues.

Objectives

This System was recommended in the Reorganization Project's report on the Executive Office of the President as a means to ensure greater Department and Agency participation in the domestic policy decision process. The System's principal objectives are to:

—Ensure that the full resources of government are brought to bear on par-

ticular domestic issues in a timely manner;

—Provide a full range of realistic and properly staffed options on an issue;

—Encourage advance planning and priority setting to promote coordination among issues;

—Establish procedures to ensure that Departments and Agencies have the opportunity to comment on issues relevant to their expertise and policy responsibilities; and,

—Provide for systematic follow-up on Presidential decisions.

Memoranda and Procedures

The System will make use of the following memoranda and procedures:

—Issue Definition Memorandum
Issues for inclusion in the Domestic Policy Review System will be selected through an Issue Definition Memorandum submitted for Presidential approval by the Assistant to the President for Domestic Affairs and Policy (at his initiative or the request of a Department or

SOURCE: *Weekly Compilation of Presidential Documents* XIII, no. 38 (September 19, 1977), pp. 1343–1344.

Agency) after full consultation with the Vice President, all affected Departments, Agencies, and senior Presidential advisers. The Issue Definition Memorandum will briefly state the questions to be covered and the Agencies to be involved, and shall designate a lead Agency and the membership of a coordinating committee at the Cabinet or sub-Cabinet level—including representatives of all participating Agencies. The memorandum shall include a date for submission of a Response to the memorandum. Upon Presidential approval, the Issue Definition Memorandum will serve as a directive for analysis to begin on the questions defined.

—Response Memorandum
The lead Agency will take responsibility, in coordination with the Domestic Policy Staff and with the full assistance and cooperation of participating Agencies, for development of a Response Memorandum providing background, analysis of decision options, and Agency recommendations on questions identified in the Issue Definition Memorandum. The Response Memorandum should analyze the issues set forth in the Issue Definition Memorandum and, in doing so, reflect the views of all Agencies represented on the review committee, as well as any other Agencies affected by the Memorandum.

—Decision Memorandum
Where appropriate, a Presidential Decision Memorandum summarizing decision options will be prepared by the Domestic Policy Staff with review by affected Departments and Agencies and Senior Presidential advisers.

—Domestic Presidential Directive
Where appropriate, Presidential decisions will be set forth through a Domestic Presidential Directive.

Organization
Because of the number of Departments and Agencies involved, there will be no permanent standing committees associated with the Domestic Policy Review System. There will, however, be a coordinating committee established for each issue and the composition of that committee will be defined in the Issue Definition Memorandum.

A member of the Domestic Policy Staff will be assigned responsibility for working with the appropriate lead Agency. In addition, these committees will normally include representatives from OMB and CEA.

Alternatives to Memoranda Process
Domestic issues which otherwise would be covered by the Domestic Policy Review System may have to be handled differently because of excessive time pressures or unusual policy sensitivity. And on some domestic policy issues, extensive and formal interagency coordination will simply not be required. However, in each of these circumstances, the intent of the System is to establish early and extensive involvement between the Domestic Policy Staff and the affected agencies, whether through the Memorandum process or more informal communication.

Confidentiality
Use of this process will result in increased circulation of domestic policy documents. Circulation of draft Memoranda must be closely supervised by all parties to maintain confidentiality and avoid premature disclosure.

Identification of current issues
As a first step in implementing the new System, I would like each of you to submit a brief list of domestic issues (indicating priorities among them) to Stu Eizenstat, for possible inclusion in the Domestic Policy Review System. The list should be limited to those issues which have substantial impact on domestic policy and which require significant interagency involvement. The list should be submitted by September 23.

JIMMY CARTER

Selected Bibliography

There is a growing body of literature on the legislative presidency. Much of it is part of the public record. Each year the *United States Government Manual* list the names and titles of top officials in the Executive Office of the President as well as the rest of the executive branch. The proposals of departments and agencies and their testimony on Capitol Hill are generally available in committee hearings and reports. The floor debates and final enactments of Congress appear in the *Congressional Record*. Legislation is also listed in the Federal Register.

All presidential signing and veto statements appear in the weekly compilation of *Presidential Documents,* as do major addresses and messages to Congress. They also appear in the *Public Papers of the Presidents of the United States*. Presidential positions on legislation can usually be found in the *Congressional Quarterly* in its listing of roll call votes. Internal executive branch memoranda may be a little more difficult to obtain although much of it is available under the Freedom of Information Act. The Presidential libraries are excellent sources for White House communications. Finally, the enrolled bill file that OMB compiles accompanies the actual parchment copy of the legislation to the archives. These files are presently accessible through the Nixon administration.

Information on the structural and functional aspects of the legislative presidency often appears in newspapers such as *The New York Times, Washington Post, Los Angeles Times, Christian Science Monitor,* and *Wall Street Journal*. The best in-depth coverage is provided by the *National Journal,* a weekly periodical focusing on the executive branch. Dom Bonafede, its senior editor, has written particularly useful accounts of the

White House organization and operation and David Havemann has done the same for the OMB. The *National Journal* also regularly reports on presidential-congressional relations as does the *Congressional Quarterly*. The most comprehensive and up-to-date listing of the presidency literature appears in *Evolution of the Modern Presidency: A Bibliographic Survey* by Fred I. Greenstein et al. (Washington, D.C.: American Enterprise Institute for Public Policy Research, 1977).

The selections that follow highlight some of the works that are devoted wholly or in part to the legislative aspects of the presidency. Both monograph and journal literature are cited. Categorized by subject area, each item is listed only once. A short section on the personalized presidency is also included but accounts that are mainly devoted to individual presidents or particular administrations are not. The Greenstein survey contains a large number of citations on the modern presidents.

The Institutionalized Presidency

Clark, Keith C. and Legere, Laurence J. *The President and the Management of National Security*. New York: Praeger, 1969.

Corwin, Edward S. *The President: Office and Powers*. New York: New York University Press, 1957.

Cronin, Thomas E. *The State of the Presidency*. Boston: Little, Brown, 1975.

Destler, I. M. *Presidents, Bureaucrats and Foreign Policy*. Princeton, N.J.: Princeton University Press, 1974.

Falk, Stanley L. "The National Security Council Under Truman, Eisenhower, and Kennedy." *Political Science Quarterly* LXXIX, no. 3 (September 1964).

Fenno, Richard F. *The President's Cabinet*. New York: Random House (Vintage Books), 1959.

Figliola, C. L. "Considerations of National Security Administration: The Presidency, Policy Making and the Military." *Public Administration Review* XXXIV, no. 1 (January/February 1974).

Flash, Edward. *Economic Advice and Presidential Leadership: The Council of Economic Advisers*. New York: Columbia University Press, 1965.

Gilmour, Robert S. "The Institutionalized Presidency: A Conceptual Clarification." In *The Presidency in Contemporary Context,* edited by Norman Thomas. New York: Dodd, Mead, 1975.

Hargrove, Erwin C. *The Power of the Modern Presidency*. New York: Knopf, 1974.

Heclo, Hugh. *A Government of Strangers: Executive Politics in Washington*. Washington, D.C.: The Brookings Institution, 1977.

Hilsman, Roger. *The Politics of Policy-Making in Defense and Foreign Affairs*. New York: Harper & Row, 1971.

Jackson, Henry M., ed. *The National Security Council*. New York: Praeger, 1965.

James, Dorothy B. *The Contemporary Presidency*. New York: Pegasus, 1974.

Janis, Irving L. *Victims of Group Think*. Boston: Houghton Mifflin, 1972.

Kallenbach, Joseph. *The American Chief Executive*. New York: Harper & Row, 1966.

Koenig, Louis. *The Chief Executive*. New York: Harcourt Brace Jovanovich, 1975.

Neustadt, Richard E. *Presidential Power*. New York: Wiley, 1960.

Reedy, George. *The Twilight of the Presidency*. New York: World, 1970.

Rourke, Francis E. *Bureaucracy, Politics and Public Policy*. Boston: Little, Brown, 1969.

Patterson, Bradley H. *The President's Cabinet: Issues and Questions*. Washington, D.C.: American Society for Public Administration, 1976.

Schlesinger, Arthur M., Jr. *The Imperial Presidency*. New York: Popular Library, 1973.

Sorensen, Theodore C. *Decision-Making in the White House*. New York: Columbia University Press, 1963.

Wann, A. J. *The President as Chief Administrator*. Washington, D.C.: Public Affairs Press, 1968.

Wolanin, Thomas R. *Presidential Advisory Commissions: Truman to Nixon*. Madison, Wisconsin: University of Wisconsin Press, 1975.

Staffing the Presidential Office

Anderson, Patrick. *The President's Men*. Garden City, N.Y.: Doubleday, 1968.

Carey, William D. "Presidential Staffing in the Sixties and Seventies." *Public Administrative Review* XXIX, no. 5 (September/October 1969).

Hess, Stephen. *Organizing the Presidency*. Washington, D.C.: The Brookings Institution, 1976.

Johnson, Richard T. *Managing the White House*. New York: Harper & Row, 1974.

Neustadt, Richard E. "Approaches to Staffing the Presidency, Notes on FDR and JFK." *American Political Science Review* LVII, no. 4 (December 1963).

Raven, B. M. "The Nixon Group." *Journal of Social Issues* XXX, no. 4 (1974).

Thomas, Norman. "Presidential Advice and Information," *Law and Contemporary Problems* XXXV, no. 3 (Summer 1970).

Development of the President's Legislative Role

Binkley, Wilfred E. *President and Congress*. New York: Random House (Vintage Books), 1962.

Chamberlain, Lawrence H. *The President, Congress and Legislation*. New York: Columbia University Press, 1946.

Edwards, George. "Presidential Influence in the House: Presidential Prestige as a Source of Presidential Power." *American Political Science Review* LXX, no. 1 (March 1976).

Fisher, Louis. *President and Congress*. New York: Free Press, 1972.

————. *Presidential Spending Power.* Princeton, N.J.: Princeton University Press, 1975.

Huntington, Samuel P. "Congressional Responses to the Twentieth Century." In *The Congress and America's Future,* edited by David B. Truman. Englewood Cliffs, N.J.: Prentice-Hall, 1965.

Johannes, John R. "Congress and the Initiation of Legislation." *Public Policy* XX (1972).

————. "The President Proposes and Congress Disposes—But Not Always." *Review of Politics* XXXVI, no. 3 (July 1974).

Lehman, John. *The Executive, Congress, and Foreign Policy.* New York: Praeger, 1976.

Mansfield, Harvey. ed. *Congress Against the President.* New York: Praeger, 1975.

Moe, Ronald C., and Teel, Steven C. "Congress as Policy-Maker: A Necessary Reappraisal." In *Congress and the President,* edited by Moe and Teel. Pacific Palisades, Calif.: Goodyear, 1971.

Schlesinger, Arthur M., Jr., and deGrazia, Alfred. *Congress and the Presidency: Their Role in Modern Times.* Washington, D.C.: American Enterprise Institute, 1967.

Sundquist, James. *Politics and Policy.* Washington, D.C.: The Brookings Institution, 1968.

Wilson, Woodrow. *Constitutional Government.* New York: Columbia University Press, 1908.

————. *Congressional Government.* New York: New American Library (Meridian Books), 1956.

Young, James S. *The Washington Community.* New York: Columbia University Press, 1966.

Legislative Clearance and Coordination

Davis, James W., and Ripley, Randell B. "The Bureau of the Budget and Executive Branch Agencies: Notes on their Interaction." *Journal of Politics* XXIX, no. 4 (November 1967).

Gilmour, Robert S. "Central Legislative Clearance: A Revised Perspective." *Public Administration Review* XXXI, no. 2 (March/April 1971).

Hanson, Donald A. "Legislative Clearance by the Bureau of the Budget." Staff monograph, Bureau of the Budget, 1940.

Heclo, Hugh. "OMB and the Presidency—the Problem of Neutral Competence." *Public Interest* 38 (Winter 1975).

Jackson, Carlton. *Presidential Vetoes, 1792–1945.* Athens: University of Georgia Press, 1967.

Neustadt, Richard E. "Presidential Clearance of Legislation." Ph.D dissertation, Harvard University, June 1950.

————. "Presidency and Legislation: The Growth of Central Clearance," *American Political Science Review* XLVIII (September 1954).

Reese, J. M. "The Role of the Bureau of the Budget in the Legislative Process." *Journal of Public Law* XV (1966).

Schick, Allen. "The Budget Bureau That Was: Thoughts on the Rise, Decline and Future of a Presidential Agency." *Law and Contemporary Problems* XXXV, no. 3 (Summer 1970).

Presidential Programing

Kessel, John H. *The Domestic Presidency.* North Scituate, Mass.: Duxbury Press, 1975.

Moe, Richard. "The Domestic Council in Perspective." *The Bureaucrat* V (October 1976).

Neustadt, Richard E. "Presidency and Legislation: Planning the President's Program." *American Political Science Review* XLIX, no. 4 (December 1955).

Thomas, Norman C., and Wolman, Harold L. "The Presidency and Policy Formulation: The Task Force Device." *Public Administration Review* XXIX, no. 5 (September/October 1969).

Waldmann, Raymond. "The Domestic Council: Innovation in Presidential Government." *Public Administration Review* XXXVI, no. 2 (May/June 1976).

Wildavsky, Aaron. *The Politics of the Budgetary Process.* 2d ed. Boston: Little, Brown, 1974.

Congressional Liaison

DeGrazia, Edward. "Congressional Liaison." In *Congress,* edited by Alfred deGrazia. Garden City, N.Y.: Doubleday, 1967.

Holtzman, Abraham. *Legislative Liaison: Executive Leadership in Congress.* Skokie, Ill.: Rand McNally, 1970.

O'Brien, Lawrence F. *No Final Victories.* Garden City, N.Y.: Doubleday, 1974.

Pipe, Russell. "Congressional Liaison." *Public Administration Review* XXVI, no. 1 (March/April 1966).

Implementation

Bernstein, Marver. "The Presidency and Management Improvement." *Law and Contemporary Problems* XXX, no. 3 (Summer 1970).

Mackenzie, G. Calvin. "The Appointment Process: The Selection and Confirmation of Federal Political Executives." Ph.D. dissertation, Harvard University, 1975.

Mansfield, Harvey. "Reorganizing the Federal Executive Branch: The Limits of Institutionalization." *Law and Contemporary Problems* XXXV, no. 3 (Summer 1970).

Nathan, Richard. *The Plot that Failed: Nixon and the Administrative Presidency.* New York: Wiley, 1975.

Neustadt, Richard. "Politicians and Bureaucrats." In *The Congress and America's Future,* edited by David B. Truman. Englewood Cliffs, N.J.: Prentice-Hall, 1965.

Rose, Richard. *Managing Presidential Objectives.* New York: Free Press, 1977.

Seidman, Harold. *Politics, Position and Power.* New York: Oxford University Press, 1970.

The Personalized Presidency

Bailey, Thomas A. *Presidential Greatness.* New York: Appleton-Century-Crofts, 1966.

Barber, James D. *The Presidential Character.* Englewood Cliffs, N.J.: Prentice-Hall, 1975.

————. "Strategies for Understanding Politicians." *American Journal of Political Science* (Spring 1974).

George, Alexander. "Assessing Presidential Character." *World Politics* XXVI (1974).

————. "Power as a Compensation for Political Leaders." *Journal of Social Issues* XXIV (July 1968).

George, Alexander and George, Juliette. *Woodrow Wilson and Colonel House: A Personality Study.* New York: John Day, 1956.

Hargrove, Erwin. *Presidential Leadership, Personality and Political Style.* New York: Macmillan, 1966.

Kearns, Doris. *Lyndon Johnson and the American Dream.* New York: Harper & Row, 1976.

Mazlish, Bruce. *In Search of Nixon: A Psychohistorical Inquiry.* New York: Basic Books, 1973.

Index